The White Image
— in the —
Black Mind

*A Study of African American
Literature*

JANE DAVIS

*Contributions in Afro-American and African Studies,
Number 194*

GREENWOOD PRESS
Westport, Connecticut • London

Library of Congress Cataloging-in-Publication Data

Davis, Jane, 1954–
   The white image in the Black mind : a study of African American
literature / Jane Davis.
      p. cm.—(Contributions in Afro-American and African
studies, ISSN 0069–9624 ; no. 194)
   Includes bibliographical references (p.) and index.
   ISBN 0–313–30464–5 (alk. paper)
   1. American literature—Afro-American authors—History and
criticism.   2. Whites in literature.   3. Race in literature.
I. Title.   II. Series.
PS173.W46D38   2000
810.9'896073—dc21   99–36173

British Library Cataloguing in Publication Data is available.

Library of Congress Catalog Card Number: 99–36173
ISBN: 0–313–30464–5
ISSN: 0069–9624

First published in 2000

Greenwood Press, 88 Post Road West, Westport, CT 06881
An imprint of Greenwood Publishing Group, Inc.
www.greenwood.com

Printed in the United States of America

The paper used in this book complies with the
Permanent Paper Standard issued by the National
Information Standards Organization (Z39.48–1984).

10 9 8 7 6 5 4 3 2

This book is dedicated
to the people of
141 Watson Avenue,
a place which exists
more strongly in my mind
precisely because it no longer
exists in the material world:

Donna Davis
Dana Davis
Ruby Davis
Ernest Davis
Josephine Welch
Sandy

and to the
St. Charles School and Church
in Newark, New Jersey

July 10, 1967

Dear Mrs. Davis:

Thanks for your nice letter which I thought was very interesting and showed much insight. I'm glad you liked the book, and I agree with you that the problem of race hatred is getting to be a very difficult one. Perhaps much of the trouble has come from the fact that people have been living in a dream world, and have imagined that they had everything under control when they did not. Hence there will be some difficult times, and everyone will blame everyone else. It remains for individuals to be as tolerant and as understanding as they can, and to be really patient in living as Christian peacemakers in spite of all the conflict around them. That is about all we can do.

Cordially yours,

Thomas Merton.

Letter from Thomas Merton to Ruby Davis.

Contents

Preface

The aims of this book have been reflected in comments by several writers who have addressed the issue of whiteness, both before and during the current interest in "whiteness studies" and "the construction of whiteness." Peggy McIntosh, for example, a central thinker on the role of white privilege, has argued that many whites "think that racism doesn't affect them because they are not people of color; they do not see whiteness as a racial identity."[1] One of McIntosh's key ideas is how the arrogance of assuming oneself to be part of a raceless norm needs to be challenged in order to combat racism. Hence, the starting point for combating racism would seem to be, according to this argument, an examination of how assumptions about identity are at the foundation of white privilege and bigotry. If race, as Mark Twain remarked in *Pudd'nhead Wilson*, is a "fiction of law and custom," it is a fiction that is lived and operationalized, and many writers have called for its unmasking. Henry A. Giroux has articulated important related points:

> Central to any pedagogical approach to race and the politics of "whiteness" is the recognition that race is a set of attitudes, values, lived experiences, and affective identifications. However arbitrary and mythic, dangerous and variable, the fact is that racial categories exist and shape the lives of people differently within existing inequalities of power and wealth. . . . Rather than proposing the eradication of the concept of race itself, educators and other cultural workers need to take a detour through race in order to decide how "whiteness" might be renegotiated as a productive force in a politics of difference linked to a radical democratic project.[2]

This passage ties the study of whiteness to the need for social change. Years before the current interest in whiteness, this need was reflected in a dialogue between anthropologist Margaret Mead and James Baldwin:

Mead: . . . the offer—which is substantially the way I would phrase it—the offer that well-intentioned white people made is: "If you will be like us—

Baldwin: "You could join our clubs and come to our houses—

Mead: "And we'll pretend that you're just like us."

Baldwin: Yeah.

Mead: Which means of course that we'll deny you.

Baldwin: Exactly.

Mead: We'll deny your hair, we'll deny your skin, we'll deny your eyes. We deny you. We deny you when we accept you; we deny the ways in which you are not exactly like us, by ignoring them.

Baldwin: Yes.

Mead: And what black power is saying is: I want to accept myself first, and my parents, and I want to enjoy the way my mother and father look and from there—

Baldwin: Then we'll see.[3]

This dialogue returns us to the arrogance of the raceless norm of which Peggy McIntosh writes; moreover, it points out how this arrogance can attempt to cancel out black identity and difference. Both Baldwin and Mead see the need for such difference to be recognized. This point leads to the main topic in this volume: while granting the importance of white writers on the subject of race, it is imperative to devote significant analysis to blacks' perspectives on whiteness.

Several black writers have indicated the need for America to deal with blacks' perceptions of race in general and whiteness in particular and with the volatile nature of the subject. Ellis Cose, for instance, speaks of a perceptual chasm between blacks and whites on matters of race: "While polls consistently show that a majority of whites believe blacks face little or no discrimination in employment, most blacks believe just the opposite. That perceptual split is evident on virtually any question where race is a factor."[4] Certainly, part of this perceptual difference would include the absence, in many whites' consciousness, of how blacks perceive whiteness. This perception is clearly not uniform; however, as pointed out by Ralph Ellison, blacks can sometimes feel that they are "a spy in the enemy's country."[5] Ellison, like the other writers under discussion in this book, calls attention to the fact that there is a continual evaluation of whites by blacks as a result, in part, of the outsider status of blacks, the denial of which has been a factor in race relations.

Jamaica Kincaid continues this theme in her novel *Lucy*. The novel, a story of a young Antiguan woman who works as an au pair for a white family in New York, calls attention to the young black woman's awareness that the whites she meets seem devoid of the knowledge that she is a thinking, analytical being who is judging their behavior (and identity) at the same time that they are both oppressing and ignoring her (at times simultaneously). "How does a person get to be that way?" is the refrain of one section of the book.[6] "How do you get to be that way?" (20). The "way" referred to by Lucy is summed up in a passage where she contemplates a woman who is a friend of the family, someone who the woman for whom Lucy works seems to admire. Yet, trapped in Lucy's gaze, a far different evaluation emerges:

> Dinah now showered the children with affection—ruffling hair, pinching cheeks, picking Miriam up out of my lap, and ignoring me. To a person like Dinah, someone like me is "the girl"—as in "the girl who takes care of the children." It would never have occurred to her that I had sized her up immediately, that I viewed her as a cliché, a something not to be, a something to rise above, a something I was very familiar with. (58–59)

Kincaid's changing of perspective in this book in giving the evaluative power to the overlooked person, the outsider, the other, is central in raising the importance of an examination of the images of whites in blacks' minds. Yet, this passage raises another issue: the touchy nature of the subject and how some may not like what they find when confronted with blacks' perceptions of whites.

In dealing with this issue, two episodes which took place in Illinois, separated by several decades, are intriguing. In *American Hunger*, Richard Wright recalls his working as a dishwasher in a cafe in Chicago. His evaluation of his white coworkers is especially interesting:

> During my lunch hour, which I spent on a bench in a near-by park, the waitresses would come and sit beside me, talking at random, laughing, joking, smoking cigarettes. I learned about their tawdry dreams, their simple hopes, their home lives, their fear of feeling anything deeply, their sex problems, their husbands. They were an eager, restless, talkative, ignorant bunch, but casually kind and impersonal for all that. They knew nothing of hate and fear, and strove instinctively to avoid all passion.
>
> I often wondered what they were trying to get out of life, but I never stumbled upon a clue, and I doubt if they themselves had any notion. They lived on the surface of their days; their smiles were surface smiles, and their tears were surface tears. . . . How far apart in culture we stood! . . . It was in the psychological distance that separated the races that the deepest meaning of the problem of the Negro lay for me. For these poor, ignorant white girls to have understood my life would have meant nothing short of a vast revolution in theirs. . . . The essence of the irony of the plight of the Negro in America, to me, is that he is doomed to live in isolation while those who condemn him seek the basest goals of any people on earth.[7]

This passage, which begins as a discussion of Wright's coworkers, widens to become a commentary on white identity in Wright's view. The women's ignorance is, for Wright, a metaphor for the sterility and small-mindedness that he sees as constituting a huge part of the psychology of white America. The "revolution" needed for whites to understand such an evaluation of them is one of Wright's main concerns. And, indeed, one must be prompted to ask who would want to know such negative judgments about themselves. This desire to hide from such a harsh reading of whites can be understood as a main motivation of Wright's publisher not to include Wright's account of his negative judgments of the North in his autobiography, thus chopping what later became *American Hunger* from *Black Boy* and leaving that work originally to end on the misleadingly optimistic note of Wright's going to the Promised Land of the North. His perceptions of what he found there certainly must strike a nerve in some readers and a chord in others. The question of whether racialized negative judgments of whites is still a volatile issue is relevant to an example in contemporary America. In the 1998 gubernatorial Democratic primary held in Illinois, black politician Roland Burris was the front-runner during much of the campaign. Then, a fatal controversy arose: a television station showed a tape of a speech Burris had made earlier in the year in which he referred to his opponents as "non-qualified whiteboys." Specifically, Burris said, "I've got twenty years' experience in Illinois government and some of those other non-qualified whiteboys ought to get out." Subsequently, it was stated that Burris "said using the word 'boy' does not carry the negative connotation for white people that it does for African Americans because of the historic use of the word since the days of slavery."[8] (That some television stations "bleeped" the word whiteboy in showing the tape of Burris' speech indicates that the word was presented to the public as being on a par with a curse word, unallowable on television.) Yet, Burris' reply seems off the mark; he seemed to apologize for the second syllable of whiteboy when, if one recalls the theories of McIntosh and Mead, in particular, it may have been the first syllable that was the real problem. That Burris lost the election is clearly relevant; was this a sign of white voters' sensitivity to having revealed to them what a black person saw when whites were trapped in his gaze?

Race is still a volatile issue in America, and sensitivity to blunt discussions of race is a significant factor. According to Michael Eric Dyson,

The tragedy of our condition is that . . . many . . . Americans . . . have ignored . . . how race continues to shape American life. Worse yet, they blame those who resist the color-blind myth for extending, rather than exposing, the hold race still has on the American character. But we cannot overcome the history of racial oppression in our nation without understanding and addressing the subtle, subversive ways race continues to poison our lives. The ostrich approach of burying our collective head in the sand of historical amnesia or political denial will not work. We must face race head on.[9]

Dyson's comments extend to the need for looking at images of whites in blacks' imagination without flinching. This point is especially relevant as it seems that the purpose of many writers was similar to Frederick Douglass' desire to "make a weapon" of bigoted whites—a weapon to be used against themselves.

I would like to make a few final comments about what this book is intended to be and what it is not intended to be. First, while it employs a taxonomic system in discussing the images of whites in the first and last chapters, it is not a taxonomy. Second, it is not intended to be an encyclopedic book report masquerading as criticism; that is, it does not merely (or primarily) summarize literature, but interprets it. On this score, the subject of ideology is relevant. As stated by W. Lawrence Hogue, "[T]he once acceptable assumptions that critical practice is an innocent activity . . . have been quelled almost completely" by the unmasking of the role of ideology in reading and interpreting literature by much critical theory.[10] Hogue also states that writing is "a way in which we attempt to establish new and relevant myths and conventions to explain our lived experiences" (ix). These comments greatly illuminate the practice of criticism. While it is a naive assumption that critics are "objective," as Hogue points out, it seems an illusion to prop up notions of infallibility.

Many years before critical theory raised the issue of ideology, Søren Kierkegaard anticipated the subject in his critique of objectivity and analysis of subjectivity. In a chapter entitled "Truth Is Subjectivity," Kierkegaard writes: "[T]he objective way deems itself to have a security which the subjective way does not have and, of course, existence and existing cannot be thought of in combination with objective security."[11] One of Kierkegaard's main ideas here is that existence is an unfolding, often seemingly irrational process; our consciousness is the mediator between facts and our arrival at what we believe to be truth. To quote a dense and amazing passage:

> When subjectivity is truth, the conceptual determination of the truth must include an expression for the antithesis to objectivity, a memento of the fork in the road where the way swings off. . . . Here is such a definition of truth: An objective uncertainty held fast in an appropriation-process of the most passionate inwardness is the truth, the highest truth attainable for an existing individual. At the point where the way swings off (and this cannot be specified objectively, since it is a matter of subjectivity), there objective knowledge is placed in abeyance. Thus the subject merely has, objectively, the uncertainty. . . . The truth is precisely the venture which chooses an objective uncertainty with the passion of the infinite. . . . But the above definition of truth is an equivalent expression for faith. Without risk there is no faith. (182)

This passage captures the paradox of interpretation (and literary criticism): the value of searching for and expressing one's beliefs in the meaning of works of literature without recourse to saying that one has arrived at a final, essentialist truth. To illustrate this idea, Hogue's discussion of his aims indicates "where the way swings off" in literary criticism: "This book is my attempt to produce new definitions of and assumptions about literature that complement my own political and social interests and concerns, my own lived experiences" (ix). To me, this is the most honest and valid statement of the concerns of the truly intriguing works of literary criticism; others may agree or disagree.

NOTES

1. Peggy McIntosh, "White Privilege: Unpacking the Invisible Knapsack," *Peace and Freedom* (July/August 1989): 12.

2. Henry A. Giroux, "Racial Politics and the Pedagogy of Whiteness," in *Whiteness*, ed. Mike Hill (New York: New York University Press, 1997), 294–95.

3. James Baldwin and Margaret Mead, *A Rap on Race* (New York: Dell Publishing, 1971), 10.

4. Ellis Cose, "To the Victor, Few Spoils," *Newsweek*, 29 March 1993, 54.

5. Ralph Ellison, *Invisible Man* (New York: Random House, 1952), 16.

6. Jamaica Kincaid, *Lucy* (New York: Farrar Straus Giroux, 1990), 17.

7. Richard Wright, *American Hunger* (New York: Harper and Row, 1977), 12–13.

8. Scott Fornek and Michael Gillis, "Burris Deflects Controversy," *Chicago Sun-Times*, 27 February 1998, 3.

9. Michael Eric Dyson, *Race Rules* (Reading, Mass.: Addison-Wesley Publishing, 1996), 223.

10. W. Lawrence Hogue, *Discourse and the Other* (Durham, N.C.: Duke University Press, 1986), 1.

11. Søren Kierkegaard, *Kierkegaard's Concluding Unscientific Postscript*, trans. David F. Swenson and Walter Lowrie (Princeton, N.J.: Princeton University Press, 1941), 182.

Acknowledgments

This book is the product of many years of reading and living; hence, there are many people to thank. First, Chris GoGwilt gets the Oscar for being one of the few and not, as the saying goes, one of the many; his insights also greatly helped this study. Some of my key ideas on race and on whiteness were inspired by a National Endowment for the Humanities (NEH) seminar directed by Eric J. Sundquist on race in American literature; thus, I thank Eric for the inspiration. My research on whiteness was also inspired by an NEH institute on postcolonial literature, given at Indiana University and directed by Albert Wertheim, and by my colleagues while I was a Mellon Fellow at the Africana Center at Cornell University. Some people who contributed significantly to my spirit during the period that this book was written deserve great thanks: Elliot Dawes, Aleah Bacquie, John Staunton, Bill Mottolese, Lisa Archibald, Jerry McGill, Heather Bernard, Gloria Parker, Kevin Gray, Stephen McHayle (for being one of the few rather than one of the many), Nancy Buckley, and Tina Andreadis. Talks with Egbert Hall lifted my spirits. An imaginary bouquet of roses goes to Sean McKenna. Denny Conley was another source of support during the period of the writing of this book. Two people who mean more than they know are Lisa Orloff and Kevin Hibbert, who were heaven-sent at a difficult time. This book reflects my understanding of that time. Eric Cliette has meant much to me and shared some of the period of the writing of this book. Moreover, Carolyn, Ayannah, and Jim Wells provided much appreciated friendship and connection over the years that spanned the writing of this book. In addition, I owe a great debt of gratitude to the professor who first showed me how exciting the study of literature could be: Dr. Richard Sypher, who endured me as an undergraduate at Hofstra University. Without Dr. Sypher I might not have discovered the personal meaning and joy that can come from the intensive study of complex issues in literature. The impact of his class on American fiction has shaped me as a reader, writer, and professor. Also, great thanks to my mother, Ruby Davis, who read the manuscript. And eternal love to those who unknowingly provided "spiritual milk" over the years: Sandy, Danny, Julie, Amalia, Emma, and Zach. Perhaps some of the most important words spoken to me in the last several years were written by Delores Morgan, whom I met at Literacy Chicago: "Don't give up before the miracles come." Finally, for his insight and professionalism, I wish to thank my editor, George F. Butler.

These and unnamed others contributed greatly to the spirit and substance of this book.

Chapter 1

The White Image in the Black Mind

In an article written about the book *A Common Destiny: Blacks and American Society*, edited by Gerald David James and Robin M. Williams, Jr., *Time* magazine writer Walter Shapiro stated, "The implicit message of *A Common Destiny* is that white America, left to its own devices, will never complete the unfinished task of creating racial equality."[1] The central thesis of this study is that black American authors have long known and expressed in their works that this apathy is a key component of most whites' identity concerning their attitudes toward blacks and that a neurotic self-righteousness among whites allows them to believe that they are not the racists that blacks perceive them to be. This denial is a crutch whites use throughout life to prop up their own self-image.

The ways in which black writers have understood white identity is a subject that illuminates both race relations and many whites' maintenance of their privileges and delusions of superiority—even while they charge that racism is a figment of blacks' imagination, a "race card" which was, in fact, invented by whites. Whites' "record," as James Baldwin sometimes called it, is represented in the many works in which black writers diagnose the identity of the whites who have held back racial progress. In such works, black writers demonstrate that racism is both a behavioral and attitudinal phenomenon and a matter of identity, thereby revealing the deep-rooted nature of bigotry. These writings reflect what *Time* stated about white apathy in the article on *A Common Destiny* written in 1989.

Forty-four years earlier, an essay written about Richard Wright states: "According to a recent survey, Wright says, 60 percent of the whites in America believe that the Negro is being fairly treated. The Negro, he is convinced, will have to assume the initiative."[2] If whites' laziness was treated as

a revelation in 1989, this statement mirrors the lack of concern about erad-
icating white bigotry that has existed among many whites for decades, to say
the least. Furthermore, the "initiative" has been assumed by black American
writers who have attempted to show whites to themselves and to nonwhite
readers who have been the targets of the aspects of white identity analyzed
in this study. These works are designed, in part, to prompt whites to assume
the initiative in examining themselves of which President Bill Clinton spoke
in 1996: "White racism may be black people's burden but it is white people's
problem. We must clean our house."[3]

    The importance of a study of the image of whites in blacks' works is made
clear in bell hooks's "Representations of Whiteness in the Black
Imagination," which is, in fact, a call for such studies. In referring to her
study of criticism (primarily postcolonial criticism), hooks states,

> I found that much writing bespeaks the continued fascination with the way
> white minds . . . perceive blackness, and very little expressed interest in rep-
> resentations of whiteness in the black imagination. Black cultural and social
> critics allude to such representations in their writing, yet only a few have dared
> to make explicit those perceptions of whiteness that they think will discomfort
> or antagonize white readers.[4]

To be sure, despite the recent interest in the topic of "the construction of
whiteness," the discussion of racial typology seems primarily to have concentrated on whites' representations of blacks; for example, in such important works as historian George Fredrickson's *The Black Image in the White
Mind*, film historian Donald Bogle's *Toms, Coons, Mulattoes, Mammies and
Bucks*, and the late filmmaker Marlon Riggs's films, *Ethnic Notions* and *Color
Adjustment*. Each of these works is a brilliant presentation of whites' stereotyping of blacks to maintain white supremacy. Yet, it is certainly past time for
us to turn our attention more fully to the nature and function of the racial
typology of whites found in black literature and understand how it serves a
different function from the advancement of racism that is at the heart of
whites' stereotyping of blacks. In short, one of the primary aims of this volume is to accomplish what hooks states at the outset of "Representations of
Whiteness":

> Although there has never been any official body of black people in the United
> States who have gathered as anthropologists and/or ethnographers whose
> central project is the study of whiteness, black folks have, from slavery on,
> shared with one another "special" knowledge of whiteness gleaned from close
> scrutiny of white people. . . . [I]ts purpose was to help black folks cope and
> survive in a white supremacist society. For years, black domestic servants,
> working in white homes, acted as informants who brought knowledge back to
> segregated communities—details, facts, observations, psychoanalytic readings
> of the white "Other." (31)

My research shows that black writers have acted as ethnographers of sorts; their works are aimed at "informing" the reader of the various guises of the identities of racist whites. This typology of whites advances the readers' understanding of the diagnosis of major black writers concerning how many whites relate to blacks and how these ways of relating are manifested in the representations of whiteness in the literature. This discussion of racial typology is focused on the manifestation of white racism because that is what the overwhelming bulk of black literature that features whites examines. Also, this presentation of the topic does not reflect an approach that had an agenda or a hypothesis that it set out to prove affirming any a priori conclusions about whites in black literature, but instead it represents my findings after having read a huge amount of black literature. It is my desire to give an accurate presentation of major trends in black literature. Furthermore, I do not define blacks' typology of whites as stereotypes, which Thomas Pettigrew, in "Prejudice," defines as "cognitive distortions" whose aim is to simplify and thus distort the "other."[5] Instead, I believe that the typology of whites under discussion are archetypes, in the sense that archetypes are recurring identity types in a culture—identity types that are often left unexamined but whose examination would be a key to freeing individuals (and thereby society) from duplicating negative forms of identity that hover as shadows over a culture, thus hindering individual and cultural progress. These concepts are essential in shedding light on the nature and purpose of black writers' exposure of recurring identity types among whites as blacks have judged them.

What follows is a list of the images of whites in black literature that I compiled after discussing black stereotypes with author Susan Witty. These are presented as manifestations of neuroses that sometimes exist alone in an individual or in combination with characteristics of another identity type. Furthermore, although there are other major images of whites in black literature, the following list represents the central, most provocative images of whites in the minds of black writers.

1. The overt white supremacist. Individuals in this category can exhibit straightforward acts of bigotry or use sneaky and duplicitous strategies to fulfill their campaign of oppression or the extermination of blacks. They attempt to justify themselves by believing that blacks earn their brutal, racist behavior.

2. The hypocrite. These internally (and perhaps, unconsciously) flaming racists project a façade of being interested in morality and justice. If conscious, their hypocrisy may be a way of gaining the fruits of acting on others' racism without risking the taint of being perceived as the first type. If unconscious, they try to convince themselves that they do not have dirty hands in promoting bigotry. This may be the most insidious type of racism because it is the most difficult to expose and, therefore, to fight.

3. The good-hearted weakling. These individuals often think that they are genuinely sympathetic to blacks' plight, but at the moment of truth,

when they must act on this self-proclaimed enlightenment, they are unable to stand up adequately for these sentiments either because of their loyalty to the dominant group or their inability to risk the condemnation of fellow whites by aligning themselves with blacks. Too often, as they have been morally castrated from years of fence-straddling, their concern for blacks is also castrated—ultimately, they fail to act on it.

4. The liberal. Liberals think that they truly care for blacks and have their best interests at heart. However, they often have an attitude of guardianship of blacks as if they are trustees of them as expressed in Nelson Mandela's *The Struggle Is My Life,* which illuminates how this aspect of white psychology was prevalent in South Africa.[6] Liberals do not consult sufficiently the objects of their do-goodism about their own feelings on how to respond to racism but instead dictate (however "kindly") to blacks how they should act and think to gain advancement—on white people's terms. In other words, they want to run the show. This is another very subtle, complex form of racism because the reference point for liberals is how they as whites think blacks should feel and behave. And no one is more defensive than liberals when blacks question their progressiveness. (The word "liberal" is used here not in the strict sense of connoting leftists but to designate self-proclaimed white progressives in general.)

These types are briefly discussed here and more fully examined in chapter 2. Works of black writers past and present, including James Baldwin and Manning Marable, who have given us insights into white psychology, will be utilized to illuminate central characteristics of black authors' perceptions of whites in the literature under discussion. For those readers who may feel that I have neglected the "good white" as represented in black literature, my response is that this type exists to such a small degree that it does not merit discussion. Even Max, the Communist lawyer in Richard Wright's *Native Son,* who seems to articulate the blacks' plight, ultimately fails to understand Bigger Thomas, the protagonist of the novel. Thus, while there may exist what the late socialist leader Michael Harrington called "decent liberalism" as opposed to the bogus kind, the failure of progressiveness among many whites is a main topic of black literature.

What follows are brief descriptions of some people or characters in black literature who exemplify the images defined above. These are certainly not the only works in which these images occur, but they are among the most striking.

IMAGES OF WHITES IN BLACK LITERATURE

The Overt White Supremacist

Lyle, the poor white storeowner in James Baldwin's *Blues for Mister Charlie,* who murders a young black man in the Civil Rights era South who confronts him about his racist attitudes. (Lyle will be discussed in greater depth in the following chapter.)

The fascist in Richard Wright's *The Outsider*, who refuses to let blacks live in his New York City apartment building and physically attacks the protagonist, Cross, when he learns that he is staying there.

The pregnant white woman in Alice Walker's first novel, *The Third Life of Grange Copeland*, who would rather drown than be pulled from the water by a black man.

The white man in Gwendolyn Brooks's poem, "The Life of Lincoln West," who sees the little boy in a movie theater and comments loudly to his friend on what he feels is the repulsiveness of the little boy's dark skin.

The whites who kill Roy in Langston Hughes's story "Home" after they see him talking innocently to a white schoolteacher. (Roy's sophistication—he is a musician who has lived in Europe—is a strong factor in the whites' hostility toward him on his return to the South because he threatens their shaky illusions of superiority.)

Most of the whites in Wright's autobiography, *Black Boy*, including those who are infuriated by Wright's desire to learn about the optical business when he is working for an optical company and those who kill his Uncle Hoskins.

Mrs. Auld in Frederick Douglass' *The Narrative of the Life of Frederick Douglass*. (Douglass traces the transformation in this woman, who is the wife of a slave owner, from being a person who is kind to blacks to becoming a person who absorbs the prevalent attitude that blacks are inferior and should simply be subservient to whites.)

Mrs. Bellmont and her daughter, wealthy New England family members, in a nineteenth-century novel written by Harriet Wilson, *Our Nig*, who despise the heroine, Frado, because of her race and physically abuse and mistreat her when she works as a servant for them.

The little white boy in Countee Cullen's poem "Incident" who, when observed by a little black boy on a train who expects a friendly greeting from him, spits out the word "nigger."

The judge (among others) in W.E.B. Du Bois' story "Of the Coming of John" in *The Souls of Black Folks*, who is shocked and appalled that John would return from college with ideas of improving the condition of blacks, without even thinking to follow the white man's direction.

Finally, and as a living illustration of many of the whites already discussed who sometimes attempt to protect their illusion of supremacy through violence, "our sick white brothers" mentioned by Dr. Martin Luther King, Jr., in his last speech.[7] (The media, which endlessly played the final part of the speech in which King talked about the possibility of being killed, mostly deleted the allusion to those whites who made threats during his trip to Memphis, although the mentioning of the threats of "our sick white brothers" is what introduces the final, famous section of the speech. As a result, viewers were given an impression that King merely had prophetic premonitions of death, as if by magic, instead of the truth: he knew that his death could very well be at hand because of the attitudes and actions of "our sick white brothers.")

The Hypocrite

Major Carteret in Charles W. Chesnutt's *The Marrow of Tradition*. (The major presents himself as a genteel aristocrat even while he mounts campaigns of white supremacy that endorse lynching and eventually result in a white riot to deprive blacks' progress toward equality in the South. Carteret will be analyzed extensively in the following chapter.)

The white members of the Brotherhood in Ralph Ellison's *Invisible Man*, who use black members to give the party greater visibility and then completely drop their interest in Harlem when they determine that the blacks are no longer useful to them—all the while demanding that black members denounce their individuality and give themselves completely to an organization that merely sees them as tools to be manipulated at will.

Mr. Dalton in Wright's *Native Son*. (While he professes to have blacks' interests at heart, he is one of the major slumlords of Chicago and consigns blacks to overpriced, overcrowded housing. He is an exploitive segregationist in sheep's clothing.)

Several characters in Ann Petry's novel *The Street*, including the white lawyer who tells the heroine, Lutie, that she must pay him two hundred dollars to get her son out of a juvenile center, smugly congratulating himself on taking advantage of the black woman's ignorance that she does not need to pay a lawyer (and may not need a lawyer) in such a case; and the owner of the club in which Lutie, desperate for money, sings, who does not (unbeknownst to her) intend to pay her but to give her trinkets to induce her into having sex with him. (This character type relies on trickery to retain power.)

The whites who run the home for disabled children in the story "Berry," by Langston Hughes, who exploitively underpay him for his somewhat menial job, thinking incorrectly that he is too ignorant to know the difference, and then fire him even though he is the only one who gives the children love, unlike the whites at the institution, on the pretext that he is harmful to the children.

The white man who comes to visit the Younger family after they plan to move into a white neighborhood in Lorraine Hansberry's *A Raisin in the Sun*. (Using a friendly façade that makes the family think that he has come to welcome them, he really wants to persuade them not to live near whites.)

The European whites in Nella Larsen's *Quicksand* who simultaneously treat the heroine, Helga, as if they adore her, but who feel this way because they see her as an exotic, emotional, impulsive black who embodies the stereotypes they impose on and expect from her.

Many of the female Civil Rights workers in Alice Walker's *Meridian* who, while pretending to be interested in black equality, feel themselves to be more desirable to black men than black women are and regard black men as sexual objects whose prowess they want to experience.

The usher in Claude McKay's autobiography, *A Long Way from Home*, who pretends that there is no seat in the orchestra for McKay when he comes to the theater (with orchestra tickets) to review a play, humiliating him by telling him that he must sit in the balcony of the New York City theater.

Lula, the white woman in LeRoi Jones's *Dutchman*, who, in the course of the play, shows her multilayered racism. (She earns her place in the category of the hypocrite because—even though she uses racial epithets when she talks to and flirts with the young black man Clay, which might seem to place her into the category of the overt white supremacist, which is manifested more fully in her murder of Clay—she uses her flirtatiousness and sexuality to draw Clay into her web. Her racism is lethal precisely because she misrepresents her motives.)

The whites discussed by Margaret Mead and James Baldwin in *A Rap on Race* who pretend to embrace blacks but whose friendliness is contingent upon blacks' never reminding them of their differences from (and with) whites.[8]

The Good-Hearted Weakling

Parnell in Baldwin's *Blues for Mister Charlie*, the seemingly progressive white man, who maintains his friendship with Lyle even while he tries to maintain his friendship with Meridian, the father of Lyle's victim. (The personal confusion and betrayal of blacks manifested in this duality will be examined in the discussion of Parnell as the quintessential good-hearted weakling in chapter 2.)

The Communist lawyer, Max, in *Native Son*, who as Bigger's lawyer, is able to articulate how racism led Bigger to a life of crime but is frightened and horrified by Bigger's affirmation of his crimes, even though he seems to have articulated these very feelings in his courtroom speech. (It seems that Max can accept Bigger only as a statistic, a representative of the "Negro problem," not as an independent human being.)

Eva, the white lover of Cross in Wright's *The Outsider*, who romanticizes blacks' suffering yet seems to identify with them only as victims; her conversations with Cross show a condescending sympathy for blacks but she, like Max, cannot accept an autonomous black person, as is shown in her suicidal rejection of her lover after she learns about his crimes. (Even the district attorney seems better able to understand Cross than Eva; Eva's "enlightened" attitude toward blacks seems to exist only as long as she can sympathize with their inferior status in American society.)

Vivaldo in James Baldwin's *Another Country*, who wants to believe that he is in love with Ida, the sister of his dead black friend, Rufus. (Baldwin's writing early in the book of Vivaldo's habitual trips to Harlem to have sex with black women make the reader wonder if he is honest and strong enough to love any black woman or if he just needs Ida as a crutch to prove his manhood to himself and to prop up his ambiguous feelings about his sexuality. One main subplot is Vivaldo's struggling to come to terms with his bisexual desires.)

The whites attacked by Era Bell Thompson in the essay "Some of My Best Friends Are White," who think of themselves as liberals and yet do such things as confess that they are afraid of what their friends will think of them if they have their black acquaintances to their homes.[9] (Thompson's point is that such gutlessness is part of an overall pattern among whites who want to think of themselves as not being racist but who will even tell their black friends that they feel they cannot withstand other whites' reactions if they act on their ideas about racial equality.)

In *The Autobiography of Malcolm X*, Malcolm elucidates the good-hearted weakling strain among whites and challenges whites (after leaving the Nation of Islam) to work among other whites to combat racism rather than join coalitions with blacks.[10] His message is that, as many examples from black literature attest, this is what many whites fail to do, which makes their desire for racial progress seem like so much hot air.

The good-hearted weakling is often a liberal.

The Liberal

The rich white couple, the Pembertons, in Langston Hughes's "Poor Little Black Fellow," whose raising of a black child, Arnie, is contingent upon their control over his identity. (The Pembertons are our representative liberals in chapter 2.)

The whites about whom Alain Locke writes in "The New Negro," who view blacks as objects to be helped and managed but not to be viewed as fully developed human beings who should aspire to psychological and material independence from them.[11]

The white husband of the female protagonist in LeRoi Jones's *The Slave*, who seems to be interested in blacks' progress until he realizes that it means an alteration in his and other whites' personal status and security.

Harriet Beecher Stowe, in James Baldwin's view in "Everybody's Protest Novel," who was a sloppy sentimentalist in her kindly view of blacks in *Uncle Tom's Cabin*. (According to Baldwin, sentimentality, by definition, is an exaggerated display of artificial emotion which is an attempt to sublimate the sentimentalist's actual hostility and disdain for the objects of his or her false sympathy.[12] Stowe's good intentions were undermined by her complete failure to see blacks as humans of any complexity but as mere objects to be categorized and contorted into semihumans.)

Mr. Norton, the white Bostonian benefactor of a black college, in Ralph Ellison's *Invisible Man*, who sees the college as a way of molding blacks into what he wants them to be and is terrified by blacks beyond his control, as is shown in his near nervous breakdown when he hears Jim Trueblood tell his tale of incest. (Beyond blacks civilized by him, Norton seems to think, is unthinkable chaos.)

Mr. Ostrowski, the schoolteacher in *The Autobiography of Malcolm X*, who seems to think it is benevolent to snatch young Malcolm's dreams of being a lawyer from him—it is only realistic for blacks to aspire to menial employment.

The benefactor in James Weldon Johnson's *The Autobiography of an Ex-Colored Man*, who also seems to think that it is benevolent to tear the title character's dreams of being part of black culture and helping to advance it, seemingly on the pretext that the soon-to-be-ex-colored man is too refined to be subjected to the indignities blacks suffer and should not align himself with other blacks. (Again, a white person's good intentions take the form of identity control over a black person.)

Mrs. Dalton in *Native Son*, who wants Bigger to be educated, he feels, not because she really cares even to know his desires, but simply because she wants to impose her view of what is good for Bigger on him—with no care to know his hopes and dreams. (Mary, her radical daughter, and Jan, Mary's Communist boyfriend, also want to direct how Bigger should think and act; they seem to think, "You must act like my equal and be my friend—whether you like it or not." Bigger's discomfort with these seemingly progressive whites conveys Wright's belief in the alienation many blacks feel at being the targets of insensitive, unempathic, and manipulative liberalism.)

Ann and Michael, the young white couple living in New York during the Harlem Renaissance in Langston Hughes's "Slave on the Block," whose desire to control blacks even as they feel that they like them is symbolized by their hiring a young black man, Luther, to pose for a picture which they mean to capture the essence of blacks: wonderful innocents. (Hughes shows that the couple is fascinated by blacks but never befriended by them. The equality of true social interaction is precluded by the control that the couple wants to have over the objects of their fascination. Thus, in this case, as in others, liberals are shown to be people who have deluded themselves into thinking that they are enlightened—when what they really want is to be guardians or keepers of blacks.)

Other writers, including Kenneth B. Clark, John O. Killens, Lerone Bennett, Jr., and Manning Marable, have also given insights into the mindset at work in the forms of identity prevalent in black literature.

UNMASKING THE ROLE OF IDEOLOGY

The need for the kind of study of which hooks writes in "Representations of Whiteness" is best expressed in James Baldwin's "White Man's Guilt," which must be one of the most important and perceptive examinations ever written about white psychology regarding racism. Baldwin begins the essay with key issues that are among the fundamental ideas of this study:

I have often wondered, and it is not a pleasant wonder, just what white Americans talk about with one another.

I wonder this because they do not, after all, seem to find very much to say to *me*, and I concluded long ago that they found the color of my skin inhibiting. This color seems to operate as a most disagreeable mirror, and a great deal of one's energy is expended in reassuring white Americans that they do not see what they do see.

This is utterly futile, of course, since they *do* see what they see. And what they see is an appallingly oppressive and bloody history known all over the world. What they see is a disastrous, continuing, present condition which menaces them, and for which they bear an inescapable responsibility. But since in the main they seem to lack the energy to change this condition they would rather not be reminded of it. Does this mean that in their conversation with one another they simply make reassuring sounds? It scarcely seems possible and yet, on the other hand, it seems all too likely. In any case, whatever they bring to one another, it is certainly not freedom from guilt. The guilt remains, more deeply rooted, more securely lodged, than the oldest of old fears.

And to have to deal with such people can be unutterably exhausting, for they, with a dazzling ingenuity . . . are defending themselves against charges which one . . . has not really, for the moment, made. One does not *have* to make them. The record is there for all the world to read. . . . One wishes that Americans—white Americans—would read, for their own sakes, this record and stop defending themselves against it. Only then will they be enabled to change their lives.[13]

The most important reasons for readers to examine blacks' images of whites are expressed in this passage: that blacks reflect to whites an image of their identity which rebukes their idealized self-image; that many whites do nothing among themselves to face their own bigotry but try to avoid recognizing their racism through evasion and repression; and that, as a result, blacks suffer from what I would call tolerance exhaustion—the feeling of being fed up and frustrated with whites' transparent refusal to assess themselves. These psychological evasions, Baldwin theorizes, have drastic effects on whites' identity which, by closing off the truth, prevent honest discussions between blacks and whites about race. Baldwin continues,

> [T]he history of white people has led them to a fearful, baffling place where they have begun to lose touch with reality—to lose touch, that is, with themselves. . . . They do not know how this came about; they do not dare examine how this came about. On the one hand, they can scarcely dare to open a dialogue [with blacks] which must, if it is honest, become a personal confession—a cry for help and healing, which is really, I think, the basis of all dialogues—and, on the other hand, the black man can scarcely dare to open a dialogue [with whites] which must, if it is honest, become a personal confession which, fatally, contains an accusation. And yet, if neither of us can do this, each of us will perish in those traps in which we have been struggling for so long. (412)

The literature of blacks concerning whites contains many of what perhaps the majority of whites might call accusations. As Baldwin points out, however, it is essential for human progress for both races (indeed, all races) to look closely at the nature of bigotry—especially bigotry that is practiced and maintained, in great part, as a result of the denial of its existence. Baldwin points out another obstacle to whites' looking in the mirror blacks hold up to them: when confronted by blacks' perceptions of them, he implies, many whites adopt a victim mentality. This mentality is expressed by Baldwin's representation of what he feels is most whites' response in such situations: "I have nothing against you, nothing! What have you *got* against me? *What* do *you* want?" (411). It is no wonder, then, that there is a general neglect in the reading and teaching of American literature concerning one of the major topics that is part of the black American tradition: white identity.

John O. Killens makes central observations about white psychology and the fear of facing what blacks think of whites. In *Black Man's Burden,* he makes statements relevant both to the white image in blacks' minds and why many educators (among others) are silent on the subject.

Can you imagine the slave master living with the fear that his liberated slave will preach at his, the master's, funeral? [White] western man lives with a built-in nightmare that the disinherited will soon and finally inherit the earth and rewrite the history of the last five hundred years and that "niggers" everywhere will be vindicated, from Birmingham to Johannesburg, which means that mankind, no matter what color, will at long last be vindicated.[14]

This passage is intriguing in at least two ways. First, one may ask if blacks' "data" (that is, writings about whites by blacks) is, in fact, a funeral oration that debunks white supremacy and claims of innocence from racism and hypocrisy. Second, the latter part of the passage is certainly relevant to current immigration debates and to white ideas that undeserving minorities have an easy road because they are given things by whites not because of merit but because these things are taken from deserving whites (e.g., Killens's remarks on minorities "inheriting the earth"). Most important, Killens's ideas that "niggers" everywhere "will be vindicated" during the blacks' funeral oration raises questions about what is the nature of this vindication. Readers may have different interpretations of this idea. For the purposes of this study, the most important form of vindication is that blacks have understood and kept literary records of the identity of white bigots—bigots who most often have as their defense mechanism the illusion that they are not being judged—and often exposed—by blacks.

Baldwin, again in "White Man's Guilt," illuminates why this defense mechanism is rooted in psychological weakness which he contends is manifested in the identity of many whites (particularly of the more liberal or seemingly progressive sort) in their conscious or unconscious racial attitudes when he states that "people who imagine that history flatters them (as it does, indeed, since they wrote it) are impaled on their history like a butterfly on a pin . . . [whites] are dimly, or vividly, aware that the history they have fed themselves is mainly a lie, but they do not know how to release themselves from it, and they suffer enormously from the resulting personal incoherence" (410–11). Baldwin continues, "This incoherence is heard nowhere more plainly than in those stammering, terrified dialogues which white Americans sometimes entertain with the black conscience, the black [person] in America. The nature of this stammering can be reduced to a plea. Do not blame me. I was not there. I did not do it" (411). The duality that Baldwin captures—guilt and self-absolution—is one of the main factors that keeps America stuck in the cycle of racism, which could be combatted, according to Baldwin, if whites would look self-critically in the "mirror" or "conscience" provided by many black people.

Comments made by Lerone Bennett, Jr., in "The White Problem in America," coupled with Baldwin's essay, make evident the importance for readers to become acquainted with and to analyze blacks' images of whites. This theme of black literature combats what I would term the myth of agentless racism, which is a particular crutch of many whites who think of themselves as progressive on racial matters. In *The Rage of a Privileged Class*, Ellis Cose illustrates that in contemporary America, whites often dismiss charges of racism, as if they were a figment of blacks' imagination (which has sent some blacks in search of a new word to replace racism). As is implicit in Bennett's essay, the purpose of such whites' defensiveness is clear: how many whites are honest enough to define racism in a way that implicates them? This dishonesty gives rise to the transparent ruse that racism must be defined only as conscious acts intentionally designed to demean blacks in quantifiable ways. Yet, how many whites sit down and think, "I am now going to do something racist?" Even George Wallace, while proudly proclaiming himself a segregationist during the Civil Rights era, did not proclaim himself to be a racist. Most blacks have, no doubt, suffered the unintentional racism of inexcusably ignorant whites, whether in white assumptions that blacks are hired for good positions only to fill quotas or in whites' telling racist jokes they think blacks will appreciate. On these topics, Bennett's words, written over thirty years ago, are especially relevant to contemporary society: "It is fashionable nowadays to think of racism as a vast impersonal system for which no one is responsible. But this is still another evasion. Racism did not fall from the sky. . . . No: racism in America was made [by whites]."[15]

This myth of agentless racism helps explain Baldwin's statement that the white person has psychologically "locked himself into a place where he is doomed to continue repeating" acts of bigotry.[16] One again sees how America is stuck in a cycle of "eternal recurrence" concerning racism. Consequently, one needs to reflect on both writers' ideas on many whites' evasion from admitting their own racism and their self-absolution. Baldwin points out, "One can measure very neatly white American's distance from his conscience—from himself—by observing the distance between himself and black people. One has only to ask oneself who established this distance. Who is this distance designed to protect? And from what is this distance designed to protect him?" (412). Who, Baldwin is asking, is responsible for racism? How can we address the issue of a white's giving responsibility to blacks? Black literature can at least help us to understand these issues and to demythologize the identities of those who—intentionally or unintentionally—keep racism alive.

Psychologist Kenneth B. Clark has fascinating theories on the issues raised by Baldwin and Bennett, particularly concerning what is at the heart of whites' "personal incoherence," in his essay "What Motivates American Whites?" Clark finds this racial schizophrenia to be at the heart of the foundation of America's and whites' professed beliefs in the concepts of equality best expressed in the Declaration of Independence. That Thomas Jefferson, in his draft of this document, denounced King George's support of slavery as "barbarous" but simultaneously was a slave owner himself and felt that

American blacks should be colonized (ironic for the intellectual giant in the fight against American colonization by England) would be consistent with Clark's ideas on the basic dichotomy within white Americans.[17] In his central thesis, Clark asserts,

> The white Americans' espousal of the American creed is real and meaningful for them. It is the expression of their desire for equality, security, and status—for themselves. . . . [Racial inequality results in] a complex, paradoxical way, a basis for subjective satisfaction. [The white person's] denial of equality to those who are visibly different is a manifestation of his desire for status, and an enhancement of his subjective feelings of having obtained a superior status. It would probably be a psychological calamity [for whites] for the Negro either to disappear or for him to succeed in translating the words and promises of democracy into day to day reality. It would then be necessary for the American whites to either find other scapegoats, or to face . . . the intolerable state of their own emptiness. In this sense, therefore, the American creed and American racism are not contradictory. Both appear to reflect the pathetic desire of insecure people to be "aristocrats" rather than peasants.[18]

On reading this passage, one can surmise that Alfred Adler's theory that compensation for a perceived weakness is, perhaps, the main feature of an individual's psychology helps explain Clark's ideas, for Clark implies that whites' conscious or unconscious need for a belief in their supremacy is a compensatory tool for their knowledge or fear of their possible inferior status—whether inferior in comparison to others or to their fantasies of what they want to be—and thus for their feelings about their position in relation to blacks.

According to Clark, a basic part of the psychology of many whites regarding racism is to maintain bigotry while using a stated belief in principles of equality to perform self-absolution and thus promote a feeling of psychological superiority. This mind-set has been so deeply ingrained in the American character from the very founding of the country, Clark seems to imply, that for many whites at this point in history, it is inescapable and unconscious (and, perhaps, even preconscious for some). In addition, Clark believes that the drive for status exists with a need for such advancement to be denied to others; thus he explains many whites' need for blacks to stay in an inferior position in American society (52–53). If one accepts these ideas, Clark seems to be asking, how could one expect anything more from many whites than an external, self-proclaimed freedom from prejudice that exists simultaneously with a desire for supremacy—a desire which is externalized in the identity of many whites in so many acts of discrimination, lack of commitment to integrated workplaces and neighborhoods, and unfair treatment of those who are not like them?

Perhaps the most devastating consequence—certainly to nonwhites—of "personal incoherence," in Clark's interpretation, is that whites who suffer from it must, very often, employ defense mechanisms to shield themselves from facing the truth about themselves. The psychological defense mechanism of denial is, according to Clark, perhaps the chief way prejudiced whites avoid confronting the cracks in the American mind concerning the coexistence of professed beliefs in equality and inner feelings of bigotry. One aspect of this denial is that it shields whites from looking into the "disagreeable mirror," to use Baldwin's phrase, held up by blacks to whites. As a result, one wonders how the moral and psychological bankruptcy of racism can be escaped, especially if the maintenance of this condition has its privileges. Yet, this situation leads to exactly what Manning Marable discusses in *Beyond Black and White*:

> To be white is not a sign of culture, or a statement of biology or genetics: it is essentially a power relationship, a statement of authority, a social construct which is perpetuated by systems of privilege, the consolidation of property and status. There is no genius behind the idea of whiteness, only an empty husk filled with a mountain of lies about superiority and a series of crimes against "nonwhite" people.[19]

The internal collapse of those who may be privileged by societal standards is powerfully illustrated by Marable. He also makes it evident that, as one's outer status may rise, if it does so on a foundation of bigotry, one's inner status crumbles. Thus, if one were to take Marable's and Clark's critiques of white prejudice, it would be interesting to do a cost–benefits analysis concerning the maintaining of white privilege and the loss of spiritual integrity that results. On these points, Baldwin, in *The Fire Next Time*, pinpoints a major aspect of one of the "losses" to whites:

> White Americans find it as difficult as white people elsewhere do to divest themselves of the notion that they are in possession of some intrinsic value that black people need, or want. And this assumption . . . is revealed in all kinds of striking ways . . . [including] the unfortunate tone of warm congratulation with which so many liberals address their Negro equals. It is the Negro, of course, who is presumed to have become equal—an achievement that . . . corroborates the white man's sense of his own value. Alas, this value can scarcely be corroborated in any other way; there is certainly little enough in the white man's public or private life that one should desire to imitate. White men, at the bottom of their hearts, know this. Therefore, a vast amount of energy that goes into what we call the Negro problem is produced by the white man's profound desire not to be judged by those who are not white, not to be seen as he is.[20]

Baldwin's and Marable's ideas on the sterility of prejudiced whites make an important commentary on the pathetic nature of the denial of which Clark writes because the transparency of the bigotry denied by such whites is more than apparent.

Yet, breaking this narcissistic cycle is much harder than diagnosing it. Bennett, for example, asserts in "The White Problem in America" that racism is an essential aspect of the psychology of many whites; it not only allows for the psychological status to which Clark and Baldwin refer, but also has clear material benefits. Hence, Bennett agrees that racism serves an important psychological function by providing affected whites with a sense of self-importance; as such, it might even be called a psychological crutch (6). Bennett elaborates on key aspects of racial neurosis by stating that racism is an externalization of the insecurities of the bigot for whom the objects of bigotry are a convenient but artificial target (6). This mind-set and the drive to be at the top of the social ladder (in the way of which Clark writes) reflect issues of identity, for the writers under discussion reflect that "the white problem" is, fundamentally, a matter of identity, not a problem that can be solved by laws or even by denunciations by blacks. Perhaps the best that can be expected, therefore, is that blacks' representations and analyses of the nature of the beast can help society to understand the starting point for an attempted resolution of racism: the white mind.

Through the provocative and perceptive theories put forth by such writers as Baldwin, Bennett, Clark, and Killens, one sees that the challenge that they themselves emphasize is that whites' sense of self-protection prevents them from analysis concerning their racial attitudes and actions. Bennett helps explain the charge that whites resort to "magical thinking" to shield themselves from examining the bigotry within themselves by employing displacement and denial to deflect attention from themselves and onto blacks. As Bennett points out, much public discussion focuses on black crime, black educational disadvantages, and the lack of adequate black leadership as if these were essential racial characteristics without these same qualities of crime, education, and inadequate leadership being critiqued in a similarly essentialist way concerning whites (4). Bennett's words are still relevant today; even a superficial examination of the white media supports these charges. From the media, one might think that blacks are wretched, criminal, ineducable welfare-mongers and that, in the presentation of crime and education regarding whites, these issues are never presented as manifesting negative racial characteristics. Furthermore, while many whites decry the role of Reverend Al Sharpton and Minister Louis Farrakhan as leaders to many blacks, how many whites can one name who have assumed leadership on racial matters in contemporary America? The mentality of many whites concerning racism, therefore, reveals that whites must be forced to look in the mirror held up to them by blacks.

In sum, as long as many whites are psychologically in denial of their racism, America will continue, in its professed dedication to equality and the factual maintenance of inequality, to suffer from what Clark calls "the extent of the pathology within" the white character, whereby whites need to employ material and technological goods to cover their feelings of deep self-doubt and insecurity (50). To Clark, these compensatory measures are a main weapon in the continuation of racism.

GOALS OF THIS STUDY

Since the topic of this book is bound to be perceived as provocative, it is important for me to define my role as a critic. What is the purpose or goal of a black person who writes about whites? Clearly, there are as many answers as there are writers, but I want to address some of the primary stances: the writer as a missionary who seeks to bring enlightenment to white people and to change them, the exposé writer who reveals the depths of the destructiveness of many whites toward blacks, and the writer as a realist who realizes the enduring nature of bigotry and wants to shed light on the problems the racial neurosis common to the white identity causes blacks.

Certainly, some readers may see any critique of whites as a so-called reverse racism. Reverse racism is a classic example of a charge that is a foundational aspect of bigotry: projection. The illogical thinking behind the charge is that "If you are doing what I have done, then you are worse than I and your criticisms have no merit." The self-defensiveness of this posture is evident to most rational human beings. Perhaps the critical stance most sweet to the ears of whites who want to hide from blacks' revelations to them of their true nature is the missionary stance. This position is best illustrated by Clark in "What Motivates American Whites?" One of the most insightful analysts of white identity vis-à-vis blacks, Clark concludes this stinging essay with the following idea: that blacks' criticisms of whites and demands for ending discrimination can help "to save white Americans whose destiny we share" (56). This salvationist ideology was refuted implicitly by Clark in an interview in the 1980s when he stated his shock that, in contrast to his Civil Rights era belief that whites could be redeemed of their racism, bigotry existed in a virulent form in contemporary society that was startling to him.[21] Thus, history proved wrong such an estimable thinker as Clark that advances in civil rights would end racism. Hence, while I believe that some white readers are prompted to self-analysis by blacks' representations of them, the goal of saving whites from themselves seems an impossible mission to me.

The other two stances—the exposé writer and the realist—provide a key not only to understanding this study but the authors examined in it. To expose the truth about how many blacks have perceived whites is an important mission. On this point, Richard Wright had several important ideas. Wright states, for instance, that for black writers on controversial or innovative issues a main factor is that readers may be more used to works that attempt to leave an analysis of whites' feelings toward blacks underexamined, making works that go against the grain seem threatening.[22] He also contends that the writer must trust his own feelings and observations concerning the subject of racism, implying the importance of the centrality of black writers' writing an experientially inspired analysis of race, regardless of the defensive posture of whites who want to deny their own bigotry and how it is all too evident to blacks (46).

Another essential idea behind this study is captured by Wright's feeling that blacks have an obligation not to "be silent about the facts of their lives."[23] Under examination in this work is how blacks have presented one of the chief "facts of their lives"—whites' attitudes toward and treatment of them—and how these writers have tried to leave clues to their fellow blacks as to the nature of the beast—the white bigot. If these ideas "annoy" some, it is far more annoying to be the subject of racism than to be the subject of literary interpretations of the identity of whites who create and maintain—however actively or passively—a climate of obstacles for blacks, the chief obstacle being the very forms of identity under discussion.

Perhaps the closest reflection of my relationship to this study and my goals for it are expressed best in a statement by Wright:

> Those ideas which I feel are harmful to man, I fight and seek to destroy. Those ideas which I feel are life-furthering, I seek to defend and extoll. From the position where I stand as a Negro writer, such questions are not abstract. Those ideas in people's minds that are against granting a fuller life to people of color, I fight.[24]

Though Wright's contention that ideas that do not conform to those embraced by the dominant society may be rejected may be true, if the ideas contained in these pages provoke thought, in the form of debate, disagreement, or agreement, I will have achieved the primary goal of this study. To be blunt, the fundamental purpose of this work is to expose and analyze the fact that black writers have very pointedly created a typology of white images; that this typology gives voice to the observations of many blacks throughout America; and that such a typology should not be ignored by those who have not fully comprehended the vast amount of material that conveys the white image in the black mind.

Clearly, racism is a question not merely of actions but of identity. Black writers have long understood that it is precisely this fact that helps make it so difficult to combat. As stated earlier, the narcissism at the heart of the identity of bigots is something black writers have been trying to demolish for decades, if not centuries. The writers under discussion in this work make this narcissism a weapon against itself to expose the sterility that underlies those who would have others imagine them to be superior. Wright and many other black writers have used their works to advance enlightenment and to attempt to contribute to the examination of racism and the long-hoped-for destruction of those who practice it.

The following chapters will analyze the typology presented and defined earlier in relation to Charles W. Chesnutt's *The Marrow of Tradition*, James Baldwin's *Blues for Mister Charlie*, and Langston Hughes's "Poor Little Black Fellow," among other works; reflect the images of white women in Hughes's "Little Dog," Wright's *The Long Dream*, *Native Son*, *Savage Holiday*, and *The Outsider*; examine some contemporary nonfiction which represents important contributions to race theory, including Derrick Bell's *Faces at the Bottom of the Well* and Ellis Cose's *The Rage of a Privileged Class*; analyze the problem of internalization among blacks of white images of them, which reflects how white identity can be absorbed by blacks, reducing them to white shadows, principally in Wright's *The Long Dream*, *Lawd Today*, and *Native Son*; and, finally, briefly discuss the images of whites in about twenty-five works by black authors.

NOTES

1. Walter Shapiro, "Unfinished Business," *Time*, 7 August 1989, 15.

2. Keneth Kinnamon and Michel Fabre, eds., *Conversations with Richard Wright* (Jackson: University Press of Mississippi, 1993), 70.

3. William J. Clinton, *ABC World News Tonight*, October 16, 1996.

4. bell hooks, "Representations of Whiteness in the Black Imagination," in *Killing Rage* (New York: Henry Holt, 1995), 33.

5. Thomas F. Pettigrew, "Prejudice," in *Prejudice*, ed. Stephan Thornstrom (Cambridge, Mass.: Harvard University Press, 1980), 7.

6. Nelson Mandela, *The Struggle Is My Life* (New York: Pathfinder Press, 1990), 13, 15.

7. Reverend Dr. Martin Luther King, Jr., "Dr. Martin Luther King, Jr., Memphis, Tennessee, April 3, 1968," *Free at Last*, audiocassette (Los Angeles: Motown Record Corporation, 1968).

8. James Baldwin and Margaret Mead, *A Rap on Race* (New York: Dell Publishing, 1971), 10.

9. Era Bell Thompson, "Some of My Best Friends Are White," in *The White Problem in America*, ed. editors of *Ebony* (Chicago: Johnson Publishing, 1966), 155–56.

10. Malcolm X and Alex Haley, *The Autobiography of Malcolm X* (New York: Grove Press, 1965), 377.

11. Alain Locke, "The New Negro," in *Black Voices*, ed. Abraham Chapman (New York: New American Library, 1968), 513.

12. James Baldwin, "Everybody's Protest Novel," in *Notes of a Native Son* (New York: Bantam Books, 1964), 10.

13. James Baldwin, "White Man's Guilt," in *The Price of the Ticket* (New York: St. Martin's/Marek, 1985), 409–10.

14. John O. Killens, *Black Man's Burden* (New York: Trident Press, 1965), 157–58.

15. Lerone Bennett, Jr., "The White Problem in America," in *The White Problem in America*, ed. editors of *Ebony* (Chicago: Johnson Publishing, 1966), 7–8.

16. James Baldwin, "Unnameable Objects, Unspeakable Crimes," in *The White Problem in America*, ed. editors of *Ebony* (Chicago: Johnson Publishing, 1966), 180.

17. Thomas Jefferson, "Original Draft of the Declaration of Independence," in *The Norton Reader: The Shorter 9th Edition*, ed. Linda H. Peterson, et al. (New York: W. W. Norton, 1996), 546.

18. Kenneth B. Clark, "What Motivates American Whites?" in *The White Problem in America*, ed. editors of *Ebony* (Chicago: Johnson Publishing, 1966), 53.

19. Manning Marable, *Beyond Black and White* (London: Verso, 1995), 6.

20. James Baldwin, *The Fire Next Time* (New York: Dell Publishing, 1962), 127–28.

21. Kenneth B. Clark, *Open Mind*, PBS, 1987; rebroadcast in New York, Channel 13, September 1996.

22. Richard Wright, "Readers and Writers," in *Conversations with Richard Wright*, ed. Keneth Kinnamon and Michel Fabre (Jackson: University Press of Mississippi, 1993), 46–47.

23. Richard Wright, "Are We Solving America's Race Problem?" in *Conversations with Richard Wright*, ed. Keneth Kinnamon and Michel Fabre (Jackson: University Press of Mississippi, 1993), 77.

24. Richard Wright, "I Curse the Day When for the First Time I Heard the Word 'Politics,'" *L'Express*, 1955; in *Conversations with Richard Wright*, ed. Keneth Kinnamon and Michel Fabre (Jackson: University Press of Mississippi, 1993), 164.

Chapter 2

White Types in Black Lives

In "Ego Development and Historical Change," Erik Erikson provides an intriguing jumping-off point for a closer examination of the white image in the black mind:

> I know of a colored boy who, like our boys, listens every night to the Lone Ranger. Then he sits up in bed, dreaming that he is the Ranger. But alas, the moment always comes when he sees himself galloping after some masked offenders and notices that in his image the Lone Ranger is a Negro. He stops his fantasies. While a child, this boy was extremely expressive, both in his pleasures and in his sorrows. Today he is calm and always smiles; and his language is soft and blurred; nobody can hurry him, or worry him, or please him. White men like him.[1]

The predictable reaction to this passage would be to investigate the black person. This chapter, however, analyzes how black writers have represented the identity type with which Erikson ends his comments: the white person who "likes" him—the white person who often demands that blacks keep him safe from the racial matters that constitute how his personality and psychology are manifested in his relations with blacks.

THE OVERT WHITE SUPREMACIST

Although this image represents a dangerous white type, it is the least complex in the literature. Moreover, Joyce Y. Rogers' essay, "An Image of Cooperation: White Volunteers in the Civil Rights Freedom Summers Projects" shows that it can also be a crutch for many whites who want to believe that only the open bigot can be called a racist. Rogers' research demonstrates that the demonization and "otherization" of this type by whites who like to think of themselves as progressive is a convenient tool: it allows the covert and unconscious racists to redirect charges of bigotry to overt racists, and it allows them a sort of strawman to look down on in an ostensible demonstration of their own racial enlightenment. These attitudes are indicated in an interview with a Northern white college student who went to the South during the Civil Rights movement:

> [T]he white Southerners . . . are just about the most physically repulsive people I've ever run into in my life . . . the women around here are pale, sickly white. Sickly white pasty bloated with self-satisfied looks on their faces—pasty is the word and they just look as if they're ready to burst and blubber would flow out of them in all directions. They are repulsive and the men are just as bad.[2]

The fact that the superiority over blacks among the white Northern volunteers helped precipitate the breakdown of the black–white coalition during the Civil Rights era makes this passage especially intriguing. The disgusting and evil nature of racism is manifested, to this no doubt liberal white, in the perception of physical monstrosity of overtly racist whites. "This is a racist," this mentality wants to claim, "And this is not me." This self-absolution hinges on such whites' defining racism in a way that never implicates them; if a racist is a consciously evil monster, only such a person could be a bigot. As James Baldwin wrote, however, "I am aware that no man is a villain in his own eyes."[3] Thus, as the literature under discussion in this chapter will show, the image of the overt bigot represents ideas that are embedded, whether consciously or unconsciously, in the minds of some whites who think of themselves as progressive or enlightened; in fact, the "evil" bigot identity type is the ego identity off-split of prejudiced whites in general, no matter how good they think they are or how unintentional is their racism.

As the image under discussion contains elements of bigotry present in the psychology of the identity types under examination in the rest of the chapter, it is important to focus briefly on key aspects of the mentality of the overt bigot as represented in works by black authors. One of the most exact and representative portraits of this type is Lyle in Baldwin's *Blues for Mister Charlie*. Inspired by Emmitt Till's murder by two whites for allegedly flirting with one of their wives, Baldwin's play dramatizes the mentality of violent white supremacy in Lyle's killing of a black man, Richard, whom he feels has been disrespectful toward him and his wife. David Leeming captures the subtlety of Baldwin's depiction of a man who, in the hands of a lesser writer, might have been presented as a mere caricature: "Lyle is depicted in his home as an ordinary individual with genuine tenderness for his wife and child. But we learn quickly that he is so thoroughly infected with the plague of racism that it is impossible to recognize the humanity of the 'niggers.'"[4] At least two aspects of this reading are relevant to the rest of this study: that the character who symbolizes the open white supremacist is a human being, not a monster about to burst open with blubber; and that he simultaneously cannot recognize blacks as fellow human beings, only as inferior objects. Perhaps the most important aspect of Lyle's murder of Richard is his reason for it: "I had to kill him. I'm a white man!" (157). This rationale makes it evident that the murder is a defense against what the white man perceives to be his very identity—that this is an extermination of a black man who seems to threaten his sense of himself and that it is the most extreme symbol of whites' need for mutuality between their self-image and blacks' image of them.

According to Erikson, the protection and maintenance of mutual agreement with others concerning one's self-interpretation is a main aspect of one's sense of identity (22), and this idea is clearly racialized in the sort of bigots symbolized by Lyle. All of these qualities are manifested in the image of the hypocrite, the good-hearted weakling, and the liberal in the works of important black writers. That they are sometimes covert or unconscious illustrates Baldwin's theory that many whites' behavior and attitudes toward blacks are marked by "personal incoherence"—the gap between their self-image and their actions toward blacks and the contradictions that arise as a result.[5] As Erikson points out, "The American group identity supports an individual's ego identity . . . as long as he can convince himself . . . that no matter where he is staying or going he always has the choice of . . . turning in the opposite direction" (43). The devastating consequences of this mentality to race relations will become eminently clear as we look at the typology of whites.

THE HYPOCRITE

In his portrayal of the hypocrite in *The Marrow of Tradition*, Charles W. Chesnutt illustrates some of the mainstays of bigotry: the fear of diminishing power and of the resultant loss of status and the need to deny recognition to blacks of their equal worth and accomplishments in comparison to whites. Ironically, in one of the true—and racist—low points in American literary history, Chesnutt's career as a fiction writer ended in part at the hands of the man who repeatedly encouraged Chesnutt to write a novel that would be an honest account of racism, William Dean Howells. Howells, the white man sometimes called the dean of American realists, asked Chesnutt to write a manuscript for *Harper's*: "[S]omething about the color line and as of actual and immediate interest as possible—that is of American life in the present rather [than] the past, even the recent past."[6] Chesnutt chose as his inspiration the white riots in Wilmington, North Carolina, in 1898 to disfranchise blacks. Chesnutt was later to learn that by taking Howells at his word, he had failed to realize the mandatory silence such whites as Howells really want on racism and the "personal incoherence" involved in Howells's asking otherwise. In *Gemini*, Nikki Giovanni best sums up the consequences to Chesnutt:

> *The Marrow of Tradition* was the beginning of the end of white folks' love affair with Chesnutt. . . . The plainer he made it, the more they hated him. The old Mammy dies in the riot. The black folks fight back. The crackers are milling around smoking cigars, deciding which black folks will have to die, while we're preparing for a siege. It's so real and so graphic.[7]

And so honest that Howells set about to silence Chesnutt as a novelist.

Chesnutt's portrayal of Major Carteret stands as a metaphor for whites who hinge their identity on their status and who are threatened by blacks who they think will encroach on their position in society. Chesnutt contextualizes Carteret in this regard from the outset of the book. Similar to William Faulkner's theme of the Civil War's having splintered and diminished the stature of the Southern aristocracy, Carteret thinks depressively,

> Long ago, while yet a mere boy in years, he had come back from Appomattox to find his family, one of the oldest and proudest in the state, hopelessly impoverished by the war—even their ancestral home swallowed up in the common ruin. His elder brother had sacrificed his life on the bloody altar of the lost cause, and his father, broken and chagrined, died not many years later, leaving the major the last of his line.[8]

This concern with position is tied by Chesnutt to Carteret's growing dedication to keeping blacks in their "place"—a place that would confirm his illusion of superiority. This theme is developed in Carteret's reaction to his son's birth, which soothes the major's fear of being the last of his family. "His regret had been more than personal at the thought that with himself an old name should be lost to the state; and now all the old pride of race, class and family welled up anew, and swelled and quickened the current of his life" (28). The centrality of superiority in race and class is further embodied in Carteret's excitement as he agrees with General Belmont's statement that "now that you have a son, major . . . you'll be all the more interested in making this town fit to live in, which is what we [he and Captain McBane] came up to talk about. Things are in an awful condition!" (33) The "condition" of which he speaks is the "spectacle of social equality and negro domination" (33). That Wellington is two-thirds black represents to Carteret (and his friends) the possible end of white domination and the continued decline in prestige and power of Carteret's family in particular and the white race in general. Black equality in the form of voting rights, improved class status, and professional opportunities represents to the whites of Chesnutt's book the "reverse racism" of black "domination," clearly showing the projection involved in this line of thinking.

This attitude among the whites leads to the importance of a second theme: nonrecognition by whites of blacks of equal or superior status, achievements, and intelligence. This topic is illustrated in an episode in which Dr. Miller, a black physician who has lived in the North, is invited by a white colleague, Dr. Price, to assist in the operation on Major Carteret's sickly son (whose weak condition is symbolic, no doubt, of the flimsy basis for white hopes of maintaining the illusion of supremacy). Carteret refuses to let Dr. Miller participate, despite the white doctor's statements about Miller's excellence. Dr. Price realizes,

> [H]e knew Carteret's unrelenting hostility to anything that savored of recognition of the negro as the equal of white men. It was traditional in Wellington that no colored person had ever entered the front door of the Carteret residence. . . . If Miller had been going as a servant, to hold a basin or a sponge, there would be no difficulty; but as a surgeon—. (68)

Chesnutt certainly uses Carteret's rejection of Miller to make some relevant points. For one thing, Miller embodies a form of identity that Carteret finds threatening. If Miller were someone who held a position inferior in status to Carteret, his presence would be tolerated or even welcomed in the household. Chesnutt uses the theme of recognition (or whites' refusal to give it to blacks as equal human beings) to exemplify the decaying state of white supremacy. At the end of the novel, Carteret needs Miller to operate on his son, and he also has to recognize Miller as being someone whom he needs and as being someone who is related to him by marriage. His wife acknowledges Miller's wife as a black relative, which shows the hypocrisy of strict segregation and racial purity that are the pillars of the white supremacy Carteret and his counterparts protect so vociferously in the face of racial progress. Hence, the themes of white protection of status at the expense of blacks and withholding recognition to blacks are intertwined—they are, Chesnutt suggests, both doomed to failure.

The brand of racism that Chesnutt represents in Carteret may seem, so far, to be straightforward. Where, one might ask, is the hypocrisy?

The hypocrisy is revealed (among other places) in a discussion with Delamere, the elderly, progressive lawyer, when Carteret states,

> You are mistaken, sir, in imagining me hostile to the negro. . . . On the contrary, I am friendly to his best interests. I give him employment; I pay taxes for schools to educate him; and for court-houses and jails to keep him in order. I merely object to being governed by a servile and inferior race. (25)

Carteret's contorted logic collapses under its own weight; while he clearly feels that it is important not to be considered (or to consider himself) a racist, his statements make it quite plain that the only blacks he finds toler-able are those who are subservient to him and to whom he can feel supe-rior. Furthermore, his identity is defined by his ability to manage blacks: blacks are merely objects for him, as a white person, to shape, direct, and keep in check. These views make Carteret's summary of blacks to Delamere to be a defense of his own identity: "No doubt the negro is capable of a cer-tain dog-like fidelity—I make the comparison in a kindly sense,—a certain personal devotion which is admirable in itself, and fits him eminently for a servile career" (24). Carteret is silent about Dr. Miller, who Delamere points to as a refutation of these remarks, for his psychological defense of his delu-sion of superiority cannot admit (to himself and others) that blacks exist who are not only his equals but even his superiors, which is clearly the case with Dr. Miller. The major's profession as founder and editor of the news-paper *The Chronicle* is a result of his wife's money and did not come through his own merit or initiative. Chesnutt emphasizes that Carteret lives in fear of social equality in another scene, in which the major and members of his family are riding in a carriage:

> Now and then one of [the blacks] would salute the party respectfully, while oth-ers glanced at them indifferently or turned away. There would have seemed, to a stranger, a lack of spontaneous friendliness between the people of these two races, as though each felt that it had no part in the other's life. At one point the carriage drew near a party of colored folks who were laughing and jesting among themselves with great glee. Paying no attention to the white people, they continued to laugh and shout boisterously as the carriage swept by.
>
> Major Carteret's countenance wore an angry look. "The negroes in this town are growing absolutely insufferable. . . . They are sadly in need of a les-son in manners. . . . They will learn their lesson in a rude school, and perhaps much sooner than they dream." (142)

Certainly, this passage conveys one of Chesnutt's main points about the kind of racism represented in Carteret. The major's sense of himself hinges to a great degree on blacks' affirming that they (and he) find him a supe-rior being, thus giving factual support for his delusions of grandeur and thereby establishing the mutuality of which Erikson writes. That Carteret cannot, in fact, own up to the fact that he despises blacks implies that he needs to believe that his feelings about them are rational and objective rather than subjective and ideological—a belief that is excessively compli-mentary to his self-image and is narcissistic in the hypocrisy of his denial of his very clear racism.

Protection from social and political equality are two of Carteret's main priorities, in keeping with key characteristics of racism throughout American history. Chesnutt also shows the role of the media, as embodied in Carteret's use of *The Chronicle,* as one of the main perpetrators of the bla-tant racism practiced by self-flattering hypocrites.

Carteret's racism is nowhere more clear than in his use of the newspaper, the most influential in the city, to inflame whites' hostility and potential violence toward blacks. Propaganda against black political empowerment is one of the main purposes of the newspaper.

> Taking for his theme the unfitness of the negro to participate in government,—an unfitness due to his limited education, his lack of experience, his criminal tendencies, and more especially to his hopeless mental and physical inferiority to the white race,—the major had demonstrated, it seemed to him clearly enough, that the ballot in the hand of the negro was a menace to the commonwealth. He had argued, with entire conviction, that the white and black races could never attain social and political equality by commingling their blood; he had proved by several historical parallels that no two unassimilable races could ever live together except in the relation of superior and inferior. (31)

Though the paper is the most powerful in the city, Chesnutt underlines the vigilance with which Carteret, who scoffed at the idea of being a racist, incites the whites of the town, most of whom are indifferent to such pronouncements as those above. It is the paper's coverage of the story (mistaken, as it turns out) that a black man, Delamere's servant Sandy, has murdered a white woman that provokes many whites to pay attention to Carteret's warnings about the "black peril" (anticipating the role of the media in inflaming the public to believe that Bigger Thomas is an animalistic killer of a white woman in Richard Wright's *Native Son*). Characterizing Mrs. Ochiltree's killer as "a brute in the lowest form," Carteret editorializes in the paper that the murder confirms

> that drastic efforts were necessary to protect the white women of the South against brutal, lascivious, and murderous assaults at the hands of negro men. . . . If an outraged people, justly infuriated, and impatient with the slow processes of the courts, should assert their inherent authority . . . [and] set aside the ordinary judicial procedure, it would serve as a warning and as an example . . . of the swift and terrible punishment which would fall, like the judgement of God, upon anyone who laid sacrilegious hands upon white womanhood. (185–86)

The power of the media to distort blacks' identity, to create stereotypes, and to use white women as a pretext for racial superiority to strip blacks of any social and political advancement are illustrated by this editorial—by one who, in his own mind, is not and could not be a racist. Chesnutt emphasizes that such pronouncements lay the groundwork not for mere character assassination, but for the continuation of the inferiorization of blacks by whites. This theme is evident in the fact that after the accused man, Sandy, is cleared by whites, and weeks go by during which whites seem to calm down from the fever induced in them by the newspaper accounts, most whites come to agree with the views Carteret expressed to keep blacks not only from social advancement but to disfranchise them. Hence, in *The Chronicle,* "Statistics of crime, ingeniously manipulated, were made to present a fearful showing of the negro" (238). In the views expressed in the paper, Chesnutt presents some of the main weapons used to argue for the continued oppression of blacks. Furthermore, it is the hypocrisy—"I think blacks are animals but I am not a racist"—that allows such bigots as Carteret to perform clear acts of bigotry while believing that they are on a noble and chivalric mission to maintain order and civilization in what to them is a degenerating society.

The hypocritical nature of the brand of racism symbolized by Carteret is made clear in two different episodes in the novel: Carteret's attitude toward Sandy's guilt or innocence even as he uses his newspaper to denounce Sandy as a symbol of the animal within blacks, and in his actions regarding the white riot that results from his campaign against blacks. In the first episode, Chesnutt underlines the dishonest nature of Carteret's treatment of Delamere. Delamere, who has long employed Sandy, swears to Carteret that he knows the black man well enough to be sure that he is incapable of murder. While Carteret seems to view the elderly gentleman with pity for his faith in Sandy (and, it seems, for his integrity in defending him), he is extremely duplicitous in his attitude toward Delamere. Making it clear that he will not be influenced by a black person's proof of Sandy's innocence, Carteret tells Delamere that a white person must offer proof of Sandy's innocence, and even then it would only be "barely possible to prevent the lynching" (214). He is perfectly content with the fact that "[w]hite men might lynch a negro on suspicion; they would not kill a man who was proven, by the word of white men, to be entirely innocent" (215). As indicated earlier by Chesnutt's showing a rush to judgement (to borrow a term popular in the O. J. Simpson trial) in Sandy's being portrayed as guilty by the newspaper and the mountain of extremist rhetoric made against blacks on the white assumption of Sandy's guilt, Carteret really does not care if Sandy is guilty or innocent. Sandy is not a human being for Carteret but a convenient tool for the aforementioned "rude lesson" he has long wanted to teach blacks. Moreover, this point is borne out by the fact that as he encourages Delamere to believe that there is some small hope of saving Sandy, and that he will wait for Delamere to return with proof of Sandy's innocence, his inner thoughts are as follows: "He did not believe that Mr. Delamere could prove an alibi for his servant, and without some possible proof the negro would surely die,—as he well deserved to die" (215). Thus, it is evident that Carteret does not really care about Sandy (or Delamere's faith in Sandy), about his guilt or innocence, or about averting the lynching, as he had led Delamere to believe. He is merely stringing the respected and prominent white man along, possibly out of deference to a fellow white whom he considers "this ideal gentleman of the ideal past" (214). Carteret's hypocrisy reaches even greater heights when Delamere tells him that his (Delamere's) own grandson committed the murder. Carteret believes Delamere, but a white murderer could seriously undermine both Carteret's status (for he assumed Sandy's guilt in his editorials against blacks) and the image of the white race as angels besieged by black devils.

> Carteret's thoughts were chasing each other tumultuously. . . . There could be no doubt that the negro was innocent . . . and he must not be lynched; but in what sort of position would the white people be placed, if the true facts [were] known? The white people had raised the issue of their own moral superiority, and had themselves made this crime a race question. . . . Even the negroes would have a laugh on them. . . . The reputation of the [white] race was threatened. (228)

This passage is intriguing in several ways. First, Carteret hypocritically displaces the blame for the growth of the issue of alleged black crime and white superiority onto whites in general, but he personally exaggerated the unproved charges against Sandy to mythic proportions and influenced the public to share his prejudices. Second, he is so concerned with saving face—his own face and the face of the white race—that he seems still to feel the need for whites to believe in a black man's guilt rather than face the truth. (In true racist fashion, an unproven belief about a black person was racialized and generalized into an innate flaw in blacks, whereas the white man's guilt is not perceived or denounced as a general racial flaw by Carteret.) Chesnutt further underlines Carteret's nature as a bigot when Carteret hires Sandy as a butler after the murder charges are dropped. Carteret's atonement—"I tried to have you lynched but you tricked me by being innocent so I will let you be my servant"—serves two purposes: it eases his conscience by doing the right thing and employs the man he mistakenly wanted killed, and it stems any self-criticism that would arise out of an honest assessment of the entire episode. Carteret emerges from his egregious blunder not only intact, but, in his own mind, morally above reproach. The ability of bigots never to face themselves and to see the evil that they do, Chesnutt seems to say, allows them to continue as they are: on a path of destruction (as further plot developments bear out).

The nature of the riot that develops as a result of the plans of Carteret (and the other two members of the Big Three, McBane and Belmont) to disfranchise blacks and to have them and progressive whites removed from office also shows Carteret's self-deluded destructiveness. "The proceedings of the day—originally planned as a 'demonstration,' dignified subsequently as a 'revolution,' under any name the culmination of the conspiracy formed by Carteret and his colleagues—had by seven o'clock developed into a murderous riot" (198). It is preposterous to think that Carteret actually thought that there would be a mere demonstration by a white community that had been aroused in great part by his rhetoric in *The Chronicle* into nearly lynching Sandy, certainly a sign of the volatility of the general hostility toward blacks mobilized primarily by Carteret's pronouncements.

Carteret's hypocritical concern after blacks are killed is also flimsy; his desire to stop the riot stems mainly from the fact that Mammy Jane, who "nursed my wife at her bosom," is shot while trying to escape from the mob into the Carteret home (305). Chesnutt makes evident the nature of Carteret's true identity—which the major seems to want to disown once the riot turns deadly (or is it mainly because his wife's mammy has been killed?)—as he tries to tell the white mob to stop rioting. "The mob had recognized the speaker. . . . 'Three cheers for Major Carteret, the champion of white supremacy!' 'No nigger domination!'" (305). The word "recognized" indicates that the mob has seen Carteret's true identity: not as a man who wants to declare peace between the races but as the primary spokesman and cause for the white violence which is a defense for an illusory superiority. In addition, Chesnutt implies the hypocrisy of Carteret's mourning for Mammy Jane and the insincerity of his wanting to stop the riot in a scene in which he ignores the murder of Jerry, one of Mammy Jane's relatives and his own loyal servant, who is perhaps the most ludicrously servile black character in all fiction (he should be the sort whose existence Carteret would want to continue, as ostensibly was the case with Mammy Jane). Jerry tries, in the midst of the riot, to flee to Carteret for protection when he sees the major: "[H]is reliance upon his white friends . . . failed him in the moment of supreme need. In that hour, as in any hour when the depths of racial hatred are stirred, a negro was no more than a brute beast, set upon by other brute beasts whose only instinct was to kill and destroy" (307).

The wording of this passage points to Carteret's culpability in arousing others to act on their racism: his editorials stereotyped blacks as animals; his paper planted the seeds of murder in whites' minds in the earlier episode with Sandy—seeds that flower in the murderous demonstration inspired by Carteret; and his claims of concern for blacks during the riot are shown to be dishonest. This dishonesty is shown in the pattern Chesnutt creates in having the riot kill two of Carteret's servants, indicating that his bigotry is destructive even to the servile blacks who he states are the acceptable members of the race and who die seeking protection from their "master," showing that Carteret does not truly care about these supposedly favored blacks.

Chesnutt causes the reader to infer that Carteret is really indifferent to the murder of any and all blacks as a result of his campaign for white supremacy. This last point seems evident when Chesnutt shows Carteret's thoughts as, unbeknownst to him, it is Jerry who is being killed by the mob: "He had become aware that a negro was being killed by the mob, though he did not know whom. 'We can do nothing. The negroes have themselves to blame,—they tempted us beyond endurance. . . . I am not responsible for these subsequent horrors,—I wash my hands of them'" (307). With these words, Chesnutt inspires the reader to reflect on Carteret's complete guilt for the violence that was sown and cultivated by him. The white man's defense against his responsibility is transparent denial—a defense mechanism clearly employed to save his ego from facing the bigotry that constitutes his identity vis-à-vis blacks.

It is poetic justice that Carteret's campaign and life are in shambles at the end of the book. He is dependent on (and thus in an inferior position to) the black man whom he had earlier rebuffed because the white doctors are casualties of the violence. On the level closest to his ego, Carteret ultimately attained nothing to advance his aristocratic pretensions and realize his ambition for political office.

In Carteret, Chesnutt represents the essential hypocrisy of "good" racists—people whose actions fairly scream bigotry but whose racial hatred is manifested in the psychology and acts that constitute their very identity. This "personal incoherence" is best illustrated in Carteret's psychological relationship to other members of the Big Three. On this theme, what Chesnutt implies is that Major Carteret, whose self-image is one of a genteel, rational aristocrat, is part of one identity shared by his more overt cohorts, Captain McBane and General Belmont. Chesnutt indicates that Carteret is the epitome of the identity type of the hypocrite by showing that the major maintains a dualistic stance in his perception of himself and overt racists. He disdains open hatred toward blacks while having the same hostility and using the power to transform his hatred into active destruction of blacks. Hence, the denial of sameness—of being as much a bigot as honest racists—is the crux of the identity of the hypocrite.

In Carteret, Chesnutt explores the psychology of one who joins with other whites because of a "spontaneous revulsion of white men against . . . an inferior race" (33). Yet, the ostensible difference among the three men is shown when Chesnutt writes of Jerry as he listens to a discussion by the Big Three:

> He could hear the major, now and then, use the word "negro" and McBane's deep voice was quite audible when he referred, it seemed to Jerry with alarming frequency, to "the damned niggers," while the general's suave tones now and then pronounced the word "niggro,"—a sort of compromise between the ethnology and the vernacular. (36)

The difference in word choice is, however, superficial in indicating the men's true feelings, for they are bonded together by a desire to eliminate blacks' voting rights and any ideas and aspirations blacks have toward equal treatment and opportunities. Indeed, the unity of the men is proved in the initial passage recounting the men's first meeting during which neither the user of the seemingly polite "negro" nor the user of the compromise "niggro" objects to the word that expresses their actual feelings toward blacks: "'Gentlemen,' exclaimed the captain lifting his glass, 'I propose a toast: No

nigger domination!' 'Amen!' said the others, and three glasses were sol-
emnly drained" (37).

Still, Carteret's inability to face his true identity remains. As McBane calls
Jerry "charcoal," for example,

> A momentary cloud of annoyance darkened Carteret's brow. McBane had al-
> ways grated upon his aristocratic susceptibilities. The captain was an upstart, a
> product of the democratic idea operating upon a poor white man, the de-
> scendant of the indentured bondservant and the socially unfit. He had wealth
> and energy, however, and it was necessary to make use of him. (86–87)

It is evident that McBane offends Carteret's sense of himself as a refined, upper-class man too genteel to say "nigger" and "charcoal" but all too ready to
feel the venom toward blacks expressed in these words. Furthermore,
Carteret and McBane's sameness is underlined at the end of the episode, for
after McBane dismisses General Belmont's delicate criticism of his words to
Jerry (as Jerry is servile enough to merit his and Carteret's tolerance) and
McBane retorts that all blacks are alike and should be eliminated, "Carteret
had nothing to say by way of dissent. McBane's sentiments, in their last analysis, were much the same as his, though he would have expressed them less
brutally" (87). One sees, therefore, that it is mere etiquette that is on the major's mind in his annoyance with McBane for calling Jerry "charcoal" to his
face. If someone wants to treat someone as a "nigger," one should at least talk
nicely and classily in performing this act, the major seems to think. Thus, it
is merely an idealized self-image that Carteret wants to maintain in his earlier
disdain for McBane's crudeness—an image that tells him that a white man of
his class and good manners simply does not talk like that. He only thinks and
acts on those feelings crudely stated by his alter-ego, regardless of the dainty
delicacy in his articulation of racial hatred concerning the use of epithets.

Chesnutt again shows the egotistical duplicity in Carteret's repugnance for
McBane in the scene where the Big Three meet to discuss what to do after
Mrs. Ochiltree is murdered. McBane is outspoken in his desire to "hang 'em
high"—any "nigger" should be lynched (182). Carteret's body language and
words show his desire to distance himself from the blunt words of McBane:

> [S]aid Carteret, who had gone to the window looking out,—"I do not believe
> that we need to trouble ourselves personally about his [Sandy's] punishment.
> I should judge, by the commotion in the street, that the public will take the
> matter into its own hands. I, for one, would prefer that any violence, however
> justifiable, should take place without my active intervention." (183)

In this instance, at least McBane is honest in owning up to his reprehensible
desires; Carteret, in contrast, feigns indifference while at the same time expressing trust that whites may well murder the black suspect. The concept

that one is innocent until proven guilty clearly does not apply to blacks in Carteret's ethics. Moreover, as discussed earlier, since Carteret is quick to use his newspaper to incite whites to want to kill the accused, his stated disdain for "active intervention" seems to mean that he does not want to perform a lynching with his own hands—even as he is confident that he can make a lynching happen if he wants. His denial of wanting active intervention, therefore, is a mere psychological trick to absolve himself of endorsing violence—first in conversation, then in print.

Carteret's denial and hypocrisy are shown again in another episode much later in the novel, again vis-à-vis McBane, this time regarding the issue of violence against blacks. As the Big Three plan to mount a campaign to inflame voters to get rid of Republicans and blacks from office and take voting rights away from blacks, McBane wholeheartedly supports lynching them. In contrast, Carteret says, "I would not advocate murder. . . . We are animated by high and holy principles. . . . I don't object to frightening the negroes, but I am opposed to any unnecessary bloodshed" (250). Two questions arise: What is the nature of the means by which whites will scare blacks—violence, perhaps? And what would "necessary bloodshed" be? These questions are answered when the Big Three's plans result in chaos during which blacks are killed for no reason at all except racist hatred—hardly a "high and holy purpose" to any rational reader.

The essential nature of Carteret's character is revealed in the same meeting of the Big Three, during which they discuss what blacks they find acceptable or unacceptable. As the major again tiptoes around the issues, nonsensically saying that he wishes to be impartial, as he participates in the consideration of which blacks to harass, McBane poses the essential question:

> "What's the use of all this hypocrisy, gentlemen? . . . This is a white man's country, and a white man's city, and no nigger has any business being here when a white man wants him gone!" Carteret frowned darkly at this brutal characterization of their motives. It robbed the enterprise of all its poetry, and put a solemn act of revolution upon the plane of a mere vulgar theft of power. (152–53)

Why the need for hypocrisy? To mask racism in "poetry" and nobility rather than unmask it for the grasping for white power that it really is. The issue is not, however, one of semantics but also one of self-image: to be a racist vulgarian is not to be the high-minded poet of racial justice and the rights of the white race to maintain their privileged position in America. Hypocrisy, therefore, is the crutch upon which the sort of whites symbolized by Carteret rest their identity.

The fictional Carteret is diminished in the end, but what about his real life counterparts? Ironically for Chesnutt, they include the dean of American realism, William Dean Howells.

   The confused mind that was William Dean Howells is revealed by his reaction to the book he solicited. In a very curious letter, Howells wrote,

> I have been reading Chesnutt's *The Marrow of Tradition*. You know he is a ne-
> gro, though you wouldn't know it from seeing him, and he writes of the black
> and white situation with an awful bitterness. But he is an artist of the first qual-
> ity . . . promising things hereafter that will scarcely be equalled in our fiction.
> Good Lord! How such a negro must hate us. And then think of the Filipinos
> and the Cubans and the Puerto Ricans whom we have added to our happy
> family.[9]

At least three aspects of this odd letter are striking. First, the strange comment about Chesnutt's looks makes it seem that Howells is implying that
Chesnutt's light skin made him forget—or overlook—the black author's
race, as if he had performed a sort of mental assimilationism which back-
fired when Chesnutt gave him the honest account of racism he had re-
quested. Second, Howells's statement that Chesnutt is one of the best
authors of any race would lead one to conclude (mistakenly) that he would
still be interested in furthering Chesnutt's career, which was his original intention in soliciting the manuscript that became *The Marrow of Tradition*.
This second point leads to the third: Howells's conclusion that he must be
hated not only by Chesnutt, but also by "such . . . negro[es]" as Chesnutt
seems to symbolize to him—talented, educated, but still targets of bigotry,
however disguised and indirect was his expression of his prejudice. Finally,
Howells's coupling of his perception of being threatened by Cubans,
Filipinos, and Puerto Ricans with his more explicit discomfort with the criticism of whites by a black writer certainly has undertones of racial intolerance. What one sees in this letter, therefore, is how profoundly disturbed
Howells was by an honest presentation of racism in America, a point which
may seem inconsistent with his support for the founding of the National
Association for the Advancement of Colored People (NAACP). By the time
we are through with our examination of Howells, we will see how consistent
his recoiling from Chesnutt is with the identity type of the high-minded, directive hypocrite.
   Both Howells's letter and his review of Chesnutt's novel indicate a problem with Howells's view of literature as noted by Vernon Louis Parrington:
"his dislike of looking ugly facts in the face."[10] While Parrington does not investigate how this attitude affected his reviews of other writers, it most certainly helps explain the somewhat schizophrenic nature of Howells's
response to Chesnutt in the *North American Review*. The essay, "A
Psychological Counter-Current in Recent Fiction," is filled with contradictory thoughts. Howells states, for example, "Though *The Marrow of Tradition*
is of the same strong material as [Chesnutt's] earlier books, it is less simple
throughout, and therefore less excellent in manner."[11] The point seems to

be that not only does Howells tie complexity to weakening a book but also that his mind could not handle a presentation of racism that was not "simple"—a thought truly at odds with the writer whom he asked to write an honest novel about race. A key passage from the review exemplifies what would truly trouble a man who thought he wanted Chesnutt to write an honest story about bigotry but who really wanted pablum: Howells' claims that Chesnutt "stands up for his own people with a courage which has more justice than mercy in it. The book is, in fact, bitter, bitter. There is no reason in history why it should not be so . . . and yet it would be better if it was not so bitter" (832).

This passage is filled with nonsensical thoughts. One sees, for example, that Howells's response to the novel was conditioned by what he perceived to be its tone: between this passage in the review and his letter about Chesnutt, the word "bitter" is used four times. In addition, in this context, one can surmise what was troubling Howells as he notes—somewhat defensively—that Chesnutt's stance in the novel has "more justice than mercy." Mercy for whom, one might rhetorically ask? The answer is clear: while Howells concedes that Chesnutt is just, he still wants mercy for white people. Yet, later in the piece, Howells seems to concede the correctness of the "bitter" and "merciless" nature of the book, which is at the heart of his derision of it.

> [W]hile [Chesnutt] recognizes pretty well all the facts in the case, he is too clearly of a judgement that is made up. One cannot blame him for that; what would one be one's self? If the tables could be turned, and it could be that it was the black race which violently and lastingly triumphed in the bloody revolution in Wilmington, North Carolina, a few years ago, what would not be the excuse to the white man who made the atrocity the argument of his fiction? (832)

Howells seems to be on the edge of empathy in this section of his review, but the fact that he emphasizes elsewhere his qualms about what he considered to be Chesnutt's anger make his statements on the book overall a rejection of it. Moreover, some of Howells' final words on the novel are consistent with the duality of his feelings about Chesnutt's work: "No one who reads the book can deny the case is presented with great power, or fail to recognize in the writer a portent of the sort of negro equality against which no series of hangings and burnings will finally avail" (883). Thus, in Howells's response to the novel in general, it is clear that he found it to be a powerful book; that he thought Chesnutt was an exceptionally talented writer; but that he did not want to be presented with a blunt view of whites by a black person perhaps because, as indicated in the letter, such a view implicated him (however unconsciously on Chesnutt's part).

Perhaps a key to Howells's inability to withstand what he saw in Chesnutt's book (i.e., whites from a black man's perspective) has been overlooked in accounts of the white man's rejection of the novel in such perceptive works as William L. Andrews's "William Dean Howells and Charles W. Chesnutt: Criticism and Race Fiction in the Age of Booker T. Washington." According to Andrews, Howells admired and felt comfortable with the sort of blacks he could consider to be assimilationists or accommodationists, but he must have been horrified by the scathing account of whites in Chesnutt's novel (Andrews 1976, 334). Perhaps the key to Howells's collapse in the face of the truth as presented by Chesnutt is in the connection among his view of realism, his questionable status as a progressive on racial issues, and his own "race novel," *An Imperative Duty* (1891).

To be brief, in *Criticism and Fiction*, Howells states a few components of his definition of realism that are crucial to his feelings about *The Marrow of Tradition*. First, the realist "feels in every nerve . . . the unity of men"; second, realism must be concerned with the "large cheerful average of health and success and happy life" (unlike European realism, which he seemed to consider sordid and pessimistic); and, centrally, realism should focus on "the more smiling aspects of life" (Parrington 1930, 249). One might ask whether he could be serious. After all, one of his books, *A Modern Instance* (1881), focuses on divorce, and one might think that perhaps he overstated the optimism his statements on realism dictate as the subject and tone of the realist. Yet, the realism that portrays upper-class, repressed white men and naively wayward white women as well as constrained white American society, which marks many of the works of such realists as Howells, Henry James, and Edith Wharton, is certainly dainty and "simple" (to borrow a word from Howells's review of *The Marrow of Tradition*) in comparison to Chesnutt's novel. Here, the focus is on the disunity of America and the tragedy of white people's quest for supremacy at the expense of blacks. If Howells thought that there could be a "smiling" book on racism, he was truly naive.

Howells's defenders would say that the man could not have been that naive; to which I would say that the record shows that, when it came to race, indeed he was.

In *An Imperative Duty*, one gets a view of what a novel about race that conforms to Howells's simplistic view of realism is like. The plot is simple: it concerns that staple of black stereotypes, the tragic mulatto, in this case a young black woman, with whom that staple of white realism, the repressed white man, falls in love. Should her true race be revealed? Should he have a relationship with her? These are the main issues of this very short novel. In her introduction to *An Imperative Duty*, Martha Banta makes several intriguing comments in her attempt to explain Howells's interest in writing about race. Banta points to the Abolitionist beliefs of Howells's family as a strong influence in creating progressive views on race[12] (a credential that can be overstated and becomes questionable in light of the fact that many, if not most, Abolitionists did not want social equality any more than their proslavery foes). Banta summarizes Howells's seemingly progressive ideology in the following passage:

> Howells' public role in assuming part of the white man's burden in the historical struggle of the Negro for his social rights is a significant one; it continually found expression, whether he was giving editorial praise for the lives of Booker T. Washington and Frederick Douglass, championing Paul L. Dunbar's poetic career, or adding his signature to the petition which led to the founding of the NAACP. (xi)

This sounds impressive if one overlooks the condescending phrase "the white man's burden," but there are problems with this litany of Howells's credentials: Booker T. Washington was a comforting figure to whites who wanted a safe, or accommodationist, black stance on race relations; Howells's view of Dunbar's writing had the same directive quality as his view of Chesnutt because Dunbar felt that Howells had tried to control and limit his style (thus, his "championing" of Dunbar is overstated); and the passage quoted earlier from his letter, with its ominous reference to Cubans, Filipinos, and Puerto Ricans, makes the depth of his commitment to the NAACP dubious inasmuch as one overlooked aspect of the history of that organization is that the word "colored" was not used because it was the word of the times for African American but because the organization wanted to combat bigotry against various nonwhite people, including those by whom Howells seemed to feel threatened. In spite of his ostensible progressiveness, therefore, it is not surprising that Howells would recoil at such a blunt presentation as that found in *The Marrow of Tradition* and write a novel on race that Chesnutt considered "very pretty" (Andrews 1976, 330).

Howells's reaction to Chesnutt's novel is also illuminated by some of the reactions to his own novel. According to Banta,

> The handful of reviewers who made note of *An Imperative Duty* . . . sharply objected to what they saw. *The Critic* (16 January 1892, p. 34) stated that the story was a failure, probably due to Howells' "ignorance of the subject. He likes the race as the Princess Napraxine likes the wolves in Russia—in theory and at a distance. Brought into actual contact with these people, the inference is that he would dislike them cordially." (ix)

This passage captures the approach–avoidance conflict exhibited by Howells in his asking for Chesnutt to write a truthful account of modern racism and then being horrified by what he saw (and his support of the NAACP when he seems threatened by minorities). He wanted the truth from Chesnutt in theory, and his cordial dislike of *The Marrow of Tradition* is marked by his confused estimation of the novel, which mixes praise with repugnance, all the while affirming Chesnutt's outstanding talent. In sum,

Chesnutt, who proved to be Howells's own Dr. Miller, embodied the spectre of independent black thinking and achievement.

Sadly, Chesnutt felt that he should "drop the attempt at realism" and "write to please editors, to please the public."[13] Whom he had to please to be a successful writer in America was clear to him. Years after the publication of the novel, in 1928, he reflected on his career: "I was writing against the trend of public opinion on the race question at that particular time. And I had to sell my books chiefly to white readers" (Hogue 1986, 34). (Ironically, he said these words while accepting an award from the NAACP.)

James Baldwin's words in an interview with Quincy Troupe on why many black writers are unread are relevant to the fate of *The Marrow of Tradition*:

> For most great black writers, in general, white and black Americans won't read us until they have nothing else to read . . . because of the entire American way of life, the marrow of the American bone. The whole [white] American mentality is based on the necessity of keeping black people out of it. We are nonexistent. Except according to their terms, and their terms are unacceptable.[14]

Chesnutt's statement made in 1928 reveals that he knew the terms of being a successful writer in America and that such whites as William Dean Howells had willed his book, for most readers, into the nonexistence of which Baldwin speaks. Nevertheless, the attempted silencing of Charles W. Chesnutt is best answered by Nikki Giovanni: "Once you write for your people others will judge that your quality is failing. . . . A true numbers system starts with the son (sun) and that would be Charles Waddell Chesnutt" (1971, 105).

THE GOOD-HEARTED WEAKLING

The good-hearted weakling identity type is best represented by Parnell in James Baldwin's play *Blues for Mister Charlie*. This play illustrates what Baldwin meant when he said,

> I've had very hard things to say about liberals. . . . I was thinking of that vast army of people whose convictions are mere quotations and whose good will costs them nothing, who are always presuming to lecture the Negro on his table manners and who are hurt, to the point of vindictiveness, whenever their utterly useless good will is questioned.[15]

Baldwin's hatred for many self-proclaimed progressive whites is evident in that it is Parnell, not the racist murderer Lyle, who is the Mister Charlie of the title. (Meridian, the black preacher whose son Richard was murdered by Lyle, says that while "All white men are Mister Charlie," "You're Mister Charlie," in answer to Parnell's question about what the term means, 59). As Baldwin makes evident in the course of the play, Parnell is a metaphor for whites who, while they may pat themselves on the back for not being prejudiced, fail to take truly significant actions to disrupt bigotry, even when these actions are well within their power. The examination of whites in this play underscores the truth in the words of the great African writer Chinua Achebe in "Postscript: James Baldwin (1924–1987)":

> [A]s long as white people who constitute a mere fraction of the human race consider it natural and even righteous to dominate the rainbow majority whenever and wherever they are thrown together . . . the words of James Baldwin will be there to bear witness and to inspire and elevate the struggle for human freedom.[16]

As Baldwin's drama underlines, this struggle includes freedom from white ignorance, arrogance, and inauthenticity.

One of the main points of Baldwin's portrayal of Parnell is that he represents the ideas that good-hearted whites who are mostly talk and little action may have a knowledge of what they can do to counter bigotry, but they do these things halfheartedly (if at all), all the while believing that they are truly progressive people of conscience. Hence, Parnell is a symbol of a white person whose idealized self-image causes him or her to be, in fact, worse— more neurotic—than the hypocrite. While the hypocrite often chooses consciously to maintain a duality between his or her self-presentation and actions, the good-hearted weakling truly believes that he or she is a friend to blacks, even while failing to act on this belief. Thus, while the hypocrite may be a liar, the good-hearted weakling is a ball of confusion and a moral washout. Perhaps the chief question concerning the good-hearted weakling is whether he or she will be what the outright bigot (e.g., Lyle) is charged with being: "an honorable tribesman . . . defend[ing] . . . the honor and purity of his tribe" (19). Indeed, Baldwin shows the distrust that many blacks have for so-called progressive whites by emphasizing the skepticism of the black students toward Parnell, in contrast to Meridian's faith in the beginning of the play that Parnell will help to convict Lyle. Countering Meridian's statement that blacks should believe in Parnell because he not only helped to bring about a trial for Lyle's murder of Richard but also since he is "a pretty good friend to us all," Lorenzo, a student who clearly symbolizes the growing militancy of many students in the 1960s, says, "We can't afford to be too trusting . . . when a white man's a good white man he's good because he wants you to be good" (17–18). This idea conveys the notion that the sort of whites embodied in Parnell exhibit the liberal qualities of guardianship of blacks, and what Baldwin indicates is that such whites want to be guardians of blacks' very identity. Moreover, this attitude is characteristic, Baldwin seems to say, of an "honorable tribesman": as long as blacks' identities stay "in their place," such whites as Parnell will help them—but inadequately and disingenuously.

The deep divisions within the good-hearted weakling are indicative of a fundamental confusion (in contrast to the honest hatred of blacks seen in the outright bigot). These divisions again show the "personal incoherence" of which Baldwin writes in "White Man's Guilt." The extremity of Parnell's personal incoherence is Baldwin's way of dramatizing that Parnell is a microcosm of a much larger neurosis in the psychology of many whites concerning race relations. Examples of these psychological and behavioral divisions abound. For example, although Parnell helps bring about Lyle's arrest, he tells Meridian, "I think I should go to Lyle's house and warn him. After all, I brought it about and he *is* a friend of mine" (18). These are astonishing words in light of to whom he is saying them. Still, Parnell's loyalty to his black friends may seem evident during his visit to Lyle as he tells him, "You may think a colored boy who gets ruined in the North then comes home to try to pull himself together deserves to die—I don't" (27). This statement, however, is prefaced by Parnell's use of the word "nigger," and he pledges to Lyle, "I'll never turn against you" (28). This passage in "White Man's Guilt" says that whites may pretend to be friends to blacks in one setting, "But, on the same day, in another gathering," such whites are "proud of that history for which [they] do not wish to pay" (Baldwin 1985, 411). Indeed, in addition to never objecting to anyone's use of the word "nigger," Parnell's weak status as a progressive white is shown in a more extreme way. Again speaking to the father of the man Lyle murdered, Parnell utters these words: "[F]rom another point of view Lyle hasn't got anything *against* colored people . . . he's not mean, he's not cruel. He's a poor white man. He's not a wicked man" (61). That Parnell knows of Lyle's hatred of blacks and strongly suspects him of murder make these words pathetically illogical. Moreover, the fact that Parnell represents whites who are fence-sitters to the point of being morally and ethically castrated even as they think of themselves as blacks' allies is evident in his refusal of Meridian's plea that he get Lyle to admit to the murder: "I can't do it. I'm his friend. I can't betray him" (62). Nevertheless, Parnell seems to claim an equal friendship with Meridian. The question that Baldwin seems to be posing is to whom is such a white person loyal? Is he loyal to the buddy—the racist murderer to whom he shows his male bonding and his tribesmanship as he listens warmly to Lyle say, "Hell, Parnell, you're smarter than me. . . . [But] hell, you ain't so different from me in *other* ways—in spite of all your *ideas.* Two things we always had in common—liquor and poon-tang. We couldn't get enough of neither one" (103)? Or is he loyal to the grieving black man who he claims is his friend and whose approval he values? The answer becomes exceedingly clear as the plot develops. On these themes, Leeming's statements are relevant:

[W]hen we see Lyle and Parnell together as old friends in Whitetown, juxtaposed with the events across the gulf in Blacktown and the friendly patronizing attitude of Parnell there, we see what Baldwin had discerned from William

Faulkner's remarks on race relations in Oxford, Mississippi [that in a hypo-
thetical race war he would join with other whites in shooting blacks in the
streets]—the fact that liberal Whitetown and bigoted Whitetown are much
closer to each other than either could be to Blacktown. (Leeming 1994, 236)

The issue of Parnell's divided loyalty is the strongest example of Baldwin's
theory of whites' personal incoherence. According to Baldwin, whites ultimately cannot be loyal to blacks because they can only accept deracialized
blacks. In fact, the climactic scene that conveys Parnell's moral and ethical
collapse occurs when Parnell begs Meridian, in essence, not to be a black
person. When Meridian refers to the hardships faced by blacks, for example, Parnell states, "I was talking about *you*—not your history" (57). He also
dismisses Meridian's references to the unjust treatment of blacks by whites
by saying, "We have to start from scratch, or do our best to start from
scratch" (61). Implicit in this statement again is the dismissal of history—
and the role that history plays in current race relations. "We have come too
far together, there is too much at stake, for you to become black now, for me
to become white," Parnell explains to Meridian (58).

Baldwin illustrates in this aspect of the play another key critique of whites
found in "White Man's Guilt."

[For] history, as no one seems to know . . . does not refer merely, or even
principally to the past. On the contrary, the great force of history comes from
the fact that we carry it within us, are unconsciously controlled by it in many
ways, and history is literally *present* in all that we do. It could scarcely be otherwise, since it is to history that we owe . . . our identities and our aspirations.
(1985, 410)

Baldwin says further that when people realize that individuals themselves
are "that great historical creation," the realization comes with "great pain
and terror" for they must face the truth about how their actions either uphold or challenge bigotry and face their complicity in the state of race relations today (410). These ideas are threatening to whites such as those
symbolized by Parnell because they force whites to challenge and change
the aspects of their identity that are part of the continuum of racism in
America rather than expect blacks to accept their inadequate self-represen-
tation as allies.

Other intriguing issues are raised by the exchange between Parnell and
Meridian in the scene under discussion. For a white person who is comfortable with the word "nigger" and devoted to "poon-tang" (indicating
Parnell's sexualized racism toward black women) to ask for nonracial relations—and identities—for himself and blacks and to ask a black man not to
"go black" on him is the height of hypocrisy and irrationality. This issue is
discussed in "Dialogue in Black and White (1964–1965)" between Baldwin

and white writer Budd Schulberg. When Schulberg asks, "[W]hich side are you on, Elijah Muhammad's side or what you call my sloppy liberal-interracial side?" Baldwin answers, "Baby, don't lay that on me. It's not for *me* to decide, it's for *you* to decide. . . . I mean you and all my well meaning white friends" (Troupe 1988, 136). This topic raises a key aspect of white denial: blacks' anger and skepticism toward whites is a *response*, not some innate free-floating black bitterness—a response to them and their actions (and inaction).

One of Baldwin's main messages in *Blues for Mister Charlie* seems to be that such self-proclaimed progressives as Parnell are completely self-deluded, and, as Baldwin and Margaret Mead discuss in *Rap on Race*, they can only accept blacks as they *reject* their race and any attitudes that differ from theirs.[17] Thus, at the heart of such self-deluded whites is a bigot—one who would scoff at the charge even while shrinking under it. Hence, Parnell and what he represents earn Baldwin's stern condemnation. This condemnation is perhaps strongest when Baldwin indicates that both Lyle and Parnell are defending their identities as whites in the way they deal with blacks. Similar to Baldwin's indication that Lyle's murder of Richard was a defense of whiteness as an identity when he exclaims, "I had to kill him. I'm a white man!" (157), Meridian concludes in the climactic scene with Parnell, "You *are* a white man, aren't you? Just another white man—after all" (62).

Obviously, a huge question remains: What does this condemnation mean? What does whiteness mean as a form of identity rather than as a mere biological fact? What Parnell clearly symbolizes is the friend who fails blacks; the crux of this failure is both the cowardice manifested in the personal incoherence of which Baldwin writes and in what South African Nobel Prize winner Nadine Gordimer has called the "sense of whiteness"—a sense of privilege and a devotion to maintaining an illusion of invulnerability regarding the consequences of white racism.[18] Such white persons, Baldwin conveys in his play, are, unlike the outright bigot, traitors to blacks; they encourage trust and meet that trust with betrayal. That is why many blacks hold good-hearted weaklings in greater contempt than outright bigots: one is the enemy you see; the other is the enemy whose failure you do not see until it is too late.

The defensiveness with which many whites respond to this feeling among many blacks is illustrated in responses to *Blues for Mister Charlie*. According to Leeming, reviews of the play were "for the most part defensive. . . . Many whites seemed to feel that Baldwin was somehow turning against them, that he was ungrateful for the white liberals' contributions to the struggle" (1994, 238). Clearly, such whites miss what they could learn about themselves by facing how they appear to blacks—and why they appear this way. This cowardice attests to the power of Baldwin's play, as illustrated by Amiri Baraka's comments about Baldwin in "Jimmy!" "Jimmy's voice, as much as Dr. King's or Malcolm X's, helped shepherd and guide us toward black liberation. . . . The celebrated James Baldwin of earlier times could not be used [by whites] to cover the undaunted freedom chants of the Jimmy who walked with King or SNCC or the evil little nigger who wrote *Blues for Mister Charlie*!" (Troupe 1988, 132). Baraka's last characterization of Baldwin's image to whites as a result of the play helps to explain why some educators who consider themselves Americanists may teach regularly the Baldwin of "earlier times" (e.g., *Giovanni's Room*, 1956) but not Baldwin's more confrontational works which try to destroy many whites' images of themselves regarding racism.

THE LIBERAL

"I can't stand white liberals. Obviously I can't stand white liberals."
—James Baldwin in *Conversations with James Baldwin*
(Standley and Pratt 1989, 51)

The problems of liberalism are best exemplified in Langston Hughes's "Poor Little Black Fellow" in *The Ways of White Folks* (1933). This story portrays the liberal's belief in guardianship and trusteeship as being deeply rooted in the fact that it seems that many liberals want to control blacks' very identity as a condition for helping them. Hughes shows the liberal attitude to be not merely "Do what I say and not what I do" but also "Be what I want and not what I am." For many writers, this attitude connotes the liberals' fundamental belief in inequality, for many liberals' progressiveness seems founded on the feelings that they know best not only how blacks should act but how they should be.

These attitudes are summarized in Louis E. Lomax's "The White Liberal." He writes a catalogue that details the gap between liberals' sentiments and their behavior citing people who wish blacks were more like the good Negro of their imaginations: businessmen who profess to welcome racial progress as long as they are not affected by it, whites who may welcome a black neighbor but wish to God that no interracial romance will be unleashed as a result, professors who make their progressiveness part of their academic persona but who automatically suspect black students to be unqualified.[19] In short, Lomax sees the white liberal as conflicted and dishonest to a neurotic degree.

These attitudes are symbolized by the white couple, the Pembertons, in Hughes's story. Hughes highlights the couple's arrogant and self-congratulatory attitudes, to which Lomax alludes, adding to the picture their missionary impulse to save a black person. The portrait of the Pembertons painted by Hughes illustrates the relevance of his work to his response to James Baldwin at a 1961 symposium. "Hughes reacted favorably to Baldwin's remark . . . that 'the Negro writer is not as interesting a subject to me as the Negro in this country in the minds of other people—the Negro character . . . and the role that he's always played in the American subconscious'" (Leeming 1994, 159). The whites of "Poor Little Black Fellow"—particularly the Pembertons—are Hughes's representation of the subconscious of the failed liberal. As a result, "Poor Little Black Fellow" makes one realize what is at stake with whites who arrogantly fail to question their own motives in their dealings with blacks: the denial of blacks' humanity and the continuance of a dynamic that causes blacks to be treated like pawns by those who may profess to be their best friends. If, as the saying goes, "An unexamined life is not worth living," Hughes shows what the consequences may be when blacks are subjected to being controlled by people with unexamined consciences.

Perhaps the best line that could be applied to the Pembertons is borrowed from Amiri Baraka's *Tales*: "WHITE PHILANTHROPY AMOK AGAIN."[20] The fact that the Pembertons are a wealthy and prominent New England family who take in Arnie, the child of their black servants, after his parents' deaths, seems designed by Hughes to delude the reader into believing that the couple's charity—or philanthropy—toward Arnie is positive. Hughes, however, conveys that the imbalance in the relationship between the white couple and Arnie is rooted in their own goodness, which is best manifested in Hughes's constant use of the word "nice" to describe their treatment of Arnie. Hughes's ironic use of this word is best shown when the couple decide to be "very nice" to the black child: "So once again the Pembertons turned loose on Arnie their niceness."[21] It seems, therefore, that Hughes wants to use the Pembertons to represent the type of whites who are condescendingly kind and charitable to blacks in return for a feeling of ownership of them, as the story goes on to illustrate.

Hughes's portrayal of the Pembertons as a symbol of a flawed white identity is clear at several points. Bringing to mind Lyle's statement about Richard's death that because he is white he felt he had to kill the black man is Hughes's presentation of the Pembertons' thoughts about why they want to keep the black child after his parents die:

> Amanda Lee had been a perfect servant. And her husband Arnold likewise.
> . . . [God] had left the Pembertons poor little black Arnie as their Christian duty. There was no other way to consider the little colored boy whom they were raising as their very own, except as a Christian duty. After all, they were white. (1933, 129)

Although Lyle's statement implying that his protection of his white identity causes his killing a black person is not comparable to such seemingly high-minded sentiments as the Pembertons', the white couple's nice feelings lead to an attempted "soul murder" (to borrow a phrase from Alice Miller's critique of authoritarian parental figures in *For Your Own Good*)[22] that is founded on the whites' belief that Arnie is a mere "duty" of which they are proprietors. Indeed, the Pembertons' and other whites' treatment of Arnie as "their very own" is, like the word "nice," repeated to the point that it becomes ominous, especially as white ownership of Arnie isolates and alienates him (Hughes 1933, 131–32). One owns a thing, not a person; and this fact explains the dehumanizing reference to Arnie as the Pembertons discuss their decision to keep him: "'Poor little black fellow,' said Grace Pemberton to her husband and her sister. . . . 'I think it is our Christian duty to keep it, and raise it up in the way it should go.' Somehow, for a long time, she called Arnie 'it'" (131). As the story progresses, Hughes makes it clear that, to the liberal white couple, Arnie is an "it": a thing to be manipulated, controlled, and used by them to feel good about themselves—a sort of human vibrator. Hughes uses this issue to address more complex ones.

One main aspect of failed liberalism is that such whites *need* to use blacks in order to affirm their sense of themselves. The attitude seems to be, "What good is believing in one's progressiveness if it is not confirmed by the object of it?" This feeling has its consequences: it boosts the egos of whites and reduces blacks to crutches used by whites to bolster their idealized self-images. According to Baldwin, "People invent categories in order to feel safe. White people invented black people in order to give white people an identity."[23] In "Poor Little Black Fellow," Hughes demonstrates the delusion of superiority that whites get from this invention of blacks as inferior objects in his portrayal of the Pembertons' and the town's self-perception as a result of their categorization of Arnie as the "poor little black" thing from which they derive their moral greatness.

Whites' (perhaps unconscious) use of blacks as crutches to hold up their delusions of adequacy is demonstrated by Hughes when the Pembertons and other citizens of the all-white town of Mapleton need Arnie psychologically. To the townspeople, Arnie is "a symbol of how Christian charity should really be administered in the true spirit of human brotherhood" (Hughes 1933, 132). Arnie is a symbol to whites of their goodness: their "charity" and their "brotherhood." Moreover, Arnie serves the same purpose to the town as Sula to the black townspeople in Toni Morrison's *Sula* (1973): proof of their worth that is so strong (to them) that they feel they no longer need to show their goodness through any other actions.

> The church and the Pembertons were really a little proud of Arnie . . . a poor little black fellow whom they, through Christ, had taken in. Throughout the years the whole of Mapleton began to preen itself on its charity and kindness to Arnie. One would think that nobody in the town need ever again do another good deed: this acceptance of a black boy was quite enough. (133)

In this passage, one can infer that the town is not really "proud of Arnie" but of themselves for this symbol—"a little black spot in a forest of white heads"—of their self-imagined racial enlightenment. Nevertheless, when

Arnie hits adolescence and is no longer a "little black boy," he becomes, as Hughes reflects the thoughts of the town, "a Negro problem" (133). They never had accepted Arnie as a fellow human being but as a lesser form of life: someone whose need for their help made him useful psychologically to them—a sort of black badge of their egotistical illusions. More complex than these feelings is the fact that they never truly accepted Arnie as a black. "To tell the truth, everybody had got so used to Arnie that nobody really thought of him as a Negro—until he put on long trousers and went to high-school. Now they noticed that he was truly very black. And his voice suddenly became deep and mannish" (134). It almost seems that Arnie, merely by growing up, became close to being a black "ape," as Bigger Thomas is described in the newspapers after he is arrested for killing Mary Dalton in Richard Wright's *Native Son* (1940). Hughes indicates that the threatening nature of Arnie's "mannish blackness" is tied to white parents' fears of his having contact with their daughters and with white girls in the town in general. "They'd have to let him go, poor little black fellow! Certainly, he was their very own! But in Mapleton, what could he do, how could he live, whom could he marry? The Pembertons were a bit worried. . . . So they decided to be extra nice to him. Indeed, everybody in Mapleton decided to be extra nice to him" (136). It is clear that this niceness is a neurotic cover for their shame. In regard to the whites' attitude toward and treatment of Arnie, Hughes implies the following: scratch the surface of many a liberal and you will find a bigot with a guilty conscience.

In addition, the white discomfort of Arnie once the people can no longer ignore his race despite their seemingly benevolent sense of ownership of him can be explained by theories offered by sociologist Erving Goffman in *Stigma.* Goffman studies what he feels is one of the chief aspects of bigotry: those who consider themselves the norm see difference as threatening and thus demand that those who are different from them minimize this aspect of their identity in order to keep the "normals" at ease.[24] (Goffman emphasizes that the ideas of who is normal and who is stigmatized are a matter of ideology; 138.) That Arnie's situation represents a fundamental characteristic of prejudice is evident when one reflects on how Goffman's ideas explain the whites' treatment of Arnie:

> That the stigmatized individual can be caught taking the tactful acceptance of himself too seriously indicates that this acceptance is conditional. It depends upon normals not being pressed past the point at which they can easily extend acceptance—or, at worst, uneasily extend it. The stigmatized are tactfully expected to be gentlemanly and not to press their luck; they should not test the limits of the acceptance shown them, nor make it the basis for still further demands.
>
> The nature of "good adjustment" is now apparent. It requires that the stigmatized individual cheerfully and unselfconsciously accept himself as essentially the same as normals, while at the same time he voluntarily withholds

himself from those situations in which normals would find it difficult to give lip service to their similar acceptance of him. (120–21)

Goffman examines the impact of this phenomenon on those who consider themselves the norm: they never have to face the intolerant nature of their alleged acceptance of those who are different, and they never have to appreciate the discomfort and suffering of those who are different. These factors contribute to how normals evaluate the behavior (and very identity) of those whom they reject even as they fool themselves into thinking they have accepted them (120–21). And what are the consequences to a black person of having to deal with such directive and hypocritical whites? Hughes answers this question in a variety of ways.

The narrative style of the story, which places most of the emphasis on the thoughts of the Pembertons via the third person limited point of view, seems designed both to explore the psychology of such whites and to reflect how overlooked and overshadowed by white narcissism blacks are when they are reduced to objects of whites' self-worship. Yet, the whites' treatment of Arnie and Hughes's portrayal of his feelings make it clear what the whites represented in the story really demand of blacks: the erasure of their identity.

One characteristic of racist whites is emphasized in Arnie's plight—that the object of their prejudice simply is not perceived by them as being able to judge what they are doing and thus to resent it. Hughes dramatizes this theme in his presentation of how Arnie is manipulated and made miserable by the good whites of Mapleton. When Arnie is a child, for example, and he feels that he is the whites' badge of superiority,

> Arnie realized how they felt, but he didn't know what to do about it. He kept himself quiet and inconspicuous, and studied hard. He was very grateful and very lonely. There were no other colored children in town. But all the grown-up white people made their children be nice to him, always very nice. . . . So even the children were over-kind to Arnie. (Hughes 1933, 133)

Furthermore, when Arnie becomes an adolescent and repels whites with his seemingly newly acquired blackness, one understands that they accepted his race only insofar as his identity could be shrunk into the role of an inferior and helpless child. When his race can no longer be dismissed, Arnie is ghettoized by whites.

> Even while the stigmatized individual is told that he is a human being like everyone else, he is being told that it would be unwise to . . . let down "his" group. In brief, he is told he is like anyone else and that he isn't. . . . This contradiction and joke is his fate and his destiny. . . . The stigmatized individual thus finds himself in an arena of detailed argument and discussion concerning what he ought to think of himself, that is, his ego identity. (Goffman 1963, 124)

The whites' determination of Arnie's identity, after they perceive his difference as disturbing (i.e., his racial difference from them), occurs at several points in the story. First, when Arnie is sixteen and the Boy Scout camp
to which the Pembertons want to send him states that it does not accept'
blacks, "The village of Mapleton and the Pembertons felt awfully apologetic
for American democracy's attitude to Arnie, whose father died in the war.
But, after all, they couldn't control the Boy Scout Camp. They were extra-
nice to Arnie, though—everybody" (Hughes 1933, 134). Arnie's misery in
the aftermath of this situation is great. The Pembertons dump Arnie into
blackness—"[H]e couldn't move in the social world of Mapleton," 135)—by
sending him to a charity camp in Boston for "black kids from the slums of
Boston who . . . made fun of him because he didn't know how to play the
dozens. So Arnie, to whom Negroes were a new nation, even if he was black,
was amazed and bewildered, and came home" (135).

The failure of Arnie's "owners" to expose him to children of his own
race until they no longer want to interact with him causes Arnie to become
an exile from both races, which puts him in a state of isolation and emotional starvation. Moreover, the Pembertons' deciding (without consulting
Arnie) to send him to Fisk—"Where those dear Jubilee singers sang so
beautifully"—and their moving him into the top floor of the garage (on
the false pretext that he could more easily entertain his nonexistent
friends there) further exile Arnie (135). While it may be arguable that it is
admirable that the Pembertons decide to send him places (e.g., the camp
and Fisk) where he will be among other blacks and to give him independence from them by letting him live along, their motivations and results
are otherwise:

> They were one of New England's oldest families, and they were raising Arnie
> as their son. But he was an African, a nice Christian African, and he ought to
> be among his own people. There he could be a good influence and have a
> place. . . . And even as a servant in Mapleton, Arnie would have been a little
> out of place [since it] was more fashionable to have white help. (137)

Hence, the Pembertons' thinking of Arnie's need to be among blacks has
nothing to do with their valuing black culture and thus feeling that Arnie
should be exposed to his own heritage. Clearly, identity control over Arnie
is at the heart of the Pembertons' plans to send him to Fisk: "Maybe he'd
marry one of those lovely brown girls who sang spirituals so beautifully, and
live like a good Christian man—occasionally visiting the Pembertons, and
telling them about his influence on the poor blacks of the South" (138).
Again, the Pembertons seem to think they have created in Arnie a missionary who will be a "civilizing" force on other blacks. Yet, as the remainder of
the story reveals, Arnie wants to decide his own life—not as an occasional
visitor to the edges of whiteness, but as an autonomous person accepted

fully by people of any race who value him as an equal, not as a target of condescending and controlling kindness.

Hughes portrays how Arnie rejects the "good adjustment" bargain with whites when he changes during a pre-college trip abroad. Arnie's feelings during a trip to France, on which the Pembertons take him as a nice gesture, should cause the reader to reflect on Arnie's feelings throughout the story about whites' treatment of him, even when the narration focuses on the whites' point of view. When Arnie is in France, his friendship with another black American, Claudina Lawrence, causes him to be "happy to be recognized by one of his own" (141). This happiness, in direct contrast to his misery when he is made by the Pembertons to go to the black charity camp, indicates that self-direction is what Arnie wants in developing relationships, not being dumped by whites into the laps of blacks. Moreover, with Claudina, "For the first time in his life Arnie was really happy. Somebody had offered him something without charity, without condescension, without prayer, without distance, without being nice" (142). This passage stands as a critique of the egotistical liberalism of the whites who are the focus of Hughes's venom. Hughes uses Arnie's growing awareness and independence as a vehicle to reveal the bigotry within the hearts of such liberals. To the Pembertons, for example, Arnie's independence (which brings him happiness for the first time in his life) is mere surliness and disrespect. And when Arnie becomes enamored of a white woman, the Pembertons are outraged—this conforms neither to their visions of his life nor their view of his place. As Arnie argues with the Pembertons, the destructiveness and indifference of their visions of him and, in fact, their treatment of him his entire life are revealed. He tells them, "I don't want to go to Fisk. . . . No . . . I don't want to go. It'll be like that camp in Boston. . . . Separate, segregated, shut-off! Black people kept away from everybody else. I go to Fisk, my classmates, Harvard and Amherst and Yale. . . . I sleep in the garage, you sleep in the house" (153). Arnie's problem, therefore, is not with Fisk—it is that the white people's choice to send him there is the latest action in their having chosen his life and his identity for him in the past and present but, Arnie is determined, not the future.

The Pembertons' responses to Arnie at this point in the story are the quintessential reactions of such liberals under attack by black writers. Reflecting the ignorant and disingenuous white defense of bigotry by saying that only actions intentionally meant to harm can be considered racist, Mrs. Pemberton responds to Arnie's speech by saying, "We didn't mean it like that!" (153) The inadequacy of this reaction in light of Arnie's presentation of the issues is monumental. The Pembertons' true inadequacy is further revealed when, in response to Arnie's feelings, Mrs. Pemberton starts crying in a passage where the third person limited point of view seems, intriguingly, to begin with Mr. Pemberton and shift to Arnie: "Anger possessed him [Pemberton], fury against this ungrateful black boy who made his wife cry. . . . And now she was crying over this . . . this. . . . In the back of his mind was the word nigger. And Arnie felt it" (154). It is evident that, for the Pembertons, an independent Arnie can have only one identity: "a black devil" (154). Liberalism, as presented in this story, never accepts a black identity that is not shaped by and approved by whites. Thus, Arnie's belief that by introducing the Pembertons to his white girlfriend and thus showing them that blacks and whites can truly care about each other he can "educate them a bit" is bound to fail (149–50). In sum, the ending of the story, in which Arnie and the Pembertons reject each other, shows that Arnie, when he becomes himself instead of an object controlled by whites, is an example of the validity of Goffman's comments on the ultimate destructiveness of identity suppression of those who are the targets of prejudice on their relationships with those who demand this suppression as the condition for ostensible acceptance:

> Control of identity information has a special bearing on relationships. Relationships can necessitate time spent together, and the more time the individual spends with another the more chance the other will acquire discrediting information about him. Further, as already suggested, every relationship obliges the related persons to exchange an appropriate amount of intimate facts about the self, as evidence of trust and mutual commitment. Close relationships that the individual had before he came to have something to conceal therefore become compromised. (Goffman 1963, 86)

This passage can help one understand why the trip to Europe is the turning point for Arnie and his white keepers. Arnie naively wants to share the new facts about himself: his love and his resentment at having always been someone to whom things were done by white people, rather than his having been allowed to be an active agent in his own life. The mature Arnie at the end of the story is one who knows that he can no longer tolerate repressing his "identity information" before those who profess to think of him as their own. At this point, the false bargain of whites' acceptance collapses for the one thing they never acknowledged—the fact that Arnie is not an "it" to be manipulated at will but someone determined to be his own person instead of their own object of charity.

The culmination of the story, the rejection by Arnie of his benefactors once he becomes independent, reflects Hughes's experience during the Harlem Renaissance. Hughes was always suspicious of the authenticity and potential endurance of whites' embracing of black culture. In *The Big Sea*, Hughes recalls, "It was a period when the Negro was in vogue. I was there. . . . But I thought it wouldn't last long. . . . For how could a large and enthusiastic number of [white] people be crazy about Negroes forever?"[25] "Poor Little Black Fellow" illustrates, therefore, a white mentality of blacks being diversions for whites, a kind of fad. Furthermore, Arnie's final break from the white couple recalls Hughes's recollections of his own breakup with his white patron. In a section entitled "Not Primitive," Hughes tells of this episode in his life:

> She possessed the power to control people's lives—pick them up and put them down when and where she wished. She wanted me to be primitive. . . . But, unfortunately, I did not feel the rhythms of the primitive surging through me, and so I could not live and write as though I did. . . . I was not what she wanted me to be. So, in the end it all came back near to the old impasse of white and Negro again, white and Negro—as do most relationships in America. (1986, 324)

In recounting this episode, Hughes makes a statement that helps explain the often sardonic (as opposed to blatantly angry) tone of "Poor Little Black Fellow." In telling his benefactor that he would no longer accept money from her but hoped to part as friends (and being rejected, similar to what happens to Arnie when he hopes to educate the Pembertons), Hughes states, "I cannot write here about that last half-hour in the big, bright drawing-room high above Park Avenue because when I think about it, even now, something happens in the pit of my stomach that makes me ill" (325). "Poor Little Black Fellow," then, seems to be Hughes's filtering of his emotions concerning his experiences and observations during the Harlem Renaissance into a story that represents a white identity type much larger than the particular time and place of the narrative. Furthermore, it is especially intriguing that while reading the story, as Arnold Ramparsad observed of Hughes's poetry, one is not struck by a tone of overt anger; the narrative pecks away at white liberalism to the point where nothing is left.[26] Hence, while Hughes may not seem to be "bitter," to borrow Howells's objection to Chesnutt's *The Marrow of Tradition*, Hughes's juxtaposition of his often sardonic tone with his portrayal of Arnie's misery, frustration, and, finally, independence makes "Poor Little Black Fellow" as powerful and complex an exposé of a white mentality dangerous to blacks as the picture of whites drawn in Chesnutt's novel.

THE LIBERAL/GOOD-HEARTED WEAKLING

The psychological failure of the good-hearted weakling and the overbearing and condescending directiveness of the liberal are illustrated in Joyce Y. Rogers's "An Image of Cooperation: White Volunteers in the Civil Rights Freedom Summers Project." Rogers's research is particularly fascinating because it focuses on transcribed interviews from Stanford University's KZSU radio station, which sent interviewers to over fifty cities in the South where white Northern college students had gone to help in the fight for voting rights and voter registration of blacks. In 1965, more than

200 interviews were conducted with the volunteers. Five hundred students, according to Rogers, went to the South as part of the Freedom Summers movement in 1964; there were 750 student volunteers in 1965 (1982, 8). The importance of Rogers's research cannot be overstated. One major goal of the Freedom Summers was to project an image of interracial cooperation in the struggle for racial progress; therefore, the strong elements of racism among what some might expect to be the most progressive whites—young, educated people from such universities as Stanford and Yale who would risk personal injury in order to advance racial progress—are evidence of a marked strain of bigotry in the white imagination with notions of racial enlightenment. Strikingly, however, Rogers argued that this dichotomy was inevitable: "Ironically, the Freedom Summers volunteers were the best and brightest products of the system that had oppressed the black race for so many centuries, therefore, it is not surprising that many of these volunteers displayed an ethnocentrism that proved inimical to the more idealistic goals of the Freedom Summers" (10). Moreover, echoing a duality that exists in many of Hughes's portrayals of whites in *The Ways of White Folks*, Rogers points out the main styles of bigotry that existed in the psychology of many of the white students: living among blacks, "many white volunteers dealt with differences by assuming the natural superiority of their own way of life. Conversely, some 'radical' white students tried to close the gap by completely adopting what they perceived as 'Negro culture,' exhibiting a 'Negrophilia' that was . . . devastating to the ideals of the summers" (11). For brevity, only a few interviews, representative of many others in Rogers's study, are considered here.

The glorification of blacks to a status beyond human—and, therefore, dehumanizing—is exposed by Langston Hughes in his story "Slave on the Block." That it finds its equivalent in the attitudes shown by some of the white volunteers makes it frighteningly evident that many ostensibly progressive whites hold onto a sickeningly sentimental image of blacks as the noble savage or the child of nature (to borrow Albert Schweitzer's characterization of Africans in *On the Edge of the Primeval Forest*[27]) which also tried to pass for enlightenment in the "romantic racism" in Harriet Beecher Stowe's *Uncle Tom's Cabin* (1852). The continuity of this mentality is evident when Rogers cites this sickeningly sentimental view in many examples from the Freedom Summers. One white student volunteer states,

We have . . . been astonished by the number of fantastic personalities who have risen out of the morass and to whom every obstacle is just a challenge, among whom are many leaders of the community and many others, many young people, many old women, who have risen out and have acquired for themselves more dignity than is possible for any white person in this society to ever acquire, by triumphing over every obstacle, fantastic women, fantastic old

men, and men who know the world this way and that way, and men who are
stern and upright and powerful in their dignity. (20)

Although many readers might find these views extremely complimentary
to blacks, such attitudes show that whites of this ideology do not accept
blacks as humans who are flawed and have both strengths and weaknesses.
Moreover, such romanticized bigotry often exiles blacks who cannot be
slavered over by whites in awestruck admiration, which is the case in Stowe's
Uncle Tom's Cabin when Stowe sends the righteously angry George to live in
Africa at the end of the book. There is no place for George in her imaginative America (or, I should say, in her good-hearted but weak imagination)
because, although George might be right in his anger at racial oppression,
he represents the kind of black person who cannot be controlled. As Rogers
points out, "The glorification of the majority of oppressed peoples and their
warmth and laughter in the midst of want and sorrow" (20) is a white rejection of blacks who cannot be viewed as simple and wondrous beings, innocent children, or the embodiment of absolute greatness, the only forms of
black identity that many good-hearted weaklings can accept. Such acceptance of blacks as pronounced by this student shows that the weakness in
those who hold such attitudes precludes their seeing blacks as equal, fellow
human beings—an attitude that reaffirms Baldwin and Mead's assertion in
Rap on Race that "benevolent" whites often refute aspects of blacks that do
not conform to their image of what blacks should be (Baldwin and Mead
1971, 10).

In sum, history confirms the view of such writers as Baldwin and Hughes
that many whites' ostensible acceptance of blacks is conditional and superficial. This aspect of Rogers's study also helps explain Lomax's idea in "The
White Liberal" that many blacks doubt the sincerity of whites' liberalism
and question their ability to follow through on their progressive sentiments
with actions (Lomax 1966, 44–45). Lomax asserts that blacks' suspicion of
liberals' dishonesty arises from the fact that it seems that many liberals accept only blacks whom they can deem extraordinary but reject ordinary
blacks. Lomax concludes that, if one cannot be accepted unless as "an exception to the rule," then the rejection of and prejudice toward blacks in
general remains in place (44–45).

These ideas help illuminate one of the problems that seems to have
plagued the Freedom Summers and contributed to the breakdown of the
black–white coalition. Rogers's study analyzes these points. While Rogers
makes a complete distinction between those white college students who exhibit romantic racism and those who came to believe in white superiority, it
can be argued, in fact, that the closet supremacist is the ego identity off split
of the sentimental racist. This connection is especially troubling for race
relations.

Rogers's discussion shows the ways in which many students interviewed came to have revulsion for blacks after living in the midst of poverty and the results of discrimination. This attitude is best exemplified in the following statement:

> I think that spending a summer in a Negro community can induce some sort of . . . sympathy for the southerners' stand. . . . [W]e have run into many disappointing things and personality traits in the Negro community which of course can be laid to the system. And I . . . have seen apathy, terrific apathy, tremendous apathy, unbelievable apathy. . . . Often we can have some sympathy for the white southerner who does not want his child to go to school with somebody who has this disease or whose morals are like this or that. (19)

This student concludes that it is absurd to argue for racial equality between people who possess such great differences in class, education, and morals (19). These perceptions clearly bear out the idea that prejudice is manifested in cognitive distortions which reduce the details of the actual character and behavior of the objects of bigotry to a blur of negative characteristics. Yet, it is fascinating in this case that the prejudice exists side by side with a belief in helping blacks and in one's own racial progressiveness. For instance, this student does not merely want to write off blacks as inferiors, as would be a logical inference from many of his stated perceptions of blacks. These negative feelings coexist with a desire to ameliorate them. The student tries to soften these vast generalizations and exaggerations by saying that "of course, this pertains only to about sixty per cent of the cases or seventy per cent" (19). This statement seems the opposite side of the same coin as the excessive admiration of blacks: both attitudes reduce blacks to simple stereotypes rather than human beings who do not look to whites for identity approval.

Furthermore, my interpretation of Rogers's research is that this revulsion exists side by side with the directiveness that characterizes the white liberal. A motif in the interviews is the desire of some whites to control the struggle for black rights and thus to control the blacks with whom they are supposedly working for equality. As one white student comments,

> I mean northern white kids have been running shows since they were in grammar school, even earlier, and they were encouraged to do that all along the line, while the Negroes North and South have not had that encouragement. And it's important for them, for their self image, that they can hold themselves on their own strength, you know. [White students should] hold back that knowledge, hold back that go-gettedness and doingness and be willing to be a foot soldier. Then I think there's a future. If they insist on usurping that kind of show, then there's going to be problems. . . . And if northern white volunteers can make their peace with that kind of thing, then they will be able to work in the South, and work effectively and be of assistance. (33)

Indeed, another student recalls that one of his main motivations in becoming a volunteer was "being able to direct things" in dealing with the blacks' struggle for civil rights (12). Once again, history confirms the controlling and narcissistic attitudes and behavior of white identity found in many black writers' images of whites.

The failure—moral, psychological, and practical—of the demeaning directiveness of liberalism is revealed by one of the white students' critiques of this very ideology:

[B]eing a northern student, all I can say is I've seen a lot of northern students come down here and screw everything up . . . there's the type of person who comes down to help raise the poor Negro, and they're the superior Great White Father carrying the white man's burden and they come down and just cause all sorts of trouble. They have this kind of superior attitude: well, I'm here to help you all and I'm white and I know what's right. (12)

CONCLUSION

The works discussed in this chapter make it clear that if more whites could be so analytical of their good intentions toward blacks and how they often undermine them by a sort of unintentional white supremacy, the strain that has marked race relations throughout American history would be less prevalent.

By examining the interviews of the white Freedom Summers volunteers, one can see that the guardianship so abhorrent to blacks in the white liberal and the good-hearted weakling are part of a continuum of how blacks have understood whites, as presented in the typology of images in the black imagination. In reflecting on the images discussed in this chapter, one should think about the source of the distrust for whites among many blacks: many if not most whites have not faced how their identities have been understood and interpreted by blacks and thus, as Baldwin argues in *The Fire Next Time*, fail to be released from "the tyranny of [their] mirror."[28]

NOTES

1. Erik H. Erikson, "Ego Development and Historical Change," in *Identity and the Life Cycle* (New York: W. W. Norton, 1980), 38.

2. Joyce Y. Rogers, "An Image of Cooperation: White Volunteers in the Civil Rights Freedom Summers Project," unpublished graduate essay (Stanford University, June 1, 1982), 14.

3. James Baldwin, "Notes for Blues," in *Blues for Mister Charlie* (New York: Dell Publishing, 1964), 6.

4. David Leeming, *James Baldwin* (New York: Henry Holt, 1994), 236.

5. James Baldwin, "White Man's Guilt," in *The Price of the Ticket* (New York: St. Martin's/Marek, 1985), 411.

6. William L. Andrews, "William Dean Howells and Charles W. Chesnutt: Criticism and Race Fiction in the Age of Booker T. Washington," *American Literature* 48 (November 1976): 331.

7. Nikki Giovanni, *Gemini* (Indianapolis: Bobbs-Merrill, 1971), 104.

8. Charles W. Chesnutt, *The Marrow of Tradition* (Ann Arbor: University of Michigan Press, 1979), 1–2.

9. Thomas Wortham, et al., eds., *W. D. Howells: Selected Letters*, vol. 4 (Boston: Twayne Publishers, 1981), 274.

10. Vernon Louis Parrington, *The Beginnings of Critical Realism in America: 1860–1920* (New York: Harcourt, Brace and World, 1930), 241.

11. William Dean Howells, "A Psychological Counter-Current in Recent Fiction," in *The North American Review*, vol. 173, ed. George Harvey (New York: Franklin Square, 1901), 832–33.

12. Martha Banta, Introduction to *The Shadow of a Dream and An Imperative Duty* by William Dean Howells (Bloomington: Indiana University Press, 1970), iii.

13. W. Lawrence Hogue, *Discourse and the Other* (Durham, N.C.: Duke University Press, 1986), 34.

14. Quincy Troupe, "The Last Interview," *Essence*, March 1988, 117.

15. James Baldwin and Budd Schulberg, "Dialogue in Black and White," in *James Baldwin: The Legacy*, ed. Quincy Troupe (New York: Simon and Schuster, 1989), 149.

16. Chinua Achebe, "Postscript: James Baldwin (1924–1987)," in *Hopes and Impediments* (New York: Doubleday, 1989), 176.

17. James Baldwin and Margaret Mead, *A Rap on Race* (New York: Dell Publishing, 1971), 10.

18. Nadine Gordimer, "A Letter from Johannesburg," in *Apartheid in Crisis*, ed. Mark Uhlig (New York: Vintage Books, 1986), 33.

19. Louis E. Lomax, "The White Liberal," in *The White Problem in America*, ed. editors of *Ebony* (Chicago: Johnson Publishing, 1966), 40–42.

20. Amiri Baraka, *Tales* (New York: Grove Press, 1967), 100.

21. Langston Hughes, "Poor Little Black Fellow," in *The Ways of White Folks* (New York: Alfred A. Knopf, 1933), 147–48.

22. Alice Miller, *For Your Own Good* (New York: Farrar, Straus and Giroux, 1983), 223.

23. James Baldwin and Nikki Giovanni, *A Dialogue* (Philadelphia: Lippincott, 1973), 88–89.

24. Erving Goffman, *Stigma* (Englewood Cliffs, N.J.: Prentice-Hall, 1963), 121–24.

25. Langston Hughes, *The Big Sea* (New York: Thunder's Mouth Press, 1986), 228.

26. Arnold Ramparsad, "Langston Hughes: The Dream Keeper," *Voices and Visions*, PBS, 1988.

27. Albert Schweitzer, *On the Edge of the Primeval Forest* (London: A. and C. Black, 1922), 133.

28. James Baldwin, *The Fire Next Time* (New York: Dell Publishing, 1962), 128.

—— *Chapter 3* ——

Lynching Gyneolatry

Birmingham Voice of the People
April 1, 1916
BUMPS INTO GIRL; IS LYNCHED
Cedar Bluff, Miss., March 31—Jeff Brown was lynched by a mob here
late Saturday afternoon. Brown was walking down the street near the
car tracks and saw a moving freight going in the direction in which he
wanted to go. He started on the run to board the moving train. On the
sidewalk was the daughter of a white farmer. Brown accidentally
brushed against her and she screamed. A gang quickly formed and ran
after him, jerking him off the moving train. He was beaten into insensi-
bility and then hung to a tree. The sheriff has made no attempt to find
out who the members of the mob were. Picture cards of the body are being sold on the street at five cents apiece.
                    —Ralph Ginzburg, *One Hundred Years of Lynchings* (1988)

"Murder, just murder, would make us all sane."
                    —Clay, a black man, to Lula, a white woman,
                              in LeRoi Jones's *Dutchman* (1964)

One of the most intriguing aspects of the white image in the black mind is
the representation of white women in fiction. Responding to the idealization—however sexist—of white women by the media and by those defending racism, black writers have clearly wanted to smash this ideal. While
white feminists have been cognizant of how ironically imprisoning it is to
be chained to a pedestal that serves the interests of white men, many
blacks have responded to the fact that this idealized white female image has
been used—both by white men and, at times, by white women (e.g., the

Scottsboro case)—against blacks, with the stakes often being the very lives of blacks. The murder of Emmett Till, which crystallized this destructive complex, leads to numerous logical questions: Is the white woman worth such psychosexual idealization? What lies beneath the myth of the purity of white womanhood and the myth of the desirability of white women to black men? Can countermyths be created to counteract the oppressive myths of whites about white women? Is the demystification by black writers of white women an attempt to create a liberating myth for blacks? Do these myths arise at the expense of white women and, if so, is this a necessary condition for a liberating mythology for blacks concerning black male–white female relations? Moreover, if the image of white women has been used as a line drawn in the dust in the defense of racism, is the effect on white women of a black liberating mythology at their expense finally irrelevant to blacks, whose creation of such a mythology is part of a quest for psychological and physical freedom from racism? Each reader will no doubt answer these questions differently after reading the black liberating mythology that acts as an exposé of white women in Langston Hughes's "Little Dog" from *The Ways of White Folks* (1933) and Richard Wright's novels *The Long Dream* (1958), *Native Son* (1940), *The Outsider* (1953), and *Savage Holiday* (1954).

The most volatile aspect of blacks' liberating mythology vis-à-vis the image of white women is the fact that, in some works, psychological liberation equals violence against white women. According to Robert Felgar, "James Baldwin charges that, where sex should be in Richard Wright's fiction, there is only violence; but Eldridge Cleaver's rejoinder is convincing: he explains that because of America's brutalization of blacks, violence does indeed reign on the holy throne of sex."[1] These ideas are very important in understanding Wright's use of violence in his fictional representations of white women. Indeed, the physical annihilation of a white woman occurs not only in *Native Son* but in two of Wright's other novels as well; both in *The Outsider* and *Savage Holiday*, the protagonist is responsible for the death of a white woman with whom he has a romantic relationship. In *The Outsider*, the relationship is between a black man and a white woman; in *Savage Holiday*, all of the significant characters are white. This may seem to suggest that *Savage Holiday* is devoid of a reading that black fictive liberation entails violence against white women. Nevertheless, to be sure, the fact that the work is a product of the imagination of a black writer indicates that it is a racial commentary on whites—an attempt to create a liberating mythology for blacks concerning white women.

Wright's stance is further complicated by the fact that both of his marriages were to white women. Wright's marriages to white women while disparaging—even killing—them in his fiction is perfectly logical within the contradictory logic of black–white relations; in his life and in his fiction, Wright is the quintessential example of the attraction/repulsion complex held by some blacks toward whites. The logic is that when a society and media simultaneously promote the white woman as the ideal but tell nonwhite citizens that they dare not try to grasp this ideal it can create within some nonwhites an attraction to white women and a feeling of resentment against and even hatred toward the idealized but actually flawed object. Moreover, the killing of Emmett Till in Mississippi in 1955 and Yusuf Hawkins in New York City in 1988 by whites, as a result of an incorrect belief that they had a sexual or romantic interest in white women, makes it evident that what is ultimately at stake for blacks in the idealization of white women is survival. Thus, the fact that Richard Wright, with all his contradictory impulses concerning white women, imagines a reversal of the traditional scenario in which a black man would be murdered because of a white woman certainly shows he was not only imagining a fictional turnabout but also envisioning a theme which, by its recurrence, is an attempt to create a countermyth: white women as well as black men are potential victims of the white psychosexual neurosis which has, as its object, the image of white women and the protection of that image. Consequently, it is fair to ask of Wright's works: is turnabout (of a racial myth) actually fair play, as the saying goes? And, in what ways is Wright's countermythology liberating for blacks, for, indeed, all of his killers of white women suffer, legally at least, as a result of their crimes. Furthermore, perhaps the most important feature of the imaginative murder of white women as a countermyth is that it reveals the logical, if terrible, results of racism: an action produces an equal and opposite reaction—an eye for an eye; a tooth for a tooth; a white life for a black life. If this cold logic has as its impetus a liberating impulse, the literature indicates the belief that we have only race hatred to thank for the genesis of the entire psychosexual drama of racism and the lingering and unanswered questions remaining in its wake.

What may be most amazing is that the fictional murder may not even be the height of the debunking of white women by black writers. For that, one may turn to Hughes's implicit condemnation of the emotional, physical, and psychological bankruptcy of the white woman as delineated in "Little Dog." While Wright imagines an apocalypse, Hughes imagines the lingering death in life of the painfully ordinary and therefore exemplary white woman. Consequently, on reading the works under discussion by Wright and Hughes, one sees the writers' belief that underneath the socially constructed facade of the attractiveness of white women are rottenness and sterility.

THE LIVING DEAD: DEBUNKING WHITE WOMEN IN "LITTLE DOG"

In "Little Dog," Langston Hughes does not focus on the seductive aspects of white women. Instead, Hughes emphasizes another aspect of the typology of whites: the emotionally lifeless, repressed white who simultaneously regards blacks as embodying a physical and emotional vitality he or she lacks and who, therefore, possesses an approach/avoidance complex toward blacks, both wanting them and fearing them.

The plot line of "Little Dog" is deceptively simple. Forty-five-year-old Miss Briggs, a single, white bookkeeper, is so isolated and friendless that she buys a little white dog, named Flips, to keep her company. She asks the janitor of her building, a young Swedish man, to buy meat and bones for her dog three times a week. Unexpectedly, the white janitor is replaced by a black man, Joe. Shortly after Joe has started delivering the meat and bones, Miss Briggs becomes flustered by her feelings of nervous anticipation and excitement as she awaits Joe's arrival with food for the dog. Miss Briggs becomes so baffled by her own reactions to Joe's brief visits that she decides she must move. "I've got to move. I can't be worried being so far from a meat shop, or where I eat my dinner. I think I'll move downtown where the shops are open at night. I can't stand this."[2] Thus, Miss Briggs plans to deliver herself from her own personal white problem: her tortured feelings of attraction to and withdrawal from a black man.

In examining the racial typology exemplified by Miss Briggs, one must rely on the mythology that has been expressed by many blacks: the white person who is emotionally withdrawn, physically unattractive, and behaviorally repressed. As explained by Frantz Fanon in *Black Skin, White Masks*, some whites know they are sterile creatures and hunger to know the "secret" which blacks, their antithesis, possess.[3] Certainly, Hughes makes it evident that, in Joe, Miss Briggs sees and is drawn to her polar opposite. Hughes repeats that Miss Briggs is "alone" (156–57), that she has sacrificed any social life to take care of her sick mother, and even six years after her mother's death (at the time of the story), she is still friendless and socially inactive. "And there was no man in view to marry. . . . Miss Briggs had nobody at all. Nobody" (158). Moreover, she is so socially repressed that although she enjoys being smiled at by people she sees in the park as she walks Flips, she shies away from conversations because "[S]he hated people to know her business. . . . You could never know who people were, Miss Briggs thought, or what they have in their minds. . . . Miss Briggs didn't trust people" (159–61). The sterility of the life of "the gaunt white lady" (163) is contrasted to the life and personality of the black janitor, who lives amid "a mighty lot of laughter and kids squalling, and people moving" (162). Hughes also calls attention to the physical qualities Miss Briggs notices in the janitor when they first meet and to which she is clearly drawn: his "gentle" face (163), his "softly beautiful voice" (163), his "rich voice" (163), and Miss Briggs's impression that he "was awfully big and brown and kind looking" (164). Hence, it is no wonder that "Flips ate an awful lot of meat that spring" (165) for Flips is the pretext for Miss Briggs to develop her attraction to the black man. Yet, as is the case in many black–white relationships in literature and life, nothing is straightforward in the relationship between the white lady and the black janitor.

Hughes makes it clear to the reader that the relationship with the janitor is part of a pattern for Miss Briggs: the main source of pleasure in this middle-aged white woman's life is black men. Actually, it would be more accurate to say that black men are the deliverers of pleasure to Miss Briggs. This aspect of race relations is first mentioned in the story in what at first might seem to be a minor detail. One of Miss Briggs's few pleasures is having dinner after work at the Rose Bud Tea Room where "the colored waiters were so nice. She had been served by Joe or Perry, flat-footed old Negro gentlemen, for three or four years now. They knew her tastes, and would get the cook to make little special dishes for her if she wasn't feeling well" (157). Miss Briggs's attachment to black men as deliverers of pleasure is made further evident by her reaction to both Joe the janitor and his wife. Noticing that Joe is "almost as old as [she] . . . but he was awfully big and brown and kind looking," Miss Briggs has him deliver the meat and bones every night (which certainly sounds like a sexual metaphor), not three times a week, as was the case with the white janitor (164). Yet, while Miss Briggs is "touched" by Joe's considerateness in bringing the meat, when his wife brings it instead, she is angry and upset in a way that reveals her attraction to the man:

> Once or twice during the spring, the janitor's wife, instead, brought the dog meat upon Saturday nights. Flips barked rudely at her. Miss Briggs didn't take to the creature, either. She was fat and yellow and certainly too old to just keep on having children as she evidently did. The janitor himself was so solid and big and strong! Miss Briggs felt better when he brought her the bones for her dog. She didn't like his wife. (165)

This passage, clearly packed with meaning, exemplifies Hughes's style of revealing the white woman's mind and her attitude toward blacks. First, one sees how Flips serves as her ego identity off-split by barking harshly to express both his and his owner's anger (Miss Briggs "didn't take to the creature, either"). Second, Miss Briggs's dislike for the woman has overtones of sexual envy, with the white woman rationalizing why the black woman should no longer have children with her (Miss Briggs's) object of desire. Thus, one sees the function of both black women and black men as givers of pleasure; and black women as either absent (they are very clearly omitted from Hughes's construction of Miss Briggs's life) or as reminders of the sexuality that is missing from the white woman's own life. Hence, in Miss Briggs's attitudes toward the blacks she encounters in the story, Hughes seems to be representing a key aspect of racism as discussed by Calvin C. Hernton in his chapter "The White Woman" in *Sex and Racism in America*:

> The Negro male became the living embodiment of not only the white woman's sense of sexual poverty, but of everything that was wrong with her life

and her society. . . . Few white women, and even fewer white men, will admit that white women feel a sexual attraction for Negro men. White people in general say that it is the Negro male who is attracted to white women; the reverse is flatly denied. . . . It is clear that somebody is lying.[4]

Hughes's story is an attempt to present the truth that stands behind the lie.

Hughes's emphasis on the defense mechanisms employed by whites to protect themselves from realizing and dealing constructively with their own flaws is a central part of "Little Dog." For example, while Miss Briggs is clearly attracted to Joe, her defense mechanisms almost reflexively start up both in reaction to this attraction and to preserve the stability of the routine life and self-image she has of herself as a "sensible" woman free of any emotional, romantic, or sexual entanglements. The first of these defense mechanisms—repression—is evident even before Joe enters the story: "Miss Briggs had nobody. Nobody. Not that she thought about it very much. Miss Briggs was too used to facing the world alone, minding her own business, going her own way" (158). Nevertheless, Hughes writes that she still cannot stop her loneliness from

> coming down on her. . . . There were some nights . . . especially summer nights, when she thought she couldn't stand it, to sit in her window and see so many people go by, couple by couple, arms locked. . . . Miss Briggs wondered why she knew no one, male or female, to walk out with, laughing and talking. (159)

This need for affection and companionship is clearly the source of conflicting emotions of loneliness and social anxiety. In addition, Miss Briggs's repression is especially evoked in response to her attraction to the black janitor. Although she has Joe deliver the meat daily and anxiously anticipates his arrival, "[O]f course, she never said more to him than good evening or thank you. Or here's a dollar for the week. Keep the change" (165). Why is she unable to treat the janitor in a casually friendly way? Why does she blush when Joe speaks and tremble when she spreads the bones on the floor for Flips? Why is she so stifled emotionally in Joe's presence? Why does her mind flip-flop as she tries to read after Joe's delivery? "She kept looking at the big kind face of the janitor in her mind, perturbed that it was a Negro face, and that it stayed with her so" (166).

Miss Briggs still cannot successfully repress her attraction which causes her to make mistakes at work and to rush home anxiously in order to be there when Joe arrives. One passage reveals the woman's repression and anxiety: "'What's the matter with me,' she said sharply to herself, 'rushing this way just to feed Flips? Whatever is the matter with me?'" (166).

> But all the way through the warm dusky streets, she seemed to hear the janitor's deep voice saying, "Good evenin'" to her. Then, when the Negro really

knocked on the door with the meat, she was trembling so that she could not go to the kitchen to get it. "Leave it there by the sink," she managed to call out. "Thank you, Joe."

She heard the man going back downstairs sort of humming to himself, a kid or so following him. Miss Briggs felt as if she were going to faint, but Flips kept jumping on her, barking for his meat. "Oh, Flips," she said, "I'm so hungry." She meant to say, "You're so hungry." So she repeated it. "You're so hungry, hey Flipsy dog?" (166)

Anxiety, attraction, and repression account for the white woman's claiming (or clinging to) ignorance as to why she hurries home and, more generally, as to "whatever is the matter" with her. Furthermore, her contradictory emotions lead to a paralysis of action, for example, her inability to open the door for Joe as she swoons over him. Her swooning and Flips's simultaneous barking at her represent her chaotic yet stymied emotions. Finally, the Freudian slip ("I'm so hungry") and her projection of her own hunger onto Flips as she corrects herself all portray the psychodrama of which the black man is the mere object.

Indeed, Hughes emphasizes that Miss Briggs's repression is futile as long as she is in the presence of the black man. This fact is shown in a passage that takes place the day after the episode just recounted, when Miss Briggs lets Joe in and she struggles "not to look at him. But as he went downstairs, she watched through the window his beautifully heavy body finding the rhythm of the steps, his big brown neck moving just a little. "Get down!" she said sharply to Flips for barking for his dinner" (167). Once again, Miss Briggs misdirects her emotions at the dog, for it is not he whom Miss Briggs wants to "get down" but the emotions stirred up by her attraction to a black man:

Miss Briggs decided that she could not bear to have this janitor come upstairs with a package of bones for Flips again. She was sure he was happy down there with his portly yellow wife and his house full of children. Let him stay in the basement, then, where he belonged. She never wanted to see him again, ever. (168)

The psychological aspect of the story is revealed in this episode. This passage raises intriguing issues. Why can Miss Briggs not bear to see Joe again? Are the first two sentences of this passage causally connectable? Does she not wish to see him because he is happy with his wife? Why does the black man "belong" in the basement? Is this idea an allusion to some whites' belief that blacks have a "place"? Moreover, why is there no middle ground for Miss Briggs between being attracted to a black man and banishing him from her mind and her life? This psychological banishment is clearly another example of repression; Miss Briggs wants the emotions aroused by her attraction to "get down" into the "basement" of her mind, banished from their destabilizing power over her routine life. Hence, though Miss Briggs takes the extreme measure of deciding to move to another building to escape from what is aroused in her by the presence of a black man on the periphery of her life, is this truly a resolution or merely an evasion? Indeed, a possible answer is indicated when she last sees Joe: "As his broad shoulders and tall brown body disappeared down the stairs, Miss Briggs slowly turned her back, shut the door, and put the bones on the floor for Flipsy. Then suddenly she began to cry" (169). Hughes emphasizes that banishing blacks from her life is Miss Briggs's loss, for while to Joe Miss Briggs is merely a "funny old white lady" (166), to her, he represents emotional and physical richness she can only desire and, as she is repulsed by her desire, shun. Ultimately, Joe is, to borrow Fanon's term for what black men often symbolize to whites, "a terrifying penis" (1967, 177). In addition, Hughes makes evident that the white woman's shunning of the black man leads to the embracing of a sterile, empty life as is, in this story, "the ways of whitefolks."

"Little Dog," which starts as a simple story, is a metaphor for many aspects of how racism works. For one thing, Hughes seems to use the character of Miss Briggs to represent the psychological bankruptcy and neuroses that a white person can sometimes bring to an interaction with a black person. Furthermore, Miss Briggs's hysterical feelings about what should be an ordinary dealing with a black man symbolizes the ways in which racism can pervade even the most casual relations between the races. Moreover, Hughes indicates that, in such cases, the black person can be entirely free of guilt in doing anything to provoke this hysteria. The story also makes one wonder about the lengths to which some whites will go to banish blacks from their lives. Thus, "Little Dog" is a representation of a white woman as the quintessence of many aspects of racism.

LYNCHING GYNEOLATRY

Boston Guardian
April 30, 1914
NEGRO YOUTH MUTILATED FOR KISSING WHITE GIRL
Marshall, Tex., April 29—Because he is alleged to have hugged and kissed a white girl, daughter of a farmer, Charles Fisher, a negro youth, was recently badly mutilated by a mob near here. According to Sheriff Sanders and County Health Officer Taylor, the mob sheared off the youth's ears, slit his lips and mutilated him in other ways below the belt.
—Ralph Ginzburg, *One Hundred Years of Lynchings* (1988)

While Langston Hughes attempts to slay the image of the white woman as in any way desirable (or even psychologically healthy), Richard Wright attempts to expose and then slay the image of white women as an idealized image that has cost many black men their lives. An important foundation for this topic is found in *The Long Dream*, in which Wright exposes how white women's sexuality has been used as a form of power over blacks. J. W. Cash, in *The Mind of the South,* locates the genesis of the racist and threatening idealization of white women in the nineteenth-century South as one of the key "defense mechanisms"[5] against racial equality employed by white men that entailed the glaring "sentimentality" that resulted in "the influence in the presence of the Negro in increasing the value attaching to Southern [white] women. As the perpetuator of white superiority in legitimate line, and as a creature absolutely inaccessible to males of the inferior group, the white woman inevitably became the focal center of the fundamental pattern of proto-Dorian pride" (1991, 84).

> [T]he upshot, in this land of spreading notions of chivalry, was downright gyneolatry. She was the South's Palladium, this Southern woman—the shield-bearing Athena gleaming whitely in the clouds, the standard for its rallying, the mystic symbol of its nationality in the face of the foe. She was the lily-pure maid of Astolat and the hunting goddess of the Boeotian hill. And—she was the pitiful Mother of God. Merely to mention her was to send strong men into tears—or shouts. There was hardly a sermon that did not begin or end with tributes in her honor, hardly a brave speech that did not open and close with the clashing of shields and the flourishing of swords for her glory. At the last, I verily believe, the ranks of the Confederacy went rolling into battle in the misty conviction that it was wholly for her that they fought. (86–87)

Cash makes clear the transformation of sentimentality into violence— violence that was part not only of a war but that continued in the form of thousands of lynchings in the nineteenth and twentieth centuries. Cash also certainly implies that, in this context, white women were—however consciously or unconsciously—mere objects to be used as weapons against blacks by the very white men who claimed to be their champions. Hence, while the mentality of which Cash writes is damaging to white women's humanity, it is completely logical that Richard Wright would emphasize the potentially catastrophic consequences to black men of violating whites' sense of gyneolatrous race worship.

In *The Long Dream,* Wright underscores how many whites made blacks internalize a view that to be attracted to a white woman—or even to evoke whites' incorrect fear on this point—was potentially lethal. The lynching of a black man, Chris, causes another black man, Tyree, to tell his son Fish, "NEVER LOOK AT A WHITE WOMAN! . . . When you in the presence of a white woman, remember, she means death."[6] Furthermore, Doc surmises that when Chris was castrated during the lynching, many white women watched excitedly (102). Doc also points out that the white woman with whom Chris was having an affair was responsible for his death, even though, as Hernton points out in *Sex and Racism in America,* during the history of vicious racism that lasted in the South until past the middle of the twentieth century, "[I]n any situation involving attraction between white women and

Negro men, it [was] the woman who must [have made] the advances" (21). Hernton's point about white female control is corroborated by Wright when he has Doc state that the woman flirted with Chris, who initially did not want to become involved with her, and after she seduced him she let her guilty conscience at violating the racial taboo cause her to inform on Chris to the whites who would murder him.

The white woman's condemnation of Chris is a sign of the psychosexual Puritanism that can characterize racism in a context in which sex itself is often considered immoral and interracial sex, the ultimate evil.[7] Thus, while the woman does desire an affair with Chris, it is her attempt to rid herself of her transgression against white society and redeem herself that lead to her attempt at atonement—causing Chris's murder. The significance of these ideas is truly frightening. According to Wright, lynching satisfied both a racist and a Puritan mythology, "cleansing" whites of their immorality, whether of their sexual transgressions or of their sinful bigotry in general. Hence, Wright makes it evident that blacks had much to fear from the psychological neurosis that found a pretext for its behavioral manifestations in the mythology of the need to punish violations against the purity of white womanhood. Wright's use of Chris's lynching illuminates the murderous consequences of the conflicted and dishonest nature of holding to an oppressive mythology as that which was a part of race relations in an era that diminished the humanity of blacks and whites alike.

Cash's points about the purpose of lynching illuminate Wright's depiction of the black male fear of white women.

> So long as the Negro had been property, worth five hundred dollars up, he had been taboo—safer from rope and faggot than any common white man, and perhaps even safer than his master himself. But with the abolition of legal slavery his immunity vanished. The economic interest of his former protectors, the master class, now stood the other way about—required that he should be promptly disabused of any illusion that his liberty was real. . . . And so the road stood all but wide open to the ignoble hate and cruel itch to take him in hand which for so long had been festering. (1991, 113)

Although Cash vastly understates the actual violence and abuse to which slaves were routinely subjected, he makes an essential point: that lynching and its usual pretext—the protection of white women—were a means of control over blacks meant to maintain white supremacy. It is no wonder that Wright underlines in his novel the fear of white women that is a consequence which some black men suffered in the face of the deadly forms white control took. This fear is seen in Fish and his friends in several passages in *The Long Dream*. For instance, when a white woman, who was dancing in a show from which the young men were turned away, makes a veiled attempt to have sex with them, they run away because the woman is "lynch-bait" (1958, 60). The young men's fear of white women is seen again when they are in Tyree's funeral parlor at night, playing jokes on people by shouting at them from a window. When they frighten a white woman so badly that she, upon hearing them, collapses convulsively to the ground, Fish and his friends fear illogically that she will tell people that she was raped. They decide fearfully not to try to scare any more people. Ironically, their fear of white women is so intense that in attempting to frighten one of them, they so frighten themselves that they become panic-stricken. Their panic is no wonder in light of what happened to Chris, which is a mere representation of such events:

BLACKS LYNCHED FOR REMARK WHICH MAY HAVE BEEN "HELLO"
Hartwell, Ga., Jan. 2—Two negroes were lynched and a negro woman badly beaten as the result of a remark to a white girl in Anderson County, South Carolina, according to reports received here last night. The three negroes were riding in a buggy when they passed the girl. One of the men made a remark to the white girl, at which she took offense. She reported the encounter to a group of white men who quickly caught up with the blacks, lynched the men, beat the woman, and ordered her out of the state.

Reports concerning the nature of the allegedly insulting remark are conflicting. Officials of Georgia County say that one of the negro men yelled out, "Hello, Sweetheart." The negro woman asserts that all they said was "Hello."[8]

In light of the reality Wright was addressing in his novel, it is perfectly understandable that white women were an object of fear and intimidation for some blacks. Yet Wright makes this subject far more complex than it might at first seem by showing that the knowledge of the power that white women had over blacks made some black men both attracted to and afraid of them. This attraction is explained in large part by Wright's contention that white women are excessively valued by the media to which Americans are exposed. Indeed, these conflicted feelings of attraction and fear are made evident in *The Long Dream* when Fish sees a photograph of a half-nude white woman in a newspaper:

She was smiling under a cluster of tumbling curls, looking straight at him, her hands on her hips, her lips pouting, ripe, sensual. A woman like this had caused Chris to die. . . . [T]hat laughing white face was so radiantly happy and at the same time so charged with dark horror. . . . Why had black men to die because of white women? The mere fact that Chris had been or would be killed . . . fastened his imagination upon that seductive white face in a way that it had never been concentrated upon any face in all his life. (89–90)

In another episode, when Fish and his friends look at pornographic pictures of white women, the thought flashes through Fish's mind that "[h]e was looking at the naked white world that had killed Chris, and the world that had killed Chris could kill him" (123). These episodes reveal the validity of Earle V. Bryant's comments that "Wright is pointing up the irony involved in white America's sexual racism, since what white America has essentially done by placing the white female on a pedestal and then issuing to black males a rigid hands-off policy is to instill into the consciousness of the black male an exaggerated sense of the white female's intrinsic worth."[9] It is a clear psychological fact that being told not to think of something can instill that very thing in one's mind. Yet, the penalty for blacks who were accused of violating white racism's ultimate taboo contributed to the fact that thousands of people were lynched from the late nineteenth to mid-twentieth centuries. Thus, it is no wonder that Wright felt the need to examine and expose the lynching power of racist gyneolatry.

Wright continues to emphasize the power of white women's sexuality in the enforcement of racism when police chief Cantley frames Fish on a rape charge because of Cantley's belief that Fish has proof that the white man was bribed by Tyree. Fish's powerlessness is made clear: he knows with certainty that "[h]e could not say that . . . [the white woman] had come into his room without uttering a dire insult against the purity of white womanhood. Indeed the anger that such a statement was capable of rousing could cause his death" (487). Even though Fish is jailed because of the charge, he is still attracted to the woman, recalling her "unreally beautiful face" and trying to recapture the feeling of being alone with a white woman (500). One passage sums up the complexity of Fish's feelings toward white women:

> White men made such a brutal point of warning black men that they would be killed if they merely touched their women that white men kept alive a sense of their women in the black men's hearts. As long as [Fish] could remember he had mulled over the balefully seductive mystery of white women, whose reality threatened his life, declared him less than a man. . . . [T]he white men's sheer prohibitions served to anchor the sense of his women in the consciousness of black men in a bizarre and distorted manner that could rarely be eradicated—a manner that placed the white female beyond the pitch of reality. (501)

The power of white women over Fish and their status as forbidden objects to him and other blacks account for Fish's simultaneous attraction to and fear of them. And this attraction—or merely the wrongful allegation of it— was often met with experiences like those collected in Ginzburg's *One Hundred Years of Lynchings*:

> The flames leaped up and licked the man's bare hands. He was held erect by one of the lynchers until his clothing was burning fairly, when he was pushed into the bed of fire. He rolled about and his contortions were terrible, but he made no sound. Suddenly the ropes on his legs parted and he sprang from the fire and started to run. A man struck him in the head with a piece of fence

rail and knocked him down. Willing hands threw him again into the flames. He rolled out several times, but was promptly returned. While this was going on, shouts, cheers and gibes went up from the crowd. (1988, 56–57)

When one knows the reality of the torture and violence that thousands of blacks have endured for whites to uphold the racist mythologies of white supremacy and the inviolate status of white womanhood, it becomes clear why Wright turns from understanding the power of the use of white women to uphold white supremacy by employing a lynching gyneolatry to himself imagining the fictional destruction of the object of this gyneolatry—the white woman herself.

In answering a question about whether he considered literature to be a weapon, Wright revealed more than he intended about his interest in creating a countermythology to the racist overvaluing of white women. He acknowledges that writers whose work reflects reality may often shock readers; yet it is justified to write about disturbing events because fictional representations not only do not exaggerate reality but may be milder than many actual incidents.

> I try to appreciate what readers are capable of taking in without feeling I am exaggerating. For instance, I went to Indonesia to report on the Bandung conference, and on that occasion I was told atrocious things. . . . For example, during the Japanese occupation, the Japanese put all the Dutch . . . into concentration camps. When the Japanese started to experience setbacks, they had to withdraw the soldiers who were guarding these camps and send them to the front. As a consequence, they used . . . Indonesians to guard the camps. But the mentality of the Dutch was such that, while they accepted being guarded by Japanese soldiers, they refused to be guarded by natives. Someone assured me that the Dutch told the native guards, "If you touch any Dutch women, if you rape them, we shall kill one thousand Indonesians for every single white woman." I was told the Indonesians were so incensed by this insult . . . that they tried to redeem themselves in the eyes of the Dutch. . . . They ordered all the white women out of the camp, lined them up against a palisade, set up a machine gun and shot every one of them. Then they asked the Dutch, "Well, now, have we touched your women? . . . [W]e are not interested in white women, but in freedom." (Van Antwerp 1982, 450–51)

Although Wright concludes by saying that he found this episode so disturbing that he could not relate to it (in spite of the shocking nature of much of his own work), it is difficult to believe that a man whose literature is so steeped in violence would be baffled by the story he recounted. One is made to feel that if Wright were being truthful in saying that he could not relate to the murder of the white women in the story he was told, it merely shows the degree to which he felt—consciously or unconsciously—that a topic about which he had written three times at this point in his career was too disturbing and toxic for American society to comprehend fully: the killing of white women as a refutation of whites' insistence that they are the ultimate untouchable object.

Native Son, Wright's first novel to explore this subject, is also his most straightforward treatment of it. Bigger Thomas inadvertently kills Mary Dalton, the rich white girl whom he chauffeurs, in order to keep her mother from finding out that he is in Mary's room after he has helped the drunken young woman get there when she was incapable of getting to her room by herself. Bigger is afraid that being caught with a white woman might result in his death, and, although this might seem like a wild leap in logic to some readers, it is important to understand the cultural memory that informs Bigger's actions in this episode. It is clear that, even without this cultural memory being explicitly stated, Bigger, a young man from Mississippi who has been in Chicago for only three years, fears being killed by whites if he is caught in Mary's room because white men use white women as a pretext for lynching blacks. Bigger's cultural memory includes such scenes as the following:

Chicago Defender
February 13, 1915
NEGRO SHOT DEAD FOR KISSING HIS WHITE GIRLFRIEND
Cedar Keys, Fla., Feb. 26—Young Reed, a Negro, of Kissimmee, was shot to death by a white mob Wednesday noon after he had been seen kissing a white woman named Belle Mann with whom he had been keeping company for the past two years.

Reed was kissing Mann good-bye when he was seen by a group of white men. The men seized him, beat him unmercifully and placed him in jail. Shortly thereafter, a lynching party was formed and Reed was shot to death. (Ginzburg 1988, 95)

Blacks, as represented by Bigger, would have known that such murders were sanctioned by white communities in many parts of the South.

New York World
May 16, 1916
15,000 WITNESS BURNING OF NEGRO IN PUBLIC SQUARE
Waco, Tex., May 15—Screaming for mercy until flames silenced him, Jesse Washington, a negro of eighteen years, was burned to death by a mob in the public square here today. Many women and children were among the 15,000 who witnessed the lynching. . . . His clothing was saturated with oil and a match was applied. At a signal the negro was hoisted further in the air, then was let fall into the flames.

After the body had been hanged to the tree it was left there for several hours and great crowds of curious visited the scene throughout the day. Everything is quiet in town tonight, the mob having dispersed soon after the lynching. (Ginzburg 1988, 141–42)

Lynchings were not merely flat words on a page to be read by blacks; the possibility of being murdered engenders the fear Wright delineates throughout Bigger's interactions with Mary Dalton.

Internalization of his inferior status and fear of white women as a danger to him inform Bigger's relationship with Mary. Bigger's fear of Mary as having power over him and his very life is evident when he first meets her. When Mary enters the room during his interview with her father, for instance, Bigger feels threatened by her questioning him about whether he belongs to a union. She imposes her leftist ideas on Bigger in front of her father, making Bigger fear that her questions may prevent him from being hired: "In his heart he cursed the crazy girl. Maybe Mr. Dalton was deciding not to hire him. . . . Goddam that woman! She spoiled everything."[10] Thus, Wright immediately establishes Mary as a threatening force in Bigger's life.

Wright then shows how this feeling of being violated by a white woman could result in a self-protective hatred in a black man. This topic is revealed in the scene where Mary and her Communist boyfriend Jan make Bigger feel humiliated by their smothering and directive attempts at friendship while he drives them around town. With Jan and Mary, leftist dilettantes that they are, Bigger feels invaded by the demands of people who are part of a race he feels is a vast force in his life, rather than fellow human beings. Hence, when Jan and Mary order Bigger to take them to a black restaurant, to come in and eat with them although he is not hungry, to let them sit with him in the front seat of the car, and even to sing, Bigger accurately takes these directives not for the friendly overtures that Jan and Mary intend them to be but for the humiliating intrusions they are. Consequently, it is understandable that Bigger wants to "blot [them] out" (1940, 70). Furthermore, in regarding Mary, as a result of her intrusiveness, Bigger realizes that leftist sympathizer though she may be, she is still part of a race of people who have the power to alter his life: "She was white and he hated her" (81). Wright therefore conveys that the seeds of Bigger's self-protective killing of Mary are embedded in the relationship from the start.

Another extremely important aspect of this section of the book is that Wright seems to want to impart that whites are culpable of the violence unleashed by a black person as a form of self-defense. More specifically, Jan and Mary are guilty of what may be termed contributory negligence in Mary's death. It is Jan, for example, in his continuing directive behavior toward Bigger, who insists that the three of them keep drinking at the restaurant, while Bigger is driving, and even just before he leaves Bigger and Mary when they drive to the Dalton home (74, 77, 79). Bigger continues to drink at Jan's insistence to alleviate his intense feelings of humiliation at the hands of these two intrusive whites. Thus, Jan is partly responsible for the inebriated state of both Mary and Bigger—the state that results in Bigger's having to help Mary to her room. Jan is therefore greatly responsible for putting Mary and Bigger in a situation that leads to the young woman's death.

This topic of Jan and Mary's contributory negligence continues in the area of sexuality. Some may object to this interpretation in an age of the belief in total male culpability and complete absolution of the female in situations that result in violence, but the text bears out this point. Indeed, a counternarrative exists: both in Wright's *Black Boy* and Hernton's *Sex and Racism in America,* the authors relate how some black men have felt that at times white females intruded their sexuality into black men's lives, promoting and parading it before blacks, for whom showing an interest in white women could be deadly. Wright, for instance, recalls in *Black Boy,* while working as a bellboy in a hotel in the South, how the white prostitutes were often naked in their rooms when the black bellboys were summoned to the rooms by either the prostitutes or their customers. What particularly bothered Wright was that the women had so little respect or consideration for the black bellboys (or plain modesty); they acted as if the blacks were mere inanimate objects before whom they could be naked and unashamed. "It was presumed that we black boys took their nakedness for granted, that it startled us no more than a blue vase or a red rug. Our presence awoke in them no shame whatever, for we blacks were not considered human anyway."[11] When Wright looked at one of the women when she walked naked across the room to pay for liquor for herself and her customer (who is watching Wright while still lying in bed), he was warned in no uncertain terms by the white man that "reckless eyeballing" will not only not be tolerated but could very well result in violence against Wright himself.

Wright realized that whites' neurotic racist mythology about sexuality could cause him to lose his life, although it is the whites who intrude sex onto him. Hence, in a counternarrative to our contemporary story, Wright suggests that whites sometimes use sex to invade and possibly to destroy black men. Hernton's research corroborates Wright's experience on this point. His chapter on "The White Woman" is filled with anecdotes and analysis of white women threatening black men in order to get these men sexually involved with them. In one representative example, a black man recalled an incident that happened when he worked as a handyman in Depression-era Florida for a fifty-three-year-old white woman and her invalid husband:

> While I was fiddling around with something in the yard, she called me up in her room. She said: "Come up here this minute, I want you to do something right away." When I got up the stairs that led right into her room—BAM—my eyes liked to have popped out: there she was lying on the bed with not a rag on her white body. Well, man, you know what I did? I ran back down those stairs like a ball of fire out of hell. But by the time I got to the bottom, she was at the top, and she said: "If you run, I'll yell and scream and say you attacked me. So you best come back up." I was trapped. (Hernton 1965, 13)

The motif in both Wright's and Hernton's narratives suggests that white women's sexuality was sometimes used to manipulate and endanger blacks. This idea makes the issue of sexuality in the scenes with Bigger and Mary especially intriguing, for part of Bigger's fear after he kills Mary is that blacks were often lynched because of false accusations of rape—an accusation he knows he was open to by his mere presence in her bedroom. The subject of sexuality runs throughout the scene in which Bigger chauffeurs Jan and Mary. For instance, as a result of Jan and Mary's insistence that they sit with him in the front seat as he drives, Bigger "smelt the odor of her hair and felt the soft pressure of his thigh against her own" (Wright 1940, 68). This motif continues when Bigger "felt Mary turn in her seat. She placed her hand on his arm" (70). The scene becomes most overt when Jan and Mary have no compunctions about "making out" when they are in the back seat while Bigger is driving them home. "Now and then he watched Jan kiss Mary in the reflection of the rear mirror above his head" (75). In an instance in which Wright brings together motifs of drinking and sexuality, he writes: "I'm almost drunk [Bigger] thought . . . he was floating in the car and Jan and Mary were in the back, kissing" (78). These scenes must be remembered when one attempts to understand how Wright uses the theme of sexuality in the novel. It seems that he is being highly ironic in his presentation of this topic: while whites, Bigger knows, are all too ready to accuse blacks by imposing sex onto white women, it is Jan and Mary who invade Bigger's imagination with their sexuality, an invasion that results in his inebriated nuzzling of Mary as he places her on the bed. Wright demonstrates that whites are guilty of the tragedy that engulfs both Bigger and Mary, corroborating Hernton's points about the role and culpability of whites in this sexual aspect of racism.

The apex of Wright's presentation of the tragedy that envelops Bigger and Mary comes with the scene following Mary's death, during which Bigger, in a panic-stricken state, disposes of Mary's body. This scene seems to be a clear and brilliant reversal of the lynching rituals that are a part of Bigger's cultural memory, a revenge fantasy in which the white woman is placed in the role of the lynched. The elaborate development of this scene is central. The scene starts with Bigger's connecting his job of taking care of the furnace with a possible way of disposing of Mary's body: "He trembled with another idea. He could—he could, he—he could put her, he could put her in the furnace. He would burn her. That was the safest thing of all to do" (89). The nervous energy Wright conveys to reflect Bigger's mind in the construction of these sentences may mirror the author's own excitement on his doing the unthinkable in the development of this scene—the idea of putting Mary in the furnace places her in one of the most widely reported situations of a lynching victim: not merely being killed but being slowly burned. "The fire seethed. Ought he to put her in head or feet first? Because he was tired and scared, and because her feet were nearer, he

pushed her in, feet first. The heat blasted his hands" (90). Bigger's decision
to put Mary into the furnace so that her head remains outside raises an interesting question: can the reader be sure that Mary is dead at this point?
Since Mary and Bigger were both inebriated when he smothered her, one
wonders if her stillness on the bed may have been a result of her drunken
state and if Bigger's quick conclusion that she is dead because she has
stopped moving and heaved a heavy sigh, which Bigger takes to be her last
breath, is incorrect. If this scene is a reverse lynching, it is essential to remember that the point of the elaborate lynching rituals conducted by
whites was to ensure that the black person suffered as much as possible
while dying a slow death. Thus, the slowness with which Bigger destroys
Mary's body may be a counternarrative to the tortures of lynching, as recounted in the following passage:

> *Chicago Record-Herald*
> May 23, 1902
> NEGRO TORTURED TO DEATH BY MOB OF 4,000
> Lansing, Tex., May 22—Dudley Morgan, a negro accused of assailing Mrs.
> McKay, wife of Section Foreman McKay, was burned to death at an iron stake
> here today. A crowd of 4,000 men, most of whom were armed, snatched him
> from the officers on the arrival of the train.
>   The husband of the woman Morgan was accused of abusing applied the
> match and the pyre was soon ablaze. Then began the torture of the negro.
> Burning pieces of pine were thrust into his eyes. Then burning timbers were
> held to his neck, and after his clothes were burned off, to other parts of his
> body. He was tortured in a horrible manner. The crowd clamored continu-
> ously for a slow death. The negro, writhing and groaning at the stake, begged
> piteously to be shot. (Ginzburg 1988, 45)

This elaborate lynching finds its counterpart in *Native Son*:

> He had all but her shoulders in. He looked into the furnace: her clothes were
> ablaze. . . . He gripped her shoulders and pushed hard, but the body would
> not go in any farther . . . her head still remained out. . . . He got his knife from
> his pocket and opened it and stood by the furnace, looking at Mary's white
> throat. . . . Gently, he sawed the blade into the flesh and struck a bone. He
> gritted his teeth and cut harder. . . . He whacked at the bone with the knife.
> The head hung limply on the newspapers, the curly black hair dragging about
> in blood. He whacked harder but the head would not come off. . . . He got the
> hatchet, held the head at a slanting angle with his left hand and, after pausing
> in an attitude of prayer, sent the blade of the hatchet into the bone of the
> throat with all the strength of his body. The head rolled off. (Wright 1940,
> 90–91)

The revulsion and shock that this scene causes some readers should be
no greater than the sorts of events that happened to blacks during lynch-

ings, which may have inspired Wright's ritualistic presentation of this
episode. Compare the violence done to Mary's body with an account of an
actual lynching:

> An eyewitness to the lynching of Luther Holbert and his wife, negroes, which
> took place in Doddsville yesterday, today gave the *Evening Post* the following
> details concerning the retribution exacted from the couple prior to their cre-
> mation yesterday:
>
> When the two negroes were captured, they were tied to trees and while the
> funeral pyres were being prepared, they were forced to hold out their hands
> while one finger at a time was chopped off. The fingers were distributed as
> souvenirs. The ears . . . were cut off. Holbert was beaten severely, his skull was
> fractured and one of his eyes, knocked out with a stick, hung by a shred from
> the socket.
>
> Some of the mob used a large corkscrew to bore into the flesh of the man
> and woman. It was applied to their arms, legs, and body, then pulled out, the
> spirals tearing out big pieces of raw, quivering flesh every time it was with-
> drawn. (Ginzburg 1988, 53)

Such accounts as this lead the reader to think that Wright's killing and disposal of Mary is an attempt to create a liberating countermythology to murderous racist ideologies. In establishing the white woman as something
worth murdering blacks for, Wright seems to imply that as long as whites insist upon making themselves into icons, blacks have no choice but to be
iconoclasts.

The liberating aspect of Mary's death is shown further in Bigger's pride
at having killed her. Hence, *Native Son*, with its concentration on a black
man's fear of lynching and his performance of a psychologically liberating
reverse lynching of the very type of creature who was the pretext for the
murder of so many black men is, perhaps, best illuminated by Claude
McKay's poem about lynching, "Baptism," which begins, "Into the furnace
let me go alone" and concludes with the narrator's saying that his spirit will
become stronger as a result of this violent ordeal.[12] This poem not only reflects the imagery of fire and the furnace relevant both to actual lynchings
and to Bigger's disposal of Mary, but it also shows why the violence against
Mary is presented by Wright as a liberating act for Bigger, one which he
commits "alone," to borrow the word from McKay's poem, and of which he
takes proud ownership, even after he is betrayed by the furnace when au-
thorities discover Mary's bones and after he is the subject of hateful white
mob demonstrations when he is in jail. Bigger's need to affirm his crime
comes from the fact that his life has been so constricted that his feelings of
autonomy redeem, for him, the horror of his actions. Hence, as in McKay's
poem, Wright illustrates the psychological strength that can come from enduring the hideous situations that can arise when one has been defined as
a mere victim of American society and finally decides to both endure and

triumph in the face of such tortures. Bigger's self-affirmation is more complex than that of the lynching victim in "Baptism" because of the moral issues involved in Wright's novel. Indeed, it seems that Bigger's final
affirmation that "[w]hat I killed for must've been good" may reflect
Wright's hope that the shocking events of the novel could possibly
awaken—and liberate—the relatively conscious Americans who knew that
we all needed to be awakened to the possible consequences of bigotry in
shaping the characters and destinies of blacks and whites alike and who
were willing to face the importance of the fact that both blacks and whites
needed to be released from a white lynching gyneolatry (Wright 1940, 392).

VARIATIONS ON A THEME

Wright's next novel after *Native Son*, *The Outsider*, focuses on the theme of
a black man's protection of his freedom at the expense of both black
women and a white woman. Indeed, Arna Bontemps wrote cynically in a review of the book, "A more hag-ridden young man than the fretting and
sweating hero of *The Outsider* is hard to imagine."[13] Certainly, Cross Damon's
plan to fake his own death in order to start a new life elsewhere is inspired
by his desire to get away from his angry wife, his pregnant mistress, and his
moralistic mother. Wright conveys Cross's thoughts in the following passage: "What greater shame was there for a man than to walk the streets
cringing with fear of grasping women? Somehow, he would shake loose of
this and never in all his life be caught again."[14] Thus, Cross abandons the
black women in his life of whom he thinks in stereotypical terms as 'bitches'
and drudges.

At first, it seems that Wright is suggesting that a white woman is the only
antidote to a black woman. Cross's only relationship with a woman (or anyone) to which he attaches any value is with Eva, the wife of a member of the
Communist party, whom Cross comes to know after his recruitment by the
party. Wright's emphasis on Eva's nonthreatening nature emphasizes her
immature "girlishness" as though Wright were actually charmed by her, especially as the antithesis of the black women introduced earlier in the novel.
Wright describes Eva, for example, as a "fragile girl" (1953, 175) and in
other passages has Cross think of her as a "child" (202), referring to her
"childishness" (202), and noticing her "schoolgirlish" handwriting (206).
To Cross, therefore, Eva is the opposite of the people (mainly black women)
who have tried to manipulate him.

There are problems, however, that make Eva seem merely a somewhat
more highly developed Mary Dalton. Like Wright himself, Eva is disillu-
sioned with the Communists; unlike Mary, who was a party sympathizer (although Wright was still in the party when he wrote *Native Son*, he had great
hostility toward its restrictive policies and lack of true interest in dealing
with racism), Eva is not directive but passive, a quality whose attractiveness

Wright seems to emphasize. Like Mary, however, she is ironically racist in her affection for blacks. Wright, for example, underscores Cross's annoyance at the importance Eva places on his blackness. At one point, for instance, Eva tells Cross, "I want your people to be my people. . . . I want to feel all the hurt and shame of being black. . . . I wish I was black, I do, I do. Let me share the fear, the humiliation" (288). Cross feels frustrated by this declaration:

> Could he allow her to love him for his color when being a negro was the least important thing in his life? . . . Yet he wanted that sensitive heart of hers to be his monitor, to check him from sinking into brutality, from succumbing to cruelty, and she wanted to love him because she thought he was an innocent victim! (288)

Cross's frustration with Eva's misinterpretation of his identity is reminiscent of his past relationships with the black women from whom he escaped: "His sorrow for Dot [his mistress], his mother, and Gladys [his wife] originated in his knowing that they had hoped for something in him which he did not possess" (107). Consequently, Cross feels that Eva's patronizing conception of him hinders him from revealing his true nature to her.

This barrier is nowhere more evident than in the section of the book that deals with Cross's hatred for and later murder of Eva's husband, Gil. Ironically, Eva and Cross share a hostility toward Gil. When Cross reads Eva's diary without her knowledge, he reads about her unhappy marriage and her feeling that "I could kill Gil" (208). Thus, after reading Eva's diary, Cross feels "a numbing sense of recognition go through him. Impulsively he wanted to run to her and talk to her, to tell her she was not alone" (212).

Despite this secret aspect of their emotional closeness, Cross's relationship with Eva is marred by his desire to have control over her. After he murders Gil, for example, and Eva tells Cross that she feels isolated and asks him to "have pity on me and let me stay near you," Cross "smiled, feeling he was listening to her words as perhaps God listens to prayers. . . . A wave of hot pride flooded him. She was laying her life at his feet. With a gesture of his hand he could own her" (260). This theme of power continues when Cross is delirious and tells Eva about his crime. Under the guise of wanting to protect Eva from the disillusionment she would feel if she knew his true nature (she does not believe him at this point), he thinks of murdering her: "Show me a way not to hurt her, not to kill this sweet girl" (322). Nevertheless, he later thinks that death is his only way of sparing her feelings: "Would it not be better for her to die now and be spared the pain and shock which he knew he had yet to bring to her? . . . [Wasn't] death better than prolonged suffering? Didn't he owe it to her to kill her and thereby guard her from the monstrousness of himself?" (327) On this theme, Wright makes it evident that Cross is merely another one of the megalomaniacs who pollute the modern world, which is perhaps the book's main theme. Certainly, Cross's kindheartedness—asserting that his thoughts of killing Eva are motivated by his love for her—is specious. Clearly, Wright underlines the fact that Cross contemplates killing Eva primarily to keep her from terminating their affair because he fears what she would do if she believed his confession.

> He strove in vain to banish from his consciousness the realization that he was the quintessence of all that Eva most deeply loathed and would flee to avoid. Eva was his kind of woman but he was not her kind of man nor would he ever be.... He ached with anxiety as he watched the flame of love and trust in her eyes, for ... when she finally gained a knowledge of what he was, it would be snuffed out. (322)

Ultimately, although Cross decides not to murder Eva, he does, in effect, kill her. Eva commits suicide in reaction to Cross's crime and deception. As Houston, the district attorney, tells Cross, "She leapt from that window to escape the kind of world you showed her! You drove her out of life!" (428). Ultimately, it seems that Eva is the victim of Cross's desire for power, which was the catalyst for his murder of her husband (and others).

The Outsider, in comparison to *Native Son*, does not affirm the protagonist's killing of a white woman or, more to the point, what this killing represents. Cross, in contrast to Bigger, is responsible for the death of a white woman not for reasons that symbolize white America's culpability for generating the fear and hatred of racism, but for reasons that are merely personal—not sociological. While Cross does think briefly of the death of Eva as being possibly liberating for him, his idea of liberation is of a piece with the tyranny that Wright so abhorred (as represented in his denunciation of communism and fascism in the novel). Thus, in contrast to Bigger's relationship with Mary in *Native Son*, *The Outsider* seems to represent that aspect of male–female relationships that Michel Fabre notes as a recurring theme in some of Wright's works: "The male desire for superiority as well as the despair at still being imprisoned in a solitude which even sexual relations cannot destroy."[15]

In contrast to *The Outsider*, Wright's next novel, *Savage Holiday*, builds up to an actual murder of a white woman. This novel, almost completely neglected by critics of Richard Wright, was first dismissed as a lurid potboiler having nothing to do with race because the characters are white (an amazing grounds for dismissal, as if whites were raceless). It finally received marginal attention as Wright's excursion into the psychological (especially Freudian) novel. This book, nevertheless, is a gold mine for Wright's critique of whites and for his attack on the idealization of white women in much of American culture. In fact, the novel is intriguing if one reads it in light of Cash's analysis, in *The Mind of the South*, that white men, in a pseudo-

chivalric gesture, elevated white women to a realm of alleged purity beyond
sexuality in their creation of the myth of the purity of white womanhood
which was, in fact, an ideology created to maintain white supremacy and a
psychological method of divesting white women of sexuality as a defense
mechanism for the widely practiced rape and sexual abuse by white men of
black women during slavery. With this defense mechanism, white men
could convince themselves that their abuse and adultery was a favor to their
wives, who were above the "beastly" practice of sex, unlike the "hot-
blooded" black women of their imagination. This psychological duplicity is
an aspect of the Puritanism condemned by Wright. As a result, *Savage
Holiday* can be read as a merciless attack both on the sexually hypocritical
white man and the lie of the purity of white women to whom men such as
the protagonist of the novel were devoted.

Erskine, perhaps the male counterpart to Hughes's Miss Briggs, and
Mabel, his promiscuous neighbor with whom he is obsessed, represent
Wright's disgust with the sexual hypocrisy of many members of the white
race—a hypocrisy which, outside of the text, Wright conveyed was a source
of much misery and violence to blacks. Moreover, as the novel is presented
completely from Erskine's point of view, although one cannot completely
separate Mabel's image from his neurosis, one can understand that Wright
is presenting an image of whites that counters the narcissistic myths that up-
held white supremacy. Indeed, Wright was aware of the meaning of *Savage
Holiday* in this regard, for the novel reflects Wright's concern with both the
cruelty and aggressiveness of some whites toward blacks and with the moral
vacuum and psychological confusion that give rise to such behavior. These
themes are reflected strikingly in Wright's complex representation of the
Puritanical and psychologically confused white man and the irresponsible
and unethical behavior of the white woman. Thus, when one reflects on
Savage Holiday, in light of the image it offers of whites and how this image is
an important part of Wright's racial typology, the book stands as a refutation
of devastating proportions of aspects of the white character that Wright
seems to feel are major aspects of white behavior and psychology.

In order to understand Wright's examination of Erskine's relationship
with Mabel, it is important to analyze what Wright emphasizes in Erskine's
character and his attitude toward women because the seeds of his murder
of Mabel are present in his repressed and Puritanical view of life. Though
Erskine is a retired successful businessman and avid churchgoer, he has a
very suspicious view of life, and much of this suspicion is focused on
women. Reflecting on his years in the insurance business, for example,
Erskine thinks:

Insurance was life itself; insurance was human nature in the raw trying to hide
itself. . . . yes, insurance was a shifty-eyed, timid, sensual, sluttish woman, trying, with all of her revolting and nauseating sexiness, to make you believe that

she'd been maimed for life in an automobile accident. . . . [I]nsurance was an old, sweet-looking woman of seventy-odd who'd insured her new daughter-in-law for a huge amount of money and then, with a stout hatchet, killed her one night in bed and had told a seemingly plausible tale . . . of finding her daughter-in-law in bed hacked to pieces.[16]

Erskine's belief that life is fowl (his last name is Fowler) is the most fundamental aspect of his view of life in general and of women in particular.

Wright emphasizes the centrality of this priggish, judgmental, defensive, and threatened view of people in the development of Erskine's relationship with Mabel. Erskine's belief that Mabel is representative of such devious and manipulative women is clear. When he suspects, for example, that she has left her son Tony alone all night, he thinks, "Women who couldn't give the right kind of attention to children oughtn't be allowed to have them" (Wright 1994, 35). Furthermore, though he is somewhat attracted to Mabel, and on two occasions has seen her from his apartment in various stages of undress, "he'd nipped in the bud the possibility of any such image haunting his mind by promptly becoming angry" (1994, 35). Thus, Erskine uses "righteous indignation" to prevent his admitting his attraction to such a woman. This is characteristic of his reaction to Mabel—especially after Tony's death. Wright emphasizes that Erskine's arrogance is a device that he uses to try to establish his superiority to, and later control over, Mabel.

Erskine's relationship with Mabel becomes central to the plot after Tony's accidental death. The circumstances surrounding the accident are essential to the understanding of Erskine's obsession with having power over Mabel. Erskine's actions lead to the boy's death. Erskine undresses for the shower and then hears the paperboy leave his paper. He decides to try to get the paper, but it is beyond his reach. Still nude, he steps outside the door, planning to pick the paper up quickly before anyone sees him. However, a gust of wind closes the door, and Erskine must find a way back into his apartment. He remembers that his bathroom window is unlocked, and he plans to climb from the balcony to his window. When he enters the balcony, Tony, who is playing by himself, is frightened by Erskine and falls off the balcony. Like Bigger, who felt that the true reason for his being in Mary's room would be disbelieved, Erskine feels that people might suspect that he was trying to do something perverse to Tony and therefore does not reveal his role in the accident to the police. It is important that Erskine first rejects his responsibility for Tony's death. In his thoughts about how the boy's death might have been prevented, Erskine blames Mabel: "[I]f only that lazy, good-for-nothing Mrs. Blake had been looking after her child properly" (79).

In Erskine's attempt to absolve himself of his responsibility and establish his superiority over Mabel, religion plays an important role. For instance,

"Since God had foreordained all," he thinks that he should not go to the police, that taking any action would be presumptuous (86). Furthermore, Erskine comes to think that Tony's death was Mabel's penalty for living an immoral life and that it is his religious duty to rehabilitate her:

> that accident was God's own way of bringing a lost woman to her senses. . . .
> [H]adn't she wallowed shamelessly in the fleshpots of nightclubs? God had
> punished her by snatching little Tony into Paradise. . . . He, Erskine, was God's
> fiery rod of anger! . . . A sense of mission seized him. Yes, God was giving him
> a mandate to face Mrs. Blake and have it out with her! (87)

Erskine's indignation is reinforced when he remembers instances of Mabel's loose behavior (seeing her drunk, hearing her having sex). Reflecting on these episodes, he was more certain than ever that the true guilt for Tony's death lay not on his, but her shoulders" (92). This belief is reaffirmed when Erskine recalls a conversation with Tony during which the little boy recalled seeing men having sex with his mother and ignorantly believed that the men were "fighting" with her (99). Consequently, Erskine thinks that when he ran into Tony on the balcony, his nudity made the boy fear that he would "fight" with him. In light of this, Erskine feels indignant.

> How right he'd been in refusing to accept blame for Tony's death. It hadn't
> been his fault at all. Only an ignorantly lustful woman could spin such spider
> webs of evil to snare men and innocent children! . . . [H]e told himself with
> the staunchest conviction of his life: "That Mrs. Blake's the guilty one." (105)

Thus, Erskine tries to convince himself of his superiority, which is crucial to his having psychological control in his relationship with Mabel.

Erskine, however, never succeeds in maintaining his command of the relationship. Erskine's confidence is shaken when he receives an anonymous phone call from a woman who says that she saw him on the balcony with Tony, and Mrs. Blake says that she also saw someone. (Mabel later reveals that she was the anonymous caller.) It is then that Erskine thinks that Mabel's death might be the only way he can control her and prevent her from raising questions that could lead to the discovery of his involvement in Tony's death. Though he is instantly horrified at having wished for her death; thereafter, Erskine's relationship with Mabel is characterized by his need to convince himself of his moral superiority and to have power over her.

Erskine's feelings toward Mabel are influenced by his belief, at times, that he has, or could have, power over her. As we have seen, his belief in her immorality makes him comfortable with his supposed moral superiority over her, which allows him to attempt to absolve himself of his guilt for Tony's death and to alleviate his feeling of being threatened somehow by Mabel. Erskine's feelings toward Mabel oscillate depending on whether he feels he has power over her. For instance, following the scene in which Erskine briefly considers how convenient it would be if Mabel were to fall over the balcony railing and die, her crying causes a radical change in his attitude: "Her grief was so genuine, so simple that his conception of her as an evil, giant, entangling spider-mother seemed remote. She was a poor woman who needed counselling and understanding and her stricken humanity appealed to him powerfully" (117). As a result, he becomes "almost hysterically anxious to help her" (118). It becomes clear, however, that this wish to aid Mabel is of a piece with his earlier arrogant desire to reform her for his actions toward her reveal that his emotions hinge upon the need to feel that she is helpless and that he can dominate—or, perhaps, he would say "help"—her.

Erskine's actions toward Mabel after Tony's death show that his need to control her is behind his seemingly affectionate behavior toward her. When he offers to make funeral arrangements for Tony, for example, she looks at him with "humble admiration" (135), and "[h]e basked in the glory of the praise in her eyes" (136). Her confession of her hard life—her bad job, her lack of intelligence—affirms his feelings of superiority. With such confidence, Erskine feels that "he could handle her. . . . She was begging for guidance" (137).

Wright emphasizes the extremity of Erskine's obsession to have power over Mabel. Not only is his help with Tony's funeral prompted by this need to establish dominance over her but his desire to marry her is also caused by this same need. He thinks of marrying her in order to prevent questions that might reveal his involvement in Tony's death and to save her: "It [marriage] solved his problems, hers, squared little Tony's death, and placed him in the role of a missionary. . . . She'd obey him! She was simple; and, above all, he'd be the boss; he'd dominate her completely" (134). One sees, therefore, the contradictory nature of Erskine's relationship with Mabel, for his actions are prompted by a self-centered desire to hide his role in her child's death and an arrogant and twisted drive to help Mabel—a drive that is, ultimately, an expression of his need to control her.

Erskine, however, is frustrated in his need to dominate Mabel by her independence. Even her appearance the day after Tony's death makes Erskine feel threatened by his loss of control over her. When he goes to see her, for example, "he was surprised by the Mabel who opened the door. She was pert, brisk; she held a detached smile on her heavily rouged lips. . . . He entered her apartment feeling that her new mood was subtly shutting him out of her life. He fought down an attitude of resentment" (142). That his emotions toward her change depending on whether he can control her is emphasized in this visit with her. His jealousy is reinforced when she glibly talks with another man on the telephone. Yet, when she cries as she talks about Tony's funeral and expresses her gratitude to Erskine and her reliance on him,

Erskine was stricken. His distrust and irritation fled. . . . He'd judged her harshly . . . and now he hated himself. Once more Mabel was redeemed in his feelings, once more she was the abandoned tragic queen of his heart—a queen whom he'd serve loyally and without reserve. She didn't even think enough of the other men she knew to invite them to the funeral. . . . Only he was being invited. (145)

Erskine's jealousy returns, however, when Mabel talks on the telephone to another man: "He felt nauseated. He should be tending to his own affairs and not meddling with this cheap woman. She wasn't worth it" (147). Erskine's feelings that Mabel is either a "cheap woman" or a "tragic queen" are bound to his ability to have power over her.

The complexity of Erskine's feelings is revealed again later in the novel. Erskine becomes jealous when Mabel is with a man in her apartment. After the man leaves, Erskine asks her about her relationships with men. He questions Mabel in such an arrogant manner that she is reduced to tears. When he realizes that he has hurt her, "Contrition gripped him. . . . Had he reduced her to this? She was his again, nobody else's" (159). Clearly, Erskine is satisfied that his ability to hurt Mabel gives him power over her. Furthermore, when she continues crying, both because of his treatment and because of Tony's death,

Erskine stood spellbound, appalled. Hot gratification suffused his body with so keen a sensation that he felt pain; he could scarcely breathe. She was his now, completely. Like this, she belonged to him. He had conquered her, humbled her. . . . Because she had been receding beyond his grasp, he had treated her abominably, had hurled at her his complaints and abuses . . . but now he could be compassionate, loving towards her, for she was prostrate and at his feet. (160)

When he hears her talking on the telephone again after he leaves and suspects that she is talking to another man, Erskine thinks that she is toying with him. This Mabel, whom he does not control, is a "bitch" and a "complete slut" (165).

Erskine's inability to maintain dominance over Mabel ultimately leads him to kill her. After Erskine reveals his responsibility in Tony's accident and convinces her that she, too, contributed to the boy's death, Mabel, in guilt and confusion, briefly considers marrying him. Again he becomes jealous when she wants to leave his apartment to answer her phone because he suspects that she will be talking to another man. Furthermore, Mabel implies that, if she and Erskine do marry, she will not be faithful unless she is satisfied with him. As a result of Mabel's refusal to accept his terms for a relationship, Erskine feels that she "loomed as the personification of an enemy" (212). When she definitely refuses to marry him, he kills her. Because of his inability to control her, Mabel falls victim to the violence that, as

Addison Gayle, Jr., points out, many of Wright's female characters suffer at the hands of his protagonists.[17]

At one point, Erskine asks himself about his relationship with Mabel: "Why did he love her one moment and hate her the next?" (186). Wright provides the answer to this question when he sums up Erskine's feelings about Mabel:

> The more distraught she seemed, the more he wanted her; the more abandoned she was, the more he yearned for her; the more dangerous she loomed for him, the more he felt that he had to remain near her for his own self-protection. His desire for her merged with his hate and fear of her and he was jealous. (155–56)

"He was jealous"—not really of the other men with whom Mabel is involved but of her own independence from him. Mabel herself—or the willful side of her personality—is the rival who prevents Erskine from controlling her and thereby having the kind of relationship he wants to have with her. He hates her both for her independence and its negation of the image he wants to cling to of himself as a morally superior human being and possible savior of this "fallen woman." She always "hovered agonizingly beyond his reach" (212). And because she is inaccessible to him in life, killing her is Erskine's only means of establishing dominance over her. Hence, as in *The Outsider*, a woman's death is part of a man's means of holding onto his sense of autonomy.

When one looks at the trajectory of Wright's trilogy on the killing of white women, it is clear that each novel has a different agenda. *Native Son* seems to be Wright's attempt to create a counternarrative to the lynching of black men with the metaphorical lynching of a white woman. The liberating aspects of Bigger's killing Mary are in contrast to the results of Cross's inspiring Eva's death in *The Outsider*, which reads like a cautionary tale on the abuse of power. *Savage Holiday*, which critiques psychosexual megalomania, acts as an exposé of the neurosis Wright believed possessed some whites, which in his other works, informs whites' psychological degeneracy in race relations. Wright's concentration on violence against white women seems, on the whole, to be related to the meaning of violence discussed by Ronald T. Takaki in *Violence in the Black Imagination*: "Violence was, in a crucial sense, an expression of rage. But the rage was complicated: it was based on an alienation from an America" to which blacks are attached.[18] Wright's attachment to and alienation from America find their greatest expression in his attachment to and alienation from white women. Thus, while Langston Hughes's implicit condemnation of the white woman as represented in "Little Dog" is unambiguous, Wright leaves the reader contemplating what exactly are the full implications of his imaginary murder of white women.

NOTES

1. Robert Felgar, *Richard Wright* (Boston: Twayne Publishers, 1980), 55.

2. Langston Hughes, "Little Dog," in *The Ways of White Folks* (New York: Alfred A. Knopf, 1933), 167.

3. Frantz Fanon, *Black Skin, White Masks* (New York: Grove Press, 1967), 128.

4. Calvin C. Hernton, *Sex and Racism in America* (New York: Grove Press, 1965), 19–21.

5. J. W. Cash, *The Mind of the South* (New York: Vintage Books, 1991), 84.

6. Richard Wright, *The Long Dream* (New York: Doubleday, 1958), 83–84.

7. Margaret A. Van Antwerp, ed., "Entretien avec Richard Wright," *L'Express*, 18 August 1960, trans. Michel Fabre, in *The Dictionary of Literary Biography: Documentary Series*, vol. 2 (Detroit: Gale Research Company, 1982), 452.

8. Ralph Ginzburg, *One Hundred Years of Lynchings* (Baltimore: Black Classic Press, 1988), 98.

9. Earle V. Bryant, "Sexual Initiation and Survival in *The Long Dream*," in *Richard Wright: Critical Perspectives Past and Present*, ed. Henry Louis Gates, Jr., and K. A. Appiah (New York: Amsterdam Press, 1993), 425.

10. Richard Wright, *Native Son* (New York: Harper and Row, 1940), 54.

11. Richard Wright, *Black Boy* (New York: Harper and Row, 1945), 221–22.

12. Claude McKay, "Baptism," in *Selected Poems of Claude McKay* (New York: Harcourt Brace Jovanovich, 1953), 35.

13. Arna Bontemps, *Saturday Review*, 28 March 1953, in *Richard Wright: The Critical Reception*, ed. John M. Reilly (New York: Burt Franklin, 1978), 208.

14. Richard Wright, *The Outsider* (New York: Harper and Row, 1953), 37.

15. Michel Fabre, *The Unfinished Quest of Richard Wright* (New York: William Morrow, 1973), 62.

16. Richard Wright, *Savage Holiday* (Jackson: University Press of Mississippi, 1994), 28–29.

17. Addison Gayle, Jr., *Richard Wright: Ordeal of a Native Son* (Garden City, N.Y.: Anchor Press/Doubleday, 1980), 108.

18. Ronald T. Takaki, *Violence in the Black Imagination* (New York: G. P. Putnam's Sons, 1972), 99.

—— *Chapter 4* ——

The White Problem
in Today's America

Though many readers may find that black fiction may provide metaphors for contemporary life, an examination of contemporary nonfiction by black writers adds to the tradition of the white image in the black mind in essential ways. Works that are particularly important in providing recurring aspects of the white image in the black mind are journalist Ellis Cose's *The Rage of a Privileged Class* (1993), which focuses on interviews with successful blacks in white-collar positions who have found their careers hindered by covert racism; Lawrence Otis Graham's *Member of the Club* (1995), which, in part, details the types of racism the author encountered while a student at Princeton University; and law professor Derrick Bell's *Faces at the Bottom of the Well* (1992), which combines short stories and essays to analyze essential features of racism and their effects on blacks, including black scholars and professors. While these works are certainly class bound, through that feature itself, the authors give an ominous and necessary message: white racists are a continual presence in blacks' lives—even in the lives of those who are thought to be successful. These racists are often covert in their actions, which are couched in the defense mechanisms of denial, silencing of blacks, and repression, among others. The authors convey to their readers that these defense mechanisms are employed mainly on an unconscious level. Hence, as bell hooks makes it clear in *Killing Rage* (1995), we must study and create a discourse that exposes hidden and insidious racism.

Perhaps the key aspect of race relations in America is what might be called neoracism or nonracist racism. Clearly, nonracist racism is an oxymoron, an impossibility. It is that very impossibility, however, that is at the heart of the good-hearted weakling and the liberal of the past and present. White "people do not have to be racist—or have any malicious intent—in order to make decisions that unfairly harm members of another race. They simply have to do what comes naturally."[1] Indeed, in *The Rage of a Privileged Class*, Cose demonstrates that what blacks often—perhaps most often—have to protect themselves from is not the foaming-in-the-mouth, Bull Connor–style racist but the person who claims that he or she is not, and, indeed, cannot be a racist: that person is the nonracist racist.

> In the past, one "knew white people didn't like black folks," which is to say that one knew how to act, how far one could go, and what would not be allowed. . . . In short, one knew one's place. For [black] parents today [who want to prepare their children for racism] such certainty does not exist. (151)

In this passage, it is made clear that overt racists policed blacks' behavior in a way that was more straightforward than covert racists. Yet, the ways in which covert racists attempt to police blacks' behavior and to maintain a system that allows them simultaneously to practice and to deny racism are of grave concern to blacks, as one sees in Cose's book, as well as in Graham's *Member of the Club*, Bell's *Faces at the Bottom of the Well*, and hooks's *Killing Rage*.

Cose builds a convincing case that many whites implement a most insidious brand of racism: hidden racism by those who claim that race plays no role in their decisions. Cose tells, for instance, the story of Lennox Joseph, a management consultant who was offered a top job at a corporation. Joseph recalls, "No one [on the board of the company] was saying 'Come on, Lennox, you'll be great'" (25). Cose continues: "Instead, at least on the part of a few board members, he sensed an attitude that he should be grateful for whatever salary and compensation package they decided to give him. He also sensed resistance from a few members of the staff. The woman in charge of marketing, for instance, could never seem to find the time to put together a press release announcing his promotion" (25). This type of reluctant and sloppy treatment, experienced by many blacks in white-collar positions, signals to the black employee, who often is one of very few black employees—a clear indicator of the lack of commitment to basic integration at many American companies, the negligence and hostility of many of the whites with and for whom he works. Cose offers the experience of black psychologist Ron Brown: "Time after time, he has encountered blacks who felt undermined in their work, or who watched less competent whites pass them by. And while they suspected race may have played a role, they could never be sure, partly because the corporations refuse to acknowledge any such possibility" (34). Cose's interviews demonstrate that the frustration experienced by such people as Brown's clients is the result of the fact that the most overt racial dynamics, which would reveal the bigotry of their white colleagues, are manifested in meetings among senior colleagues—often all white—at which evaluations and decisions about the few blacks are made, thus allowing the whites to avoid confrontation with the bigotry in their perceptions of and actions toward their black colleagues. Thus, nonracist racism performs the same function as the more honest and open brand of racism: the maintenance of white power, privilege, and homogeneity.

As a result of the consequences of nonracist racism, blacks' trust of "nice" whites is low indeed. "What is one to make, for instance, of the black law partner who laments that in today's gentler climate 'white folks ain't saying what they mean,' and who yearns for the brutal honesty of the past, when it was clear that 'white people didn't like black folks?'" (Cose 1993, 148). This episode leads one to infer that in order to understand blacks' mistrust, whites need to answer this question for themselves, for related to the answer to this question is the fact that covert racism keeps whites in power and blacks the objects of discrimination, in spite of the appearance of racial progress. This fact is made clear by Cose:

> [E]ven though the gates of the corporation have swung open, many doors are still marked "Whites only." At the same time, armies of white men have convinced themselves . . . that marginally competent minorities, pushed along by quotas, are snatching up every decent job and promotion in sight, leaving nothing worth having to hard working whites who only want a fair shake. (1993, 171)

Hence, as whites pat themselves on the back for not being racists and indeed put energy into the maintenance of an idealized self-image concerning their feelings about blacks, they promote both the continuation of racism and the feeling among themselves that racism is a mere neurosis that exists in the black mind. These are some of Cose's main points.

Cose sums up nonracist racism by quoting sociologist Joe Feagin: "[E]ven the subtle displays of prejudice blacks today are more likely to encounter can be devastating" (159). Cose continues: "Today white discrimination less often involves blatant door-slamming exclusion, for many blacks have been allowed in the corporate door. Modern discrimination more often takes the form of tracking, limiting or blocking promotions, harassment and other differential treatment signalling disrespect" (159). When whites wonder scoffingly why blacks sometimes say that they prefer outright bigots to nice whites, Feagin's point conveys that all they have to do is look at the practice and results of the nice, nonracist racism to see blacks' point.

Derrick Bell also writes about the preeminence of nonracist racism. He makes it clear, for instance, that while one no longer sees the "for whites" and "for coloreds" signs of the Jim Crow South, the absence of such overt symbols of racism while racism still exists can cause whites to claim that racism is not an important factor in American life.[2] Thus, while discrimination continues and can even flourish, according to Bell, with the erosion of active efforts to include more minorities in education and businesses, blacks can find themselves not knowing when such bigotry will arise to shut them out of opportunities necessary for educational and professional advancement (Bell 1992, 6). Hence, while Bell is certainly not calling for a return to Jim Crow, he does make the point that when discrimination is open, it not only can be fought but it also does not give people a false sense of security or deniability where racism is concerned. As Bell contends, "Today . . . bias is masked in unofficial practices" (1992, 6). One major point made by Bell is that many whites have abandoned any commitment not only to affirmative action but to mere integration (in any meaningful sense) in workplaces and educational institutions even while proclaiming a commitment to non-racialism. Hence, Bell and Cose concur: covert racism is one of the primary barriers to blacks' progress.

Moreover, Bell illustrates that a major aspect of nonracist racism is that whites may be motivated less by hostility toward blacks than by a tribe mentality that results in a desire for racial hegemony. This tribe mentality is not better than the more uncomplicated blanket hostility toward blacks; it is merely another less discussed aspect of racism. As Bell quotes Matthew S. Goldberg's "Discrimination, Nepotism, and Long-Run Wage Differentials," "Racial nepotism rather than racial animus is the major motivation for much of the discrimination blacks experience."[3] Continuing this idea, Bell says to fictional character Geneva Crenshaw,

> You're suggesting that whites tend to treat one another like family, at least when there's a choice between them and us. So terms like "merit" and "best qualified" are infinitely manipulable if and when whites must explain why they reject blacks to hire "relatives"—even when the only relationship is that of race. (56)

Bell's statements help to explain the feelings of many blacks in workplaces and educational institutions that they are the unwanted stepchild who lives in the basement while their white colleagues bond with each other based solely on race and thus on the assumption that they are similar in some fundamental way that blacks cannot share. Moreover, Bell's statements shed light on many of the experiences of the blacks interviewed by Cose in *The Rage of a Privileged Class* who feel stalemated in their careers as white colleagues who are quantifiably less qualified and less competent than they are given both social acceptance and professional advancement. (These things are often linked.) Furthermore, as many of Cose's subjects make it clear, it is the racism that is manifested in such situations that is hard to address: "Today even the worst racist denies being a racist. Most whites pay a tremendous price for their reflexive and often unconscious racism" (Cose 1993, 56). Hence, in discussing contemporary racism, one must pay close attention to the price paid by blacks as a result of the racism practiced by our modern-day good-hearted weaklings and liberals.

Related to such discussions of racism is a question raised by Lawrence Otis Graham in *Member of the Club* about whether it is harder to combat overt or covert racism. Reflecting on his years as an undergraduate at Princeton University in the early 1980s, Graham writes,

> As bad as relations were with whites, I realize that the covert nature of racism at Princeton was easier to tolerate than the vicious, overt bigotry that occurs on college campuses such as Michigan State, University of Michigan, or Rider College, where the fraternities sponsored a 1992 "Dress Like a Nigger Night" and paraded around dressed like black slave mammies and butlers. Princeton was a polite place. Few would ever call you a nigger to your face. Maybe behind your back. Instead they treated you like one. They ignored you. And if you pointed out their bigotry, they called you oversensitive. Formality and politeness were the rule. Perhaps that is why it was so hard to fight—because, like smoke, it was hard to get your arms around it.[4]

The development of this passage is intriguing, for Graham seems to argue that covert racism, while perhaps easier for blacks to bear, is much harder to address and combat than overt racism. Graham's ideas ultimately support those of Bell and Cose that "polite racism" inhibits and harms blacks' lives as it provides whites with psychological protection from having to confront their own racism or accept being confronted with it by blacks.

It is now important to look more closely at how racism is conceived of and operationalized by whites. A key component of modern-day racism, especially of the nonracist kind, is how whites employ the defense mechanism of denial. According to Cose, "[W]e live in an age where legions of white men have concluded they are the group most discriminated against" (1993, 36). He continues, "America likes success stories. We also prefer to believe that our country—give or take a David Duke or two—is well on the road to being colorblind" (38). Optimistic as this view may be, Cose makes it clear that it is part of the denial of racism by many whites. Indeed, a significant number of whites seem to believe that racism does not exist to a significant degree and that blacks who complain about its continuation are merely whiners. Another issue raised by Cose is the connection between denial and displacement in the belief in a new victimology whereby whites feel that they are the true victims of racism insofar as they believe such a thing exists: "To the extent that racism is perceived as a problem by whites it is increasingly perceived as an evil perpetuated by blacks—with whites (particularly Jews) serving principally as victims" (153). Hence, Cose believes that, in one flight of fancy, whites can both deny that white racism exists and claim to be the targets of black racism. Cose quotes one of his interviewees, a law school dean, who says that most white Americans are in denial when it comes to acknowledging their own racism.

It is essential for Americans to study "why the nation is in such a state of denial, why so many whites find it hard to believe that blacks experience what blacks clearly do" (163). Moreover, though one reason for whites' denial and demand for silence about racism is that many whites "idealize an abstract fairness" by whites for blacks, other reasons are more ominous (143). For example, based on a poll of Americans aged from fifteen to twenty-four, Cose writes that many blacks are frustrated that many whites refuse to give validity to blacks' experiences of racism (143–44). This rejection by whites of the credibility of blacks' perceptions of and experiences with racism caused many blacks polled to feel that they could not trust their peers to acknowledge and to want to combat the racism perpetuated by themselves and others (144). Thus, whites' commitment to racial advancement was thought to be highly suspect by the blacks polled (144). Consequently, white denial further damages race relations.

As bell hooks points out in *Killing Rage*,

> [W]hite folks are into "denial" bigtime. . . . Overt racism is not as fashionable as it once was and that is why everyone can pretend racism does not exist. . . . [Thus] everyone in this society, women and men, boys and girls, who want to see an end to racism, an end to white supremacy, must begin to engage in a counter hegemonic "race talk" that is fiercely and passionately calling for change.[5]

Without honest discussions of racism, denial takes place: "Racism then can be presented [by whites] as an issue for blacks only, a mere figment of our perverse paranoid imaginations, while all whites continue to be brainwashed to deny the existence of an institutionalized racist structure that they work to perpetuate and maintain" (hooks 1995, 26). Hooks and Cose thus seem to concur that one of the primary consequences of denial is that it provides for whites a pretense of a resolution to racism—even as blacks experience it otherwise.

> [P]retending (or convincing ourselves) that race no longer matters (or wouldn't if minorities would stop demanding special treatment) is not quite the same as making it not matter. Creating a color-blind society on a foundation saturated with the venom of racism requires something more than merely proclaiming that the age of brotherhood has arrived. . . . The problem is . . . that so many [whites] are in denial. And though denial may be a great way to avoid an unpleasant reality, it is no substitute for changing that reality. (Cose 1993, 188, 191)

Hence, the point is made that for whites to pretend that racism is solved by maintaining denial and silence about it is merely a disingenuous way to convince themselves that racism has nothing to do with them, which may be the ultimate slap in the faces of black people.

Coupled with denial is the white demand that blacks be silent about racism. Cose's discussions with those involved in politics make this demand for silence evident. The experience of former New York mayor David

Dinkins is illustrative of this point. Cose recalls, for example, a letter from a New York *Daily News* reader who dismissed Dinkins's anger about an anti-Dinkins police demonstration in front of City Hall where police referred to the mayor as a "nigger." What Cose felt the reader was really saying by dismissing Dinkins's anger at indisputable racism was "that whatever reactions he might have to racism were inconsequential, certainly nothing she wanted to hear. And she was not alone" (Cose 1993, 29). Moreover, still discussing Dinkins, Cose writes, "[T]o speak frankly and honestly about race would be to anger . . . those whites who preferred to believe that racism, by and large, had disappeared" (1993, 30). In addition, former New York politician Basil Patterson states that black politicians are inhibited in their ability to be honest about racism, as many whites become annoyed by what they perceive to be blacks' exaggerated concern with racism (31). Thus, whites' expectations that blacks will be silent about racism diminishes the degree to which both politicians and other blacks can combat racism by being honest about it.

Moreover, the white demand for silence certainly extends beyond the political arena. Cose, for instance, recalls the experience of a fellow writer, an editor at an important newspaper. The man wanted to write an article about the anger of members of the black middle class, a relevant topic because he had the idea soon after the first verdict concerning Rodney King's beating by police and the ensuing Los Angeles riot. The man was advised by a colleague not to do the story because high-ranking whites at the newspaper might feel that he was writing about his own anger, and they might label him an "angry black man." It "was only a small step from being seen as an angry black man to being labelled a troublemaker" (32). Lest this connection seem farfetched, Cose offers many examples of blacks to whom it has been made clear by whites that honesty about racism is converted by whites into a belief that such blacks are merely being confrontational, or troublemakers, when they openly talk about racism. For instance, Cose writes about a man who was retiring as vice president for personnel at one of America's largest companies. He

> had been moderately outspoken about what he saw as racism within and outside his former corporation. He had learned, however, that his honest attempts at advocacy got him typecast as an undesirable. So when he changed jobs, he decided to disassociate himself from any hint of racial agenda. The strategy had clearly furthered his career, even though other blacks in the company labeled him as an Uncle Tom. (66)

Thus, it seems that whites sometimes offer blacks a spurious choice: be a "safe," silent black person or be willing to earn animosity and pay the price for showing that most threatening trait of all: honesty.

One of the most important quotes of *The Rage of a Privileged Class* is that the white demand for silence calls for blacks to perform identity management around whites. According to Cose, "Putting aside for the moment what it means to be 'black,' the fear of being forced to shed one's identity in order to prosper is not at all uncommon" (66). To illustrate this point, Cose tells the story of a black man whose agreement with the white demand for silence clearly affects both his identity and his career. This story concerns a police officer who makes detective after nineteen years of seeing less qualified whites get promoted. Upon seeing whites bypass him, he does a smiling, Uncle Tom act, "so determined was he to avoid being categorized as a race-obsessed troublemaker" (67). Though his career advances, this man's tale illustrates what whites really do by demanding that blacks not be honest about racism:

> Even though he made detective years ago, and even though, on the side, he managed to become a successful businessman and an exemplary member of the upwardly striving middle class, he says the anger still simmers within him. He worries that someday it will come pouring out, that some luckless white person will tick him off, and he will explode, with tragic results. (67)

This man's repression of his feelings and the resultant hidden rage, probably against the very whites who like him as a nonthreatening black man, indicate the high emotional price blacks can pay for managing their identity in front of whites so that their careers can advance with the help of the whites who have the power to promote them and decide on their continued employment. Thus, while there may be a pleasant facade between blacks and whites, underneath is the racial division that is the hallmark of a racist society. As bell hooks explains in *Killing Rage,*

> To perpetuate and maintain white supremacy, white folks have colonized black Americans, and a part of that colonizing process has been teaching us to repress our rage, to never make them the targets of any anger we feel about racism. Most black people internalize this message well [because] we know that one can be exiled forever from the promise of economic well-being if that rage is not permanently silenced. (hooks 1995, 14)

Consequently, in order to have a career at all in fields dominated by whites, blacks very often learn that they should check their true identity at the door and stuff inside themselves their justified anger at prejudicial treatment by whites.

Cose makes two essential points in discussing whites' desire not to hear blacks' honest feelings about race. First is the whites' blame the victim attitude toward blacks who are honest. As a result of this attitude,

> [S]ophisticated blacks have learned that to suggest that whites are racist is not a useful exercise in the current climate—at least when talking to whites. Indeed, a murderer who blamed the devil for his crime would likely receive a

more sympathetic hearing from many whites these days than a black intellectual who railed against racism. (Cose 1993, 153)

Hence, Cose seems to convey that whites, whether they want to face it or not, by silencing blacks merely confirm that they are more afraid of being confronted by their own racism than of practicing it.

In a central passage in *The Rage of a Privileged Class,* Cose sums up the major effects on both whites and blacks of the white demand for silence about racism: "[W]hites tend not to understand what [blacks'] anger is about. As a result they are likely to dismiss the complainer as a chronic malcontent or a maladjusted person who perhaps needs to be eased out" (32). Thus, the stakes for blacks who do not repress their true feelings about race can include their ability to make a living at what they want to do. Moreover, the lack of honesty that many whites demand from blacks results in a lack of empathy for blacks by whites, a mainstay of racism, whether intentional or unintentional. According to Cose, "The inability to talk about race in anything resembling honest terms compounds the very misunderstanding that renders silence necessary. For those blacks and whites who come into closest contact, it stands as a huge barrier to their ever truly accepting one another or finding common ground" (33). Consequently, as whites try to impose a no-talk rule on blacks, they guarantee the perpetuation of what so many deny they are guilty: racism.

Perhaps the most maddening aspect of both white denial and the demand for silence is that these attitudes are designed to enable whites to feel that their views on race are the only valid ones, that their racism is not racism, and that they can say anything to blacks with the assurance that blacks will—or should—be silent and in denial. Two incidents from Cose's book support these points. One incident concerns a woman who worked in public relations at Dow Chemical Company. The woman recalls

attending a training session headed by a veteran [white] manager who declared, totally out of the blue, that he had absolutely no idea why anyone in a white neighborhood would vote for a certain black mayoral candidate in Chicago. She was the only black in the room and was so troubled by the attitude that seemed to underlie his comment that she walked out. (64)

When the woman hit the glass ceiling for blacks in the company, it was clear that white attitudes toward her had deteriorated and that this deterioration was certainly due to racism: "Even her way of talking drew attention [from whites]. Upon meeting her, one colleague remarked with evident pleasure and astonishment, 'You don't speak ghettoese.' She had an overwhelming sense that what he meant was 'You're almost like us, but not enough like us to be acceptable'" (61). This passage illustrates the point that while blacks are expected to maintain a white-imposed silence on race, whites express openly their race-centered thinking. Thus, if whites refuse honesty and dialogue, dishonesty and racist monologues will remain prevalent and maintain the racial divide.

Related to the denial and silencing that many whites employ concerning racism is the demand for sameness and safety from blacks. By this phrase, I mean that whites demand that blacks downplay their differences from them, thus emphasizing the ways in which blacks can pretend to be similar to whites. Ideas similar to these are expressed by Erving Goffman in *Stigma* (1963) and James Baldwin and Margaret Mead in *Rap on Race* (1971). Moreover, Cose's book has countless examples of how blacks face whites' demands for sameness and safety—which again means identity management for blacks—primarily in their places of employment.

Cose offers many stories of whites' demanding that blacks make them feel safe from their (whites') own racism. This demand is one of the main demons that Cose cites as recurring for blacks in their places of employment. The particular demon relevant here is "the inability [for blacks] to fit in" (56). Cose recalls a white newsroom recruiter who spoke with him about potential black candidates for employment by the *New York Times*. "He was concerned about an attribute that was tortuously difficult to gauge: the ability to fit into the often bewildering culture of the *Times*. . . . He wanted . . . people who could be 'Times people'" (56). The type of identity the recruiter wanted a black *Times* employee to have was evidently a combination of Bill Cosby and William F. Buckley (57). The recruiter clearly thought that only a seriously deracialized black person could "fit in" with the *New York Times*. The racism here is made further evident when Cose states that the man did not look for a similarly bizarre stereotype in whites who work for the paper: he "and many similarly placed executives almost instinctively screened minority candidates according to criteria they did not apply to whites" (57). That such demanded for black identity management are race bound to a degree that endangers many blacks' ability to gain and maintain employment in predominantly white settings is abundantly clear.

Cose continues to show white demands for sameness and safety when he states that many blacks need to "expend an inordinate amount of effort trying to make whites feel 'comfortable' with them" (77). He also states that many blacks feel that their white colleagues want them to downplay their assertiveness, especially when dealing with topics that entail issues of white fairness to blacks, or risk being thought of as people who are looking for trouble (77). Furthermore, Cose makes it evident that his interviews with blacks show that the white demand for sameness and safety is also, in effect, a demand for white supremacy. This fact stands out in key examples from Cose's text. A black female lawyer, for example, states that she sensed on the part of some of her white colleagues, "How dare you put yourself on the same plane with me! How dare you challenge me! How dare you think that you have the option to question my power and my authority!" (83). The woman goes on to state that such defenses of white superiority are often communicated in a way that is

> very subtle. . . . It's communicated when there's a meeting and there are discussions going on and you express a dissenting opinion. . . . I see a very different reaction from my challenging them than I've seen with white females. . . . I don't see it [such disapproval] with a lot of white men. . . . But it is an attitude and it is present in white males of power who can influence your career. (84)

This episode clarifies that some whites need to recognize that blacks who have such experiences know that whites are really working out in such situations as the meetings she recalls that blacks who are not safe threaten their egotistical and racist feelings of power.

A supreme example of the connection for whites among safety, sameness, and superiority can be seen in law school dean Ulrich Haynes's recollections of his days with a management recruiting firm in the 1960s. According to Haynes, whites wanted from minority job candidates "somebody who, by and large, they could feel a little bit sorry for, who would be so happy to have the position that he was entering into [that he] would not cause them any problems in terms of professional advancement" (124). Ironically enough, whites with such attitudes often wanted to hire the least qualified black person for the job; they obviously did not want their sense of superiority threatened and therefore rejected qualified minorities who might feel as confident and assertive as the black female lawyer who caused white consternation by acting as if she were the whites' equal. Such employers as those described by Haynes often put blacks into the "last hired, first fired" category because the real qualification for a job with such whites is that blacks not threaten their safety.

From these examples, one can see that whites often demand that blacks manage—or manipulate—their identity in a vain effort to make whites forget about their race and thus feel comfortable—at least to make whites feel safe in their presence, not really from blacks but from their own undealt with bigotry. This fact helps to explain the experiences of several of Cose's interviewees who were told by whites to be team players, partly by not acting as confident and assertive as their white colleagues (68). This demand is made evident by business professor Ella Bell when she speaks about blacks from the top law schools:

> They'll make it [into a company] in one or two years, and then all of a sudden they start getting this real fuzzy feedback—what I call static feedback—from their supervisors. Somehow they're "not team players." They're "too outspoken, too aggressive." . . . All of this is subjective, nothing you can fix. . . . And when you ask for examples it gets even flimsier. (78)

The idea that blacks must be docile and safe is also indicated by another story about a black lawyer. This story is perhaps the most powerful in Cose's book concerning whites' bigotry toward their black colleagues.

> When he was made a partner, a little less than three years after signing up, his first act was to request his personnel file. What he saw astounded him and confirmed his impression that many factors considered relevant to partnership were idiotically idiosyncratic. He discovered that one partner, disapproving of his Afro hairstyle, fretted over his "bushy" appearance. Another worried that clients might not accept him. Yet another, noting that he had worked for a civil rights agency, wondered whether his politics might not be too radical.
>
> At partnership meetings where the future of associates is determined, he still sees evidence of subjective criteria being used to weed blacks out. (17)

This man was extremely fortunate not to be "weeded out" himself, since his colleagues considered their own racism above his merit in some of their evaluations of him. It is no wonder that because of such racism this man fears that his children "may not be ready for the 'street fight'" they may face in trying to address such bigotry. Moreover, the lawyer's story validates the experience of many blacks who discern that whites, both secretly and overtly, judge them according to race-based standards that are not applied to whites.

At this point it is important to consider what is revealed by the examples under discussion about what whites are truly demanding from blacks by looking for black character manipulation that would produce blacks who try to reduce their racial difference from whites and thereby be nonthreatening to them. Such whites might seem to stress the need for racial sameness; however, they do not want this sameness to translate into equality. Hence, the true requirement for blacks in the incidents under discussion seems to be that blacks must accept being, to coin a phrase, the humble, docile, smiling "Negro" who stands tentatively at the threshold of American society, never presuming to come in without an invitation.

Whereas Cose studies race relations in the workplace in *The Rage of a Privileged Class*, Graham focuses on racism in the university as he meditates on "The Underside of Paradise: Being Black at Princeton" in *Member of the Club*. His experiences as a student make it evident that blacks in educational institutions often meet with the same demand as blacks in the workplace for identity management, predictability, safety, and downplaying their differences from whites. Graham recalls, for instance, being asked to join an eating club by a white student whom he had just met who tells him that he is the right type to join the club. Graham critiques the boy's alleged friendliness by exposing his racism:

> Imagine, after knowing me for only fifteen minutes, he had already determined that I was his type: safe, predictable, respectable, tame, docile—the

kind who he could understand and whose actions could easily be anticipated. I was the sort of black that didn't live in the Princeton Inn—the down-campus dorm where many of the non-integrating blacks lived. I was an up-campus black, the kind who understood the nuances of black–white relations. The kind who saved black slang for those deep and gritty moments with my own people. The kind who roomed with white guys yet didn't date white girls. The kind who would volunteer time to help plan the club's monthly parties yet not insist on attending or bringing black friends to them. (Graham 1995, 186–87)

This passage conveys the idea that such a white person really wants a black person who will not awaken his or her preexisting prejudices against blacks. Thus, Graham exposes the bigotry that lurks beneath the surface of many nice whites.

Identity management continues to be a factor in what at first may seem to be an innocuous exchange. The white person who would like Graham to join the eating club asks Graham if he likes steak. "Lying, I gave him the answer I assumed he wanted. 'Sure, who doesn't?' . . . I gave Hal a corny good-old-boy thumbs up gesture that should have gotten me kicked out of the black race on the spot. 'Awesome!'" (190). Yet, such acting makes no inroads into the overall campus racism. Graham recalls an incident that happened when he went to a dining hall without his friends, who had eaten earlier:

After standing in line for my food and then finding a space at a long wooden table populated by fourteen or fifteen very WASP-y looking men and women whom I'd never seen before (virtually everyone in the room was blonde) I put down my tray of food and walked back through the crowded room to get a glass of milk.

After getting the milk and turning back toward the table, I realized I'd missed a round of musical chairs. Except for my green tray and the knapsack on the back of my high-backed wooden seat, the trays, the knapsacks, even the chairs—except mine—were now gone.

As I stood there, glass in hand, contemplating the now vacated table, it occurred to me that more than a few people were amused by this scene. (203–4)

Graham's point seems to be that while blacks sometimes divest themselves of their very identity in order to fit in with whites, there is no reciprocity in this aspect of black–white relations. The boy who invites Graham to join the eating club and the students who leave the table merely practice different rejection styles toward a black person whom they do not know and whose feelings and very identity they do not care to know.

The connection between whites' demands for safety and predictability and their racism is clear in another episode, one which involves Graham and his white roommate. He tells of a time when he was involved in the campus antiapartheid movement and his roommate, Steve, says, "I heard what you were saying out there, about how Americans shouldn't support and invest in places like South Africa. Please don't get offended by this, but do blacks really think Americans are so terrible, and that things are so racist and unfair in the United States?" (214) Graham recalls with ennui and faint disappointment his reactions to Steve's words:

> Well, why wasn't I surprised to hear this? Although I knew Steve was open-minded and friendly to black people, I always thought that most other white people secretly wished that all black people would disappear, taking our problems and their guilt with us. . . . It was the first time I had done something to cause my white peers to say, "Oh, so he is just like the rest of them." (214–15)

In this episode, as well as the one involving the student who asked him to join the eating club, Graham makes it evident that an important component in many whites' feelings toward blacks entails a kind of false bargaining: "If you do not remind us that you are not like us, we may tolerate you; as long as you do not burden us with your racial identity, we may even like you. If you refuse this bargain, we will throw you on the junkheap with the rest of the ni . . . uh, blacks."

The failure of universities to combat racism adequately is especially sad in that they have a population that is there to learn—to be educated. While not all universities are equally negligent, both Graham's *Member of the Club* and Bell's *Faces at the Bottom of the Well* show the serious failures of white-dominated places of higher education to deal with their own racism. In fact, it seems that both authors would agree that universities often perpetuate racism by employing the tried and true defense mechanisms meant to deal with racism: denial, repression, silence, and the demand that blacks deemphasize racial differences.

Graham incisively critiques the failure of white university leaders to live up to their obligation to address racism:

> The best American universities have always been laboratories for the social and political changes that sweep the country from time to time. . . . [A student] needs the university and its administration to act both as provocateur and moral compass.
>
> Race is a subject that desperately needs the informed and authoritative voice of the college community. Most black and white students leave their homogeneous communities and arrive on campus curious, intimidated, or even repulsed by the students of the other race. . . . Filled with doubt, or even worse, derogatory stereotypes regarding the other, they are at a loss about how to treat or identify with those different from them. Without guidance or a higher moral vision from university leaders, the course of least resistance is for that student to re-create that homogeneous community on campus. Unless a university instills a vision of diversity as somehow better, more desirable than

homogeneity, a campus naturally begins to mimic the outside world, with its sturdy, racially defined barriers. (217–18)

Graham gives a case in point: the handling by white administrators of black students who were planning to bring Minister Louis Farrakhan to speak at Princeton in 1989. The administration acted with duplicity in caus-ing the students to cancel the speech at the last minute by demanding that they put up an additional five thousand dollars for security. "The university missed an ideal opportunity to take a stand on the issue of racial problems on campus and beyond. But, instead, it took the easy, passive-aggressive route it always has. It said nothing about the nature of the speech but in-stead used a shopworn ploy to prevent it from happening" (220). Consequently, blacks and whites remained locked in an adversarial position as a result of the duplicity and failure to talk honestly about racism which are the main ingredients in the mishandling of racial issues. The issue here goes beyond Farrakahn: universities sometimes contribute to the inertia that guarantees the continuance of racism which is a sad commentary on higher education.

Derrick Bell attacks universities from another angle in *Faces at the Bottom of the Well*. Bell, who left Harvard Law School because of its lack of inclusion for most of its history (until recently) of black female faculty, is highly aware of how white professors and administrators can maintain racial homogene-ity among faculty by the veiled and unyielding demand for blacks to be pre-dictable and safe in their scholarship and in their dealings with white colleagues. Moreover, Bell makes it clear that the white intolerance for dif-ference is often evident in whites' stance during tenure decisions involving blacks. Bell points out that tenure may be an even greater obstacle for blacks than open bigotry although the two are connected (1992, 139). He states that tenured faculty sometimes act as "guardians at the gates" to refuse entry to those whose backgrounds, interests, and opinions are not like theirs; in fact, Bell seems to state that merit is a much less significant fac-tor than sameness or assimilation. Furthermore, this desire by whites for blacks who will "fit in" as a result of seeming "like us" is an important exclu-sionary barrier to many if not most blacks (139). As a result, it is no wonder that near 1990, the percentage of black professors at universities and col-leges, other than historically black schools, stood at about 1 percent. It is not surprising, therefore, that in *Killing Rage*, bell hooks states,

> While it is true that the nature of racist oppression and exploitation has changed as slavery has ended and the apartheid structure of Jim Crow has legally changed, white supremacy continues . . . to inform the social status of black people and all people of color. Nowhere is this more evident than in university settings. And it is often liberal folks in those settings who are un-willing to acknowledge this truth. (hooks 1995, 187)

Bell's ideas help to explain hooks's feelings when he discusses the white attitude that often rejects black professors and scholars as a result of the unyielding refusal to tolerate difference: he states that even excellent scholarship by minorities can be rejected by whites for discriminatory reasons, barring many minorities from being hired or promoted (Bell 1992, 140). Threatened by challenges to their assumptions in works that raise political or reality-based issues, whites can dismiss such work as being simply "ideological" rantings (as if this judgment were not itself ideological), claims Bell (140). Hence, Bell concludes that the hiring and tenure process favor blacks who downplay their blackness—or, echoing the terms of acceptance discussed by Mead and Baldwin in *Rap on Race* and Goffman in *Stigma*—minimize their difference from whites. It seems, therefore, that Bell picks up on the idea that blacks in university settings are held accountable for the degree to which they are assimilable—a notion that is one of the foundations of racism and one of the key obstacles not only to diversity but also to adequate integration (however amazing it may seem that integration is still an issue to be argued for at the turn of the twentieth century). Indeed, many blacks who have experienced the racism in such evaluations as those referred to by Bell know that their white colleagues claim to be nonideological and therefore objective and fair in their rejections of their black colleagues' work. Furthermore, Bell's experiences corroborate the idea that whites who perpetuate such behind-the-scenes racism, as they almost never have to take accountability for their prejudice, are often the first to deny that race plays any role in their systematic rejection of black scholars. Yet, this denial is merely another defense mechanism: the minimizing and downplaying of the black candidates' race and of whites' own racism. Nevertheless, as whites claim a nonideological objectivity in their evaluations of their black colleagues' ideological work, they betray the fact that their stated freedom from prejudice is merely the mental trick that bigots perform when they refuse to face their own inner racism.

Finally, Bell makes another point relevant to whites' evaluations of their black colleagues' work which extends to a general commentary on the handicap many whites have in being able to respond intelligently to black scholarship and criticism. Stating ideas that are relevant to black literature, art, and music, Bell writes that innovative work can meet with a response from those who resist difference as if it smells bad, reflecting such people's "offensiveness response" to things that challenge them (143). Bell again implicitly challenges the notion that color-blind assessments of merit decide the fate of those whose work challenges the norm and for which new standards of evaluation may be in order (143). Bell's comments make it evident that, when white readers evaluate works by blacks that critique them, it is essential for those whites to ask themselves whether their estimation of such works hinges on whether the works affirm or question their view of the world and of themselves concerning blacks. They then need to ask themselves if they feel that the world is not big enough for themselves and those who question them because that is the issue that results in whites' failure to hire and promote blacks in many academic settings. As hooks points out, "Often we [blacks who work in colleges and universities] work in environments predominantly peopled by white folks (some of whom are well-meaning and concerned) who are not committed to working to end white supremacy, or who are unsure about what that commitment means" (1995, 192).

When one reads the works under discussion by Cose, Graham, Bell, and hooks, it becomes clear that a typology of whites emerges that is consistent with those in black fiction. The works by Cose, Bell, and Graham, in particular, continue the discussions begun by earlier authors of the main components of the white identity that emphasize the ways in which many whites create an armor of defense mechanisms that enable them to practice racism and to protect their self-image from being affected by charges of bigotry. Moreover, as a result, as hooks points out in *Killing Rage*, it is imperative that society become aware of and produce, when possible, "counter hegemonic race talk" which can be a liberating discourse for blacks and for relatively enlightened people of all races to "bear witness to the reality . . . that this nation can be transformed, that we can resist racism and in the act of resistance recover ourselves and be renewed" (1995, 7).

NOTES

1. Ellis Cose, *The Rage of a Privileged Class* (New York: HarperCollins, 1993), 4.

2. Derrick Bell, *Faces at the Bottom of the Well* (New York: Basic Books, 1992), 6.

3. Matthew S. Goldberg, "Discrimination, Nepotism, and Long-Run Wage Differentials," in *Faces at the Bottom of the Well* by Derrick Bell (New York: Basic Books, 1992), 47.

4. Lawrence Otis Graham, *Member of the Club* (New York: HarperCollins, 1995), 211–12.

5. bell hooks, *Killing Rage* (New York: Henry Holt, 1995), 4.

—— Chapter 5 ——

A Dirty Rag in White People's Hands: The White Image Deep Inside the Black Mind

The hardships that face blacks, which are written about by such authors as Ellis Cose and Derrick Bell, are part of a continuum of black writers' representations of blacks' inferior treatment by whites. How does this continuum reveal the impact upon the self-image of blacks and the degree to which they value being part of a race that has been the target of centuries of bigotry? Certainly, many oppressed people believe in and act on their value of themselves, not being defeated by the disdain directed against their group by members of the dominant society. What happens, however, when the oppressed person accepts the view of the oppressor? What happens when one's mind is invaded by an alien denigration of oneself and one's very existence? This chapter explores what happens when the mind of blacks, like black slums, is "a white-made thing."[1]

Self-hatred, self-rejection, and the acceptance of whites as the primary beings of one's existence result from the internalization of racism by blacks who suffer from these conditions. Such blacks live as psychological exiles from themselves and from other blacks, facts that are most clearly represented in the intraracial hostility and violence which are, in fact, manifestations of what could be termed interactive self-hatred. The writer who presents these topics and other related issues in their greatest complexity is Richard Wright. An examination of Wright's career as a novelist as a whole reveals that internalization of white bigotry by blacks recurs throughout his career and is a central feature of his first novel, the posthumously published *Lawd Today* (1963); his most acclaimed novel, *Native Son* (1940); and his last novel, *The Long Dream* (1958). Moreover, Wright's treatment of the subject of internalization and other related neuroses is both tied to and illuminated by one of America's most influential psychologists,

Kenneth B. Clark, whose work on internalization and self-image was cited by the U.S. Supreme Court in its decision on *Brown v. the Board of Education,* which established the principle that "separate is inherently unequal." While both Wright's and Clark's ideas have been controversial for the authors' concentration on self-alienation among blacks, this topic is an essential aspect of how white racism has affected blacks' identity and self-perception. This chapter analyzes the increasing complexity with which Wright treated the subject of what happens when the white image—of blacks—invades the black mind in Wright's first novel, his best novel, and his last novel. Moreover, such social scientists as Clark, particularly in *Prejudice and Your Child* (1955), Stanley Milgram in *Obedience to Authority* (1974), and Richard Sennett in *Authority* (1980) lend important insights into such psychological complexes as those that occur when the oppressed is invaded psychologically by the oppressor.

The protagonist's self-perception is an integral part of Richard Wright's fiction. This leads to a controversy involving Wright that first surfaced in regard to his autobiography, *Black Boy* (1945).

> [A]fter the habit of reflection had been born in me, I used to mull over the strange absence of real kindness in Negroes, how unstable was our tenderness, how lacking in genuine passion we were, how void of great hope, how timid our joy, how bare our traditions, how hollow our memories, how lacking we were in those intangible sentiments which bind man to man, and how shallow was our despair.[2]

This passage is but one aspect of the controversy that has surrounded Wright's attitude toward blacks. Indeed, much critical work on Wright (primarily his nonfiction, for example, *Black Boy* and *Black Power,* his book about his visit to Africa) and reminiscences of the man himself raise the issue of whether Wright was guilty of hostility toward blacks. James Baldwin's "Alas, Poor Richard" shows Wright to have been disdainful toward his black fellow expatriates in France.[3] W.E.B. Du Bois reacted angrily to the passage quoted from *Black Boy,* as well as to the book in general: "The Negroes whom he paints have almost no redeeming qualities . . . there is none who is ambitious, successful, or really intelligent."[4] Robert B. Stepto has proclaimed Wright to be a "confused" man who, either by ignorance or design, was alienated from blacks and whose alienation is reflected in his "limited depiction of the Negro."[5] Agreeing with Ralph Ellison that Wright was unable to portray blacks as intellectual and creative, Stepto echoes both Du Bois' and Margaret Walker's criticisms of Wright. According to Walker, "Black people were never his ideals. He championed the cause of the black man but he never idealized or glorified him. His black men as characters were always seen as the victims of society, demeaned and destroyed and corrupted to animal status."[6] Houston A. Baker, Jr., seems to be one of the few critics to defend Wright against the charge of possessing a hostility toward blacks which handicapped his artistry.

> Wright's works are generally celebrations of life, particularly the complex life lived by black Americans. Wright repeatedly declares that blacks are affirmers: every imaginable pressure has been asserted against them while they have continued to assert the principles of humanity vested in the American Constitution and the Bill of Rights more fully and effectively than any other group on the continent.[7]

Baker's thoughts are provocative in the face of so much criticism which views Wright from the opposing angle. Baker's view prompts one to wonder who has made the more accurate assessment of Wright: those who find his feelings toward and depictions of blacks limited and hostile, or one who finds value in Wright's portrayals of and attitude toward blacks? An examination of Wright's ideas is an essential step in dealing with these questions.

Those who complain about a perceptible self-loathing in Wright's works—his characters' disdain for other blacks and their desire to divorce themselves from blacks—should consider that Wright is illuminating a very complex frame of mind. This emotional situation is best expressed in Barry D. Adam's *The Survival of Domination*:

> The person who discovers himself or herself as a member of an inferiorized group is presented with a "composite portrait" which purports to define him or her. . . . Inferiorized identity [can appear to a member of the group] as an iron cage negating one's freedom. . . . The inferiorized person perceives an initial choice: (1) acceptance of categorization as an inferiorized member with the composite portrait of undesirable traits, or (2) rejection or lack of recognition of the self in the composite portrait, with lack of identification with the inferiorized group. This pseudochoice . . . [can] lead to one of two debilitating results, and, frequently, oscillation between the two: (1) guilt [and] self-hatred . . . or (2) flight from identity [and] denial.[8]

The hostility toward blacks that many readers notice in Wright's works is part of the self-rejection that can result from attempting to repudiate a racist view of blacks that one has internalized. Wright dramatizes, with growing sophistication, the self-hatred and rejection of identity that can be a consequence of blacks' being successfully inferiorized by accepting a white racist image of themselves in *Lawd Today*, *Native Son*, and *The Long Dream*.

In his first two novels, *Lawd Today* and *Native Son*, Wright portrays the self-loathing and hostility toward other blacks that are a consequence of his protagonists' powerlessness. *Lawd Today* begins the saga.

The racism that the protagonist, Jake, faces at his job is a major source of his self-rejection and his rejection of other blacks. *Lawd Today*, which Wright worked on from the late 1920s to 1936, was inspired in part by his experiences as a postal clerk in Chicago. The novel details a day in the wretched life of Jake Jackson, whose bleak existence consists of a job that he hates, a wife whom he loathes, and friends with whom he has superficial relationships. According to Michel Fabre in *The Unfinished Quest of Richard Wright*,

> Wright used the details of his duty at the central post office in his novel *Lawd Today*. The enormous brick building [had] the worst conditions of all United States post offices. The discipline was worthy of a penitentiary. The chapter entitled "Squirrel's Cage" follows each step of the character's eight hour shift and accurately describes Wright's daily routine and drudgery in 1928. Having become a mere number after passing the armed identification control guards, he would first sort the mail by category, then the letters by destination, then cancel the stamps before finally putting the mail into bags, all under the constant supervision of a foreman. Dust rose from the bags, the lighting was harsh. The constant noise from stamping machines and the fumes from the ink only made matters worse. Every minute spent in the bathroom was recorded, and the penalty for being caught dawdling or smoking a cigarette was two hundred demerits.[9]

In the novel, Wright dramatizes how his frustration with white supervision and the limitations put on his existence by a racist society cause Jake to misdirect his anger toward his wife as he attempts to compensate for his white-created inferior position in American society. Hence, *Lawd Today* foreshadows both *Native Son* and *The Long Dream* in showing how blacks sometimes offset their inferior position to whites by displacing their hostility onto themselves and onto other blacks.

One incident that demonstrates Jake's feelings of anxiety, dread, and rebelliousness occurs when Jake puts a few letters into an incorrect stack of mail, a white inspector gives him demerits for his mistake, and Jake feels he is singled out because he is black. When Jake things about the incident,

> He did not know of any other way that things could be if not this way; yet he longed for them not to be this way. He felt something vast and implacable was crushing him; and he felt angry with himself because he had to stand it. He had an impulse to brush . . . away everything. But there was nothing he could solve by doing that; he would only get into more trouble. And the feeling that he could do nothing doubled back upon him, fanning the ashes of other dead feelings of not being able to do anything, and he was consumed in a fever of bitterness.[10]

Reflecting on his frustration, Jake thinks that he would like to destroy the building in which he works. "If there was only something he could do to pay the whitefolks back for all they had ever done! Even if he lost his own life doing it! But what could he do? He felt the loneliness of his black skin"

(125). From these passages, one can see that through Jake Wright illustrates a psychological complex which has hostility toward white racism as its foundation but which rebounds on the impotent person to evoke self-alienation that later will be metamorphosed into alienation from and hostility toward other blacks.

Self-alienation and alienation from one's own racial group, about which Adam writes in *The Survival of Domination,* are shown by Wright in *Lawd Today* when Jake's and his friends' envy of whites brings forth feelings of self-hatred. The men seem to believe that if only they were white, all of their problems would be solved. They talk dreamily, for example, about a rich white man about whom they have read in the newspapers, and Jake even idolizes the gangsters about whom he has read: "Them gangsters is sports . . . all the time they's alive, they walk around knowing that any time somebody might shoot 'em down. Jesus, those gangsters is sports" (130). Reflecting on their situation, the men sing what they believe to be "the truth" (153) about their condition:

> A naught's a naught
> A figger's a figger
> All for the white man
> None for the nigger. (153)

Moreover, comparing the harshness of their lives to their image of how white people live, Jake says, "Sometimes when I think about it I almost hate myself" (145). The men's envy of whites and their resultant self-hatred reflect their feeling that if one has nothing, one is nothing. Thus, their anger toward whites is not manifested in actions toward whites but in self-denigration.

Wright's representation of black self-hatred in *Lawd Today* and elsewhere can be illuminated by Sennett's assertion in *Authority* that many studies show that, in the nineteenth and twentieth centuries, many people have felt that hardship was a sign of their inadequacy, that "[i]f you experience misfortune, you are personally responsible for being weak."[11] Furthermore, "Studies of poor urban blacks, for instance, testify to their belief that to be on welfare, to be dependent upon people who are judging your weakness in order to decide how much you need, is an intensely humiliating experience. For all that these blacks may know that the deck may be stacked against them, the internalizing of dependence as shame occurs" (Sennett 1980, 47). Thus, it becomes evident why Wright represents Jake as alienated from himself and from other blacks: they are as guilty of residing in a "cesspool" as whites are of putting them there (*Cesspool* was the original title of the novel.)

Wright underlines the displacement of anger onto other blacks in Jake's abuse of his wife. Jake feels that the only outlet for his anger is his plan to "stomp [his wife's] guts out," though by doing this he certainly never has any effect on the actual forces that are oppressing him (111). This destructiveness clarifies the relevance of Wright's use of a quotation from Waldo Frank's *Our America* as an epigraph: "When you study these long rows of desiccated men and women, you feel that you are in the presence of some form of life that has hardened but not grown" (108). That statement, as well as the fact that the action of the novel takes place on Abraham Lincoln's birthday, emphasizes that these characters, whose lives do not progress, remain, in fact, inert, no matter how much they may talk about rebelling or striking out in violence. Hence, *Lawd Today* represents, in a simplified form, a complex which Wright develops in more complexity in his next novel, *Native Son*, and in his last novel, *The Long Dream*: that white-inspired self-hatred and hostility toward blacks can trap blacks in a negative cycle of violence and ultimate self-destruction, even as white racism and the harm it causes to blacks continue to flourish.

Native Son, the first novel by Wright published during his lifetime, is a great leap forward from *Lawd Today*. While *Lawd Today* handles the themes of internalization and inferiorization in a bare-bones, day in the life of an angry postal worker, neorealistic way, *Native Son*'s naturalistic and existential exploration of the experience of a poor young black man has greater depth and intricacy, both in plot and in characterization.

Kenneth B. Clark wrote about the importance of Wright's tale of Bigger Thomas, an alienated young man who kills both a white woman, Mary Dalton, and a black woman, his girlfriend, Bessie. While Clark had reservations about the sensational nature of the plot, he recognized its contribution to the literature on self-rejection and the resultant hostility toward oneself and others.

> Hostile and aggressive reactions to the inferior status imposed upon the Negro have sometimes received over-dramatic descriptions in the public press and in novels. Richard Wright's *Native Son*—as well as other descriptions of Negroes who react to racial frustrations by blind expressions of hostility and aggressions towards any convenient person in the environment—may stimulate the interests of the layman and make him aware of the high human costs of racial prejudice. . . . Regardless of how [such stories] are interpreted, these patterns of reaction to racial frustration exist; they are a part of the high human and social costs of racial oppression.[12]

What is worth emphasizing in this passage is Clark's mention of how racism—and, therefore, white people—is the key to the hostility and self-rejection depicted by Wright in his novel and the real-life stories symbolized by the novel. Wright clarifies this connection in *Twelve Million Black Voices* when he points to white slumlords, such as those represented by the man for whom Bigger works, as bearing guilt for the warping of many blacks' personalities, which he felt resulted in great part from the wretched housing to which whites consigned many blacks who came to live in Northern cities. Speaking of such housing, Wright states,

> The kitchenette blights the personalities of our growing children, disorganizes them, blinds them to hope, creates problems whose effects can be traced in the characters of its child victims for years afterward.
>
> The kitchenette fills our black boys with longing and restlessness, urging them to run off from home, to join together with other restless black boys in gangs, that brutal form of city courage.
>
> The kitchenette piles up mountains of profits for the Bosses of the Buildings [white slumlords] and makes them ever more determined to keep things as they are.[13]

The reader of *Native Son* sees the decrepit and rat-infested conditions in which Bigger and his family live and sees the result of these conditions in his alienation from his family, his involvement in a gang, and the murders that lead him to death row. It is essential to remember that Wright understood the ghettoization of blacks to be the Northern whites' form of lynching (Wright 1978, 212). Wright seems to believe, therefore, that Bigger's troubled psychology, his alienation, and his aggressions are, like the ghetto, a "white-made thing," to borrow a term from Lerone Bennett, Jr.

Wright's emphasis on the connection among Bigger's oppressed status, his self-rejection, and his hostility toward others is best expressed in the scene in which Bigger chauffeurs Mary and Jan. Unable to respond to their friendliness (however directive and patronizing), Bigger is so conditioned to see himself as he thinks whites see him—as inferior—as he sits in the car with them, he wishes he could "with one final blow blot it out—with himself and them in it."[14] It is fascinating that Wright emphasizes Bigger's hatred of these two progressive whites for their making him feel intensely and humiliatingly uncomfortable as being linked to his own self-hatred, for Bigger feels that he is a thing to be hated. Clark illuminates the psychological condition represented by Bigger:

> The rejected individual must either construct for himself or acquire from his narrow environment new values appropriate to his restricted and inferior status. These new values may be anti-social. But they strengthen his ego. They tend to give him some security, prestige and status within the caste to which he has been relegated. It is possible that his disregard for property rights stems from a basic desire for revenge and aggression against something considered so important by the society which has humiliated him. (1955, 53)

To continue this line of thinking, it is more than possible that Bigger values his killing of Mary for similar ego-enhancing and vengeful reasons as those described by Clark. Hence, Wright makes it evident that Bigger's feeling that whites have made his blackness "a badge of shame," which he carries into the "shadowy region, a No Man's Land," offers him, to use Adam's word, a "pseudo-choice": acceptance of the ego-destroying inferiorization to which whites have subjected him, or an ego- and identity-salvaging move to drag whites into the "shadowy region" while he escapes this emotional zone with his new-found feelings of power (Wright 1940, 67).

In *Native Son*, Wright gives readers possibly the most alienated character in American literature. Bigger is alienated from his family, from other blacks against whom he and his gang commit such crimes as robbery, from whites whom he views with both fear and envy, and, most devastatingly, from himself. This alienation is developed further in Wright's final novel, *The Long Dream*. *The Long Dream* focuses on a father, Tyree, and his son, nick-named Fish, who live in a small Mississippi town. The self-hatred and aggressive impulses which Wright analyzes in *Lawd Today* and *Native Son* are manifested in both the father and son in *The Long Dream*. In fact, *The Long Dream* stands as a psychological novel which focuses on the tragedy of blacks who are so inferiorized that they, like Bigger, consider themselves to inhabit a shadow world, and self-aggrandizing and futile gestures are their only compensation for a devastated ego and deprived social status.

It is clear that Tyree accepts the white-created racist circumstances which determine both his status and his identity. In fact, all Tyree wants is to flourish within a separate and unequal society, not to change it. This acceptance of white racism leads to one of Tyree's main conflicts: he is equally afraid of racism and of losing the status that he has earned by complying with the racist system that could result from challenging it. For example, by paying off the white police chief, Cantley, Tyree is allowed to run a brothel, the Grove, that is in violation of the fire code. Thus, as much as Tyree resents racism, he has a vested interest in maintaining the status quo: he can benefit from doing so. Furthermore, Tyree's self-interest in maintaining his status within the racist system is shown dramatically when he is somewhat relieved after Chris is lynched, thinking that now that whites have "had their . . . fun . . . [they will be] nice and quiet . . . for a little while."[15] Tyree's "security could only be had by making victims of black men" (1958, 93). Hence, one sees that Tyree represents a psychology that has internalized a fear and acceptance of the negative and even deadly ways that racism can limit black people.

Tyree's internalization of racism is such that he manipulates his identity in the presence of whites. This identity management is evident in his radical shift in manner whenever whites are near. Though outspoken and self-confident when he is with other blacks, his son, Fish, notices that when Tyree is in the presence of whites, he becomes

> stiff and unnatural in his manner. . . . [He was] paying humble deference to the white man and his 'acting' was so flawless that Fishbelly was stupefied. This was a father whom he had never known, whom he did not want to know. . . .

When the white man had turned a corner in the corridor . . . a change en-
gulf[ed] his father's face and body; his knees lost their bent posture, his back
straightened, his arms fell normally to his side, and that distracted, foolish,
noncommittal expression vanished. (Wright 1958, 168–69)

At this point, Tyree attempts to teach his son his rule for dealing with
whites: "Obey 'em!" (170). On this point, Stanley Milgram's comments on
such behavior in *Obedience to Authority* are relevant. Tyree, when with whites
"becomes something different from his former self, with new properties not
easily traced to his usual personality."[16] Thus, although Tyree tries to salvage
his self-image by thinking of himself as successful and crafty, and as perceiv-
ing himself as having independence from whites as a result of having bribed
the police chief into letting him own the Grove, he is, in fact, trapped in his
assigned role. Nevertheless, Tyree's delusion of independence is manifested
when he says, "I could almost git away with murder in this town. But you got
to know how! . . . [A] white man always wants to see a black man either crying or grinning. I can't cry, ain't the crying type. So I grin and git anything
I want" (Wright 1958, 192). This passage is central to several points. First,
here Tyree clearly represents an idea that Wright stated in an interview:
America appreciates blacks as entertainers and objects of amusement, but it
cannot coexist equally with its black citizens.[17] Tyree's thought patterns,
moreover, illustrate other key ideas held by Wright: oppression has so al-
tered the personality of many blacks that they merely present themselves as
images of what they surmise would be pleasing to whites. Wright concluded
that what many whites feel is the natural good nature of many blacks is actually a mere facade that belies the true internal dissatisfaction in the hearts
of much of the black race. Still, since blacks, in Wright's view, are good per-
formers, the act that such people as those represented by Tyree substitute
for their true character traps them in a demeaning position (Kinnamon
and Fabre 1993, 108). In Tyree, therefore, Wright dramatizes that blacks
whose identity is shaped by white expectations are mere shadows without
substance, robbed of any authenticity as their lives become a mere performance for whites who cannot accept them as fully realized human beings.

The significance of Tyree's delusion of power and his true condition are
clarified by looking more closely at his psychology. In Tyree, Wright has created a character of frightening servility and deep complexity. In fact, Tyree
may be as complex a character as Bigger Thomas. Tyree's complexity is obvious when one considers his mentality alongside Sennett's discussion of
"disobedient dependence. It is based on a compulsive focusing of attention:
what would [authority figures] want? Once their will is known, a person can
act—even against them. But they are the central characters. . . . [This sort of
behavior] has very little to do with . . . autonomy" (Sennett 1980, 33). One
sees that in Tyree Wright shows the kind of behavior exhibited by those who
maintain their status within an oppressive society by capitulating to whites.

Their delusions of power are merely compensatory gestures that maintain a positive self-image.

Wright also uses Tyree as a vehicle to represent how some blacks default whatever power they may have to whites, showing what a "white-made thing" their very identity is. This aspect of Tyree's identity is seen in his cringing at the thought of white supremacy and his resultant hatred of blacks. In fact, this aspect of Tyree's character is one of the main lessons given to his son in teaching him about racism. The behavior modeled by Tyree is especially significant if one considers it in light of Clark's comments on parental behavior in educating children about racism.

> A direct statement of elementary truth can be one of a child's first lessons in social ethics. Similar statements, geared to the child's level of understanding, can help him to realize that he is not to blame when people hate or reject him for personal characteristics over which he has no control. He can be helped to understand that prejudice against him is not a sign of his own inferiority. With sympathetic understanding and guidance, the child can come to realize that prejudice is primarily a symptom of the inadequacy of those who hold the prejudice.
>
> When a child is struggling for self-esteem, he may sometimes be helped by identification with one of his parents. (Clark 1955, 118)

Clark makes it clear that a black parent's attitudes and behavior serve as a model on which children may base their understanding of racism and feelings about themselves and others as targets of bigotry. On all these points, Wright uses Tyree to exhibit how internalization results in self-hatred and hostility toward blacks in general, which are passed on to the next generation.

That Tyree has internalized racism toward other blacks is made evident at several points. Noticing his father's relief at Chris's lynching, for example, "Fishbelly felt that his father hated the black people now" (Wright 1958, 93). Fish is right: Tyree seems to have internalized hatred toward blacks to such a degree that he clearly feels that blacks deserve whatever mistreatment they get. This attitude is obviously a rationale for Tyree's callous and exploitive treatment of blacks, even as he grins and shuffles before whites. This mentality represents how those who internalize racism elevate themselves above other blacks and thus try to have power over them, even when they know that whites hold the greatest power. That Tyree models this mentality and behavior to Fish is evident when he gives Fish the responsibility of collecting rent from his tenants, telling the boy not to grant any extensions on payments: "[I]f you let a nigger bitch owe you fifty dollars and give her five days to git out, she just might have enough sense to go and find another place to stay. Make 'em pay. . . . Remember, we black and we can't rent to white folks. So we have to be hard on our own folks to make money" (1958, 273). One can see, therefore, that one of Tyree's chief characteristics is his contempt for black people, whom he feels must suffer to compensate for the inadequacies of his own life. Tyree, therefore, can be understood to illustrate Clark's comments that "Low racial status . . . requires the individual to show deference and restrict his open aggressiveness against the dominant group" and to displace his aggression onto members of his own, already oppressed, group.

> [I]n view of the general social reality in which whites have superior power and generally are in control of political and law enforcement agencies of the community, Negroes are rarely able to express their hostility and aggressive impulses directly against them. In his relations with whites, therefore, the Negro is required to adopt substitute or indirect forms of aggression. The larger culture frequently encourages—or certainly does not discourage—substitution of other Negroes as victims of the repressed aggressions against whites. The relatively large incidence of violence within the Negro group itself tends to support this observation. Other ways in which the Negro may disguise his aggressions [include] . . . an assumption of the role of the meek, humble, and unaggressive Negro who makes a point of being deferential to whites. He learns what role is expected of him by observing and participating in the larger culture. (Clark 1955, 56)

Hence, the white-made thing that is Tyree embodies the neurosis described above by Clark and models it for his son.

Tyree's hostility toward other blacks is, perhaps, a psychological justification for exploiting them (e.g., owning a brothel, keeping it open even though he knows it is a firetrap, and not feeling responsible when many blacks die in a fire there) and being happy with other blacks' misfortune. Milgram illuminates the complexity of the attitudes and behavior represented in Tyree. The major goal of Milgram's experiment was to find out how far people would go in harming others in order to obey an authority figure (1974, xiii). One factor that causes people to take an irresponsible attitude toward hurting others is "[s]ystematic devaluation of the victim [which] provides a measure of psychological justification for brutal treatment of the victim. . . . [M]any subjects [of the experiment] harshly devalue the victim *as a consequence* of acting against him" (9–10). This factor can be related to another factor explored by Milgram: self-image. The subject who chooses to obey orders that seem to inflict harm on another, in order to absolve himself of responsibility,

> shift[s] responsibility to the victim, who is seen as bringing on his own punishment. The victim is blamed for having volunteered for the experiment, and more viciously, for stupidity and obstinacy. Here we move from the shifting of responsibility to the gratuitous depreciation of the victim. The psychological mechanism is transparent: if the victim is an unworthy person, one need not be concerned about inflicting pain upon him. (10)

Clearly, Tyree is using this line of thinking; to him, there is nothing wrong with victimizing a "damn fool" like Chris or "nigger bitch[es]." Tyree, therefore, in effect teaches his son that one can reap the benefits of other blacks' misfortune without damaging one's own self-image.

The most significant example of Tyree's hostile, exploitive, and irresponsible attitude and actions toward blacks appears in his discussion with a white, progressive lawyer, MacWilliams, after the deadly fire at the Grove. Here, Tyree attempts to absolve himself of the responsibility of owning a brothel, doing nothing about its fire code violations, and bribing the police chief to keep the brothel open. Tyree is bold (or twisted) enough to try to convince MacWilliams of his innocence by saying, "Sure, I did wrong. But my kind of wrong is right; when you have to do wrong to live, wrong is right. . . . I took the white man's law and lived under it. It was bad law, but I made it work for me and my family" (Wright 1958, 374–75). In arguing for his immoral actions to the white man Tyree not only shows his incorrigible self-centeredness but also his need to have his actions validated by a white authority figure, all of which bears out Clark's and Milgram's observations on a psychology such as Tyree's, whose mind and identity are, as another black character says of him, "a dirty rag in other people's hands" (426).

Tyree's identity is such a white-made thing that he even seems to fear the power that he may have over whites. This aspect of his character is clear when he deal with Cantley, the police chief, after the fire at the Grove kills scores of people. Cantley asks Tyree how he will explain to the district attorney how the Grove remained open in spite of its fire violations. In order to try to ensure that Cantley will help him, Tyree again acts the role of the deferential "Negro" by saying that he will not reveal that he bribed Cantley and by lying to him that he had burned the canceled checks which would prove both that he bribed the chief and that Cantley shares the responsibility for the deaths that resulted from the fire. Though Tyree can prove the police chief's wrongdoing, which he could threaten to do to enlist Cantley's help in protecting him from the law, Tyree is so afraid to assert himself that even after Cantley tells him that he will be indicted, he "threw himself tentatively on the mercy of the white man he trusted least on earth" (331). This incident shows Tyree's internalization of his powerlessness and subordinate status before whites because he feels that remaining powerless is safer than exercising his own power.

Tyree again defaults his power when he pleads with Cantley to help him: "I'm lost! . . . I been your friend for twenty years and you done turned your back on me. You can't let this [indictment] happen to me" (340–41). It is significant that Tyree—for the first time—seems to assert himself against a white person and shows "an almost human dignity" (341). "With all the strength of his being, the slave was fighting with the master" (342). Yet, Tyree's flicker of self-assertion soon dies, and he begs Cantley either to help him or kill him. This obviously exaggerated bit of acting causes Fish to feel

that "he was watching something obscene" (343). Indeed, Tyree further reveals his contradictory feelings of subservience and manipulation of whites
when he tells Fish, after the incident, "You got to know how to handle these
goddam white folks. . . . Hell, I done saved up enough evidence against the
goddam chief to send 'im to jail for years!" (343). Still, Tyree relies on
Cantley to protect him when he asks the chief to arrange to have blacks on
the jury at his trial—in a small Mississippi town in the pre–civil rights era!
This line of thinking is clearly ludicrous. Why doesn't Tyree blackmail the
police chief, since he says he has the power to do so? One explanation is
that he is still, to borrow Sennett's phrase, in a state of "disobedient dependence," for although he thinks that he has a degree of power over whites,
Tyree, as Wright says, "automatically accepted his situation and worked will-
ingly within it" (380). Another explanation for Tyree's continuing to obey
and accept his role in spite of his potential power is, as Milgram says, that
"[t]here must be a competing drive, tendency, or inhibition that precludes
activation of the disobedient response. The strength of the inhibiting factor
must be of greater magnitude than the stress experienced [the stress of
wanting to disobey but not being psychologically ready to do so] or else the
terminating act would occur" (43). For Tyree, the inhibiting factor is his inability to change his perception of and to defy the racial definitions of the
South; Tyree believes that "Niggers ain't got no rights but them they buy
. . . for years I done bought my rights from the white man and I done built
a business. I got a home. A car" (474–75). Furthermore, years of condition-
ing that his "disobedient dependence" is the only way to have a degree of
power causes Tyree to feel that he will lose power by asserting himself and
thereby lose the fruits of submission. Tyree is psychologically unable, therefore, to utilize openly his own power—even when he has the means with
which to do it.

Only when Cantley double-crosses Tyree and spreads the rumor that
Tyree is agitating to have blacks put on the jury does Tyree fight back (349).
Only then does he understand that he is certainly doomed by choosing
powerlessness. By finally acting (as opposed to "acting") by revealing to
MacWilliams Cantley's complicity in the fire, Tyree at least seems to have
the chance to see that there may be some justice in that he is not solely responsible for the Grove's having been a death trap.

At this point, however, it seems that Wright wants to use Tyree's story as a
cautionary tale for blacks who may be following the same road of internalization and inferiorization: Tyree's self-assertion comes too late—too late to
save him. Even though MacWilliams vows to help Tyree, it is certain that
Cantley will kill him. Wright describes the results of Tyree's lone, inadequate attempt to assert himself against a white person:

You ate, slept, breathed, and lived fear. Somewhere out there in the grey void
was the ever-lurking enemy who shaped your destiny, curbed your ends, who

determined your aims, who stamped your every action with alien meanings. You existed in the bosom of the enemy, shared his ideals, spoke his tongue, fought with his weapons, and died a death usually of his choosing. (397)

Tyree's fears are well-founded: he is ambushed and killed by the police.

Tyree's tale and his ultimate fate are vehicles through which Wright reveals many complex psychological truths. The importance of internalization, inferiorization, and alienation from and hostility toward one's own group as a result of their inferior status vis-à-vis whites are all illustrated by Wright's characterization of Tyree in *The Long Dream.* Moreover, that he is a father ensures a multigenerational dysfunction, for his son shows that he has learned well his father's neurosis.

To understand why Fish inherits his father's internalization and the resultant damage to his own psychological makeup, refer to Clark's "What Can Parents Do" in *Prejudice and Your Child*, which provides incisive answers about how black parents can influence their children's feelings about race.

> Parents from minority groups in general have an even greater responsibility to their children than other parents. They must be sensitive to the necessity of counteracting the social forces that ordinarily tend to rob their children of self-esteem. . . . Paradoxically, the social forces that necessitate this relationship in the Negro family may interfere with the ability of these parents . . . to express warmth, love, and acceptance for their children—for the Negro parent is himself the product of racial pressures and frustrations. It is imperative, however, that this cycle be broken. Because it cannot be broken by the child, it must be broken by the parents and by the larger society. (Clark 1955, 115)

Because Fish's parents, particularly Tyree, fail on every count mentioned by Clark, the unbroken cycle of racial pathology continues.

Clark's analysis of the role of black parents is essential to understanding *The Long Dream* because Fish's estrangement from blacks has as its genesis his estrangement from his family. Here it is important to take a closer look at the dynamics within the family and how they affect the son, Fish, during and after the lynching of Chris. Much as Wright recalls in *Black Boy* his confusion about why his family was leaving town after the murder of his uncle, Hoskins, he emphasizes how Fish, as a panic-stricken Tyree hurries home, wonders "why they were running instead of fighting? Pity for his father dawned in him. . . . He swallowed a lump of shame in his throat . . . as there flashed in him a picture of thousands of black people running" (Wright 1958, 81–82). This incident is the greatest factor in provoking Fish's rejection of blacks because of their powerlessness and, more important, his even stronger internalization of white racist values in judging other blacks. Witnessing his parents' fear, "[s]uddenly he saw his parents as he felt and thought that the white people saw them and he felt toward them some of the contempt that the white people felt for them. . . . [H]e was ashamed of his father's fear. . . . [Tyree] was lost, and so were all black people" (82, 86). The impact of his parents' behavior on Fish is profound. According to Clark, "Some parents are more active and direct than others in influencing their racial attitudes; but every parent has some degree of influence. . . . Parents who do not take a conscious stand may still exert an influence on their children by their passive acceptance of the prevailing racial myths and customs" (121). The prevailing myths and customs Fish's parents model for him include the ideas that blacks are helpless victims, toys in the hands of a great white force. Thus, Fish's internalization of white racist evaluations of blacks and his shame are inspired by his family, mainly his father, who loudly blames the victim of the lynching for his own murder.

Fish's parents are also essential in inspiring their son's maladjusted attitudes because, as Fish reflects on his parents' fear of whites, he feels compelled to judge blacks in the same way that he feels whites do:

> He was beginning to look at his people through alien eyes and what he saw evoked in him a distance between himself and his people that baffled and worried him.
>
> One thing he now knew: the real reality of the lives of his people was negated; the real world lay over there somewhere—in a place where white people lived, people who had the power to say who could or could not live and on what terms; and the world in which his family lived was a kind of shadow world. (87)

Hence, a foundation of Fish's internalization and inferiorization is, in great part, his parents' failure to try to pass on an adequate understanding of racial victimization and hatred to their son.

In the story of Fish, Wright illustrates the complex psychological dynamics of how and why some black people manifest a self-alienated hatred of other blacks which results from their internalization of whites' hatred of blacks, filtered, in Fish's case, through his parents, especially Tyree. Moreover, that Fish represents the perils of internalization is clear in Wright's feelings about the meaning of Fishbelly's name: explaining the meaning of the fact that, as one of Fish's friends states, the stomach of a fish is white, Wright clearly uses the nickname to reflect Fishbelly's almost complete psychological immersion in and acceptance of the values of white society (Kinnamon and Fabre 1993, 205).

The depth of Fish's corruption is the crux of what Wright wants to critique in his character. Fish's inferiorized psychological state is an especially haunting and tragic aspect of the novel. The extent of Fish's debilitated sense of self-worth and his internalization of white racism is shown in what is, perhaps, the most powerful scene in the novel. In a central incident, Fish and a friend are arrested by the police for trespassing. While they are riding in the police car on the way to the station, Fish remembers that in his billfold he has a picture of a white woman in her underwear that he had torn from a newspaper. Aware that Chris was killed because of his involvement with a white woman (and of his father's feeling that Chris deserved to die), Fish thinks the police might kill him if they find the picture. In order to destroy the picture, he eats it: "Yes, he had eaten it; it was inside of him now, a part of him, invisible. . . . [H]e felt guilty in a way that they [the police] could never imagine or understand" (Wright 1958, 152–53). This passage demonstrates that the internalization of white values and white racism can become an insurmountable and inextricable part of a black person's being. According to Robert Felgar, "Wright implies in *The Long Dream* and elsewhere that the worst emasculation of the blacks by the whites takes place above the eyes rather than below the belt; for Fishbelly is all too ready to accept white culture's definition of him as a nonman, a 'nigger.'"[18] It is no wonder that, after Fish is arrested, he

> longed hotly for the sanctuary of his Black Belt, for the protection of familiar black faces; but, while yearning for his absent world, he knew that that world had lost its status and importance in his life. The world he now saw was the real one: that other world in which he had been born and in which he had lived was a listless shadow and already he was ashamed of its feebleness, of the bane of fear under which it lived, labored, hungered, and died. (Wright 1958, 147–48)

This psychological castration is depicted further in the internalization and self-hatred exhibited by Fish and his friends. That Wright changes the focus from Fish's parents to his companions is important in showing, as Clark indicates, that black children's racial attitudes are first influenced by their parents and then reinforced by their peer group (Clark 1955, 57). In *The Long Dream*, one reason for the boys' low self-esteem is their ignorance about their racial heritage—certainly a fault of the dominant society, the educational system, and their parents as products of the first two factors. According to Clark,

> As children develop an awareness of racial differences and of their racial identity, they also develop an awareness and acceptance of the prevailing social attitudes and values attached to race and skin color. . . . Another important discovery is that these young children begin to develop techniques for self-protection in an effort to cope with developing racial conflicts and threats to the personality. (1955, 46)

Unfortunately, the protective strategy used by Fish and his friends seems to be scorn for blacks and acceptance of their marginalized status. These factors are part of Wright's intention in the novel to show that America keeps blacks on the periphery of American life, both physically and psychologically, unlike most white immigrants who can become assimilated into the mainstream of the society. Wright clearly believed that this rejection of blacks by the dominant society could result in feelings of self-rejection

(Kinnamon and Fabre 1993, 194). The consequence of this experience is dramatized in the alienation of Fish and his friends from both their African and American heritages.

This internalized bigotry toward and estrangement from blacks is shown in several scenes involving Fish and his friends. For example, when Sam says that his father believes that blacks should go to Africa, Zeke says, "Sam wants us to git naked and run wild and eat with our hands and live in mud huts!" (Wright 1958, 41). Compounding this alienation from their African heritage is their alienation from American life and the society in which they live. Talking about Jim Crow laws with their friends, Sam says, "You can't live like no American, cause you ain't no American! And you ain't African neither! So what is you? Nothing! Just nothing" (41–42). Adding to the boys' alienation is their feeling that being black is a punishment. Fish, for instance, in response to Sam's statement that "to white folks, you a nigger," says, "That's only cause some of us acts bad" (42). Clearly, Fish believes that some blacks deserve to be considered "niggers" and accepts the validity of racist standards in judging blacks. Another example of this belief that racism is something that blacks earn appears in the riot after Chris's lynching. Though Fish does not know the cause of the riot, he asks if blacks have caused trouble, "accepting guilt before he knew the facts" (81). These feelings are illuminated in Clark's discussion of "The Negro Child and Race Prejudice" in *Prejudice and Your Child*:

> As minority-group children learn the inferior status to which they are assigned and observe that they are usually segregated and isolated from the more privileged members of their society, they react with deep feelings of inferiority and with a sense of personal humiliation. Many of them become confused about their own personal worth. Like all other human beings, they require a sense of personal dignity and social support for positive self-esteem. Almost nowhere in the larger society, however, do they find their own dignity as human beings respected and protected. Under these circumstances, minority-group children develop conflicts with regard to their feelings about themselves and about the value of the group with which they are identified. Understandably they begin to question whether they themselves and their group are worthy of no more respect from the larger society than they receive. These conflicts, confusions, and doubts give rise under certain circumstances to self-hatred and rejection of their own group. (1955, 63–64)

Bleak as this picture may be, *The Long Dream* seems to be the novelistic counterpart to Clark's psychological theories. Fish comes to feel that "the Black Belt was a kind of purgatory, a pit of shame to which he had been unjustifiably consigned" after witnessing his parents' fear of whites and knowing about his father's dependence on them (Wright 1958, 220). Thus, Fish and his friends interpret racial victimization to be the penalties that result from being black, and this ultimately makes them feel that being black is, in itself, a punishment. According to Clark,

> [V]arious studies and interpretations contribute to an understanding of the problem of self-hatred among Negroes. . . . [S]elf-rejection begins to occur at an early age and becomes embedded in the personality. This self-rejection is part of the total pattern of ideas and attitudes that American Negro children learn from the larger society. It demonstrates the power of the prevailing attitudes, and their influence on the individual even when these attitudes run counter to his need for self-esteem. Self-hatred is found among individuals who belong to any group that is rejected or relegated to an inferior status by the larger society. . . . The barriers against assimilation are more formidable for the Negro child and are further complicated by the fact that everyone can see his color. (1955, 50)

This passage demonstrates that the flawed psychology of the blacks in Wright's novel has its genesis in the dominant society, which should prevent readers from thinking that the sole responsibility for black self-hatred rests with blacks themselves. *The Long Dream*, therefore, emphasizes the complicated and convoluted nature of the reasons for and manifestations of the internalization of white racism by blacks.

This very complex theme of self-hatred and hostility toward other blacks is continued in the novel by the depiction of Fish's and his friends' hatred of blacks in powerless situations. For instance, as the boys play a game at a fair, "Hit the Nigger Head," the object of which is to hit a black man in the face with a ball, the boys' shame at the helplessness of the man who is the object of the game is greater than their anger at the whites who are responsible for the game (Wright 1958, 57). Wright emphasizes that the boys identify with the man and see him as a symbol of blacks in general. Thus, Fish's hatred of the man and his desire to play the game show his—and many blacks'—dilemma: "That obscene black face was his own and, to quell the war in his heart, he had to either reject it in hate or accept it in love. It was easier to hate that degraded black face than to love it" (57). This rejection is precisely what is dramatized in Fish's friends, in Fish himself, and in Fish's home situation: shame at and hatred of blacks' inferiorized position in a racist society, causing feelings of worthlessness, self-hatred, and hostility toward other blacks.

A key aspect of Wright's portrayal of self-hatred and intraracial hostility in *The Long Dream* is the combined internalized racism and sexism Fish and his friends have toward black women. In presenting this theme, Wright reveals the characters' debased self-images and acceptance of the dominant society's values in the contrast of the boys' attitudes toward white women and black women. In a statement that reveals the relationships among the internalization of racism, self-rejection, and the sexist rejection of black women, Wright declared that, in the novel, he wanted to show that the media's promotion of the image of white women can result in some blacks internalizing the view of white women as both the pinnacle of eroticism and forbidden objects whose attraction lies in part in their off-limits status (Kinnamon and Fabre 1993, 198). Reflecting the white woman's status as "lynch bait" in the old South, Wright conveys the idea that an exaggerated status gave white women a powerful psychological status to many black men, perhaps representing the blacks' own relative powerlessness—a powerlessness for which blacks futilely attempt to be compensated, Wright seems to suggest, by the desire for and attainment of a white woman.

Several instances illustrate how Wright dramatizes these concerns in the novel. When Fish and his friends go to the fair, for example, they feel "excitement" and they are "entranced" when they come upon a show where seminude white women are dancing (Wright 1958, 53). The boys are turned away from the show, but when they go to a show where black women are dancing, no mention is made of their being excited. Wright describes the black girls as "dancing trancelike" whereas the white dancers are described as "dancing swayingly," thus emphasizing their sensuality and appeal for the boys (53). The denigration of black women in the mind of Fish and his friends outlasts their adolescence and seems to be an essential part of their psyches when they become adults. Wright underscores the denigration of black women by Fish and his friends in a scene where the young men are flirting with black women, and Fish is attracted to the "near white" Gladys (220). Both she and the "yellow" one, Beth, are asked to dance while the "black girl," Maybelle, is ignored by the men; and Wright states ominously, "the cause was clear" (228). Wright describes Maybelle as having "thick lips," "bulbous eyes," and a "sweating black face" (230). Fish feels ashamed when Maybelle becomes angry and lashes out at him and his friends for ignoring her because they are attracted to women whose features are more Caucasian than hers; he is ashamed because he knows she is right. Wright, therefore, shows how color prejudice against black women is part of a larger psychological complex which has its foundation in the internalization of bigotry. Wright also uses this theme to show in Fish that if one rejects oneself, one will also reject others who remind one of oneself; if they hold a mirror to the features—and the identity—self-alienated blacks want to escape.

Similar to Wright's illustration of the intraracial prejudice discussed above is a section of the novel that was no doubt inspired by the author's own experience in the South (described in *Black Boy*) when he worked for an insurance agent. Here, Fish disdains many of the blacks he meets while collecting rent for his father. Wright calls attention to the "greasy black fingers," "flattened brown nose," (268) and "kinky, greasy tufts of hair of some of the tenants" (262). Fish's disgust is so strong that even Tyree has to tell him to hide his critical attitude. (Wright's point here seems to be that, in the multigenerational cycle of internalized racism, bigotry can become even stronger when passed from parent to child.) Nevertheless, Wright illustrates that one can superimpose one's own bigoted preconceptions onto the targets of one's bigotry when Fish feels that his negative prejudices of blacks are confirmed by his encounters. He states, for example, that he has learned by being exposed to his father's tenants that blacks are "sick" and that "[t]hese niggers are walking around in their sleep" (270). Commenting on Fish's disdain for blacks, Wright emphasizes how far Fish's internalization of white racist views of blacks has alienated him from the black race: "[T]he outlook of that alien [white] world had spoiled his own for him. Grudgingly, accepting being classed with his people, he was, deep in him, somewhat afraid of them; though he spoke their language, shared their pleasures and sorrows, there was in him some element that stood aside as though in shame" (270).

Ironically, Fish's relationship with Gladys and others to whom he turns as a result of his rejection of blackness intensifies his own self-consciousness and shame at being black. Similar to Bigger's discomfort when in the car with Mary, Fish, when he is with Gladys, "could almost feel the crown of hair on his head, hair that was straightened, and he was ashamed of it. 'Bet she sure loves that damned hair of hers,' he growled silently to himself" (280). Moreover, an incident that takes place on the plane when he is leaving the country again shows that he is attracted to white women and, consequently, is repelled by his own black skin. Of the blonde flight attendant, Wright states that Fish "let her strap him into the seat of the plane, holding his breath as he watched her head of golden hair, her white skin. . . . Finally [when he looks at another woman] he stared directly at the object that rested under that dreadful taboo. . . . [S]he had a head full of luxuriant, dark brown hair, the wispy curls of which nestled clingingly at the nape of her white, well-modeled neck" (523–25). This is certainly a far cry from the "kinky, greasy tufts of hair . . . [that has to be] killed . . . [to] make it straight, straight like the hair of white folks" (262). Fish's attraction to whites is not merely sexual. When he is sitting next to a white man on the plane, he notices the man's hand and stares. Then, "Unconsciously, stealthily, Fishbelly drew his hand in, covering his right black hand with his left black hand, trying vainly to blot out the shameful blackness on him" (526).

The rejection of blackness that Fish had directed outward (in ignoring Maybelle, in preferring Gladys, in rejecting his parents, and in being disdainful toward the tenants) is, when he is with Gladys and with whites, directed inward, for in comparing himself to them, he comes to the same conclusion as he had when he and his friends compared Maybelle to the lighter-skinned girls: blackness, whether his own or others', is inferior. Clark lends validity to this aspect of the tragedy related by Wright,

As the Negro observes the society in which he lives, he associates whiteness with superior advantage, achievement, progress, and power, all of which are essential to successful competition in the American culture. The degree of whiteness that the individual prefers may be considered an indication of the intensity of his anxiety and of his need to compensate for what he considers to be the deficiencies of his own skin color. (1955, 49)

In Fish, Wright delineates a mentality that is trapped in a cycle of self-hatred, aspiring toward ever-elusive whiteness.

Mirroring Adam's analysis of self-rejection as a result of this internalization of racism, Wright states,

> Fishbelly hotly rejected the terms in which white people weighed him or saw him, for those terms made him feel agonizingly inferior; then, in his acting against the feeling of inferiority, he had to try to be like them in order to prove to himself and to them that he was not inferior. Yet in his trying to be like them he was trapping himself. (1958, 282)

This passage is, in fact, a bit confusingly written. Fish does not "reject" the whites' view of him; he believes that whites constitute the "real world" and that blacks are mere "shadows." Furthermore, in addition to Fish's earlier acceptance of white racist standards in evaluating blacks, the belief that he must "try to be like" whites to prove his equality makes it evident that he accepts, rather than rejects, their view of blacks. Ironically, therefore, his intense desire to repudiate the racist view of blacks causes him to implant his belief of how racist whites perceive blacks in his mind and, consequently, to validate their prejudiced image of blacks as the standard for judging them. Clark's example of the cycle expressed by Wright in *The Long Dream* brings home the tragic complexity of internalized racism:

> The problem of self-hatred among Negroes must be understood as one aspect of the pattern of feelings and attitudes of minority-group members toward all other members of the society which relegates them to an inferior and humiliating status. Self-hatred is not an isolated phenomenon. It cannot be understood in terms only of the minority-group member's reactions to other members of his group. . . . As he learns from the whites the stereotypes about himself which form the substance of his self-hatred, he begins at the same time to resent the whites for imposing this stigma upon him. If there are to be significant changes in the Negro's attitude toward himself, these changes can only come from positive changes in the way in which the larger society views and treats the Negro. (1955, 51)

Though Clark's proposed solution to the problem of self-hatred may seem to some to be overly dependent on a change in whites' attitudes, perhaps Wright's novel attests to the psychological dependence on whites some blacks have regarding their self-esteem and, consequently, their estimation of other blacks. In any case, Clark's repeated call for a change in the fabric of race relations in American society in order to improve blacks' material

and psychological lives finds strong validation in the psychological shambles
Wright describes in *The Long Dream* and elsewhere.

In a passage similar to the controversial one in *Black Boy* about blacks' deficiencies, Wright states that Fish

> began to realize dimly that there was something missing in him. . . . There was
> some quality of character that the conditions under which he had lived had
> failed to give him. . . . Other than a self-satisfying yen for imitating the stan-
> dards of the white world above him, there had not come within the range of
> his experience any ideal that could have captured his imagination. Other than
> a defensive callousness toward his own people . . . other than the masked be-
> havior he had adopted toward the whites . . . he had no traditions, no mores
> to sustain him. (1958, 492)

Having a distorted view of his own heritage, seeing blacks mainly in situations
in which they are powerless and being a part of a society whose media promote white women as desirable make Fish believe in the allure of the white
world and make him reject the world of blacks. In a sense, what is "missing" is
a view of the world that is more inclusive than this one. Thus, it seems that the
characters in *The Long Dream*, and many of Wright's other characters, no matter how resentful they are of whites are, at bottom, envious of them.

Summing up the complexity of Fish's feelings, Wright states, "When he
thought of that white world he hated it, but when he daydreamed of it, he
loved it . . . he revered that white world and . . . [held] toward it an attitude
of mute awe" (238). Like Bigger, who fantasizes that perhaps Mary Dalton
will be like a woman he has seen in a movie and who plays games with his
friends in which they pretend they are white (as do the boys in *The Long
Dream*), Fish does not want so much to eradicate the white power structure
as to attain the image and lifestyle of the dominant society.

The depth of Wright's understanding of the impact of the internalization of prejudice and self-rejection certainly grew throughout his life. In
The Long Dream, for example, Wright analyzes the sort of alienation from
blacks he himself had voiced in *Black Boy*. An important indication of
Wright's increased understanding and his ability to portray the problem of
self-rejection is that the passage in which Fish uses whites as a measuring
stick for blacks' self-worth and the self-hatred that results are a far cry from
the comparative simplicity of the way in which the theme is handled in
Lawd Today, with Jake's childish admiration of gangsters, for example.
Thus, those who dismiss *The Long Dream* as a mere rehash of Wright's old
theme of Southern racism and consider the book a failure fail to realize
the newness of the book in Wright's increased perception in this very important regard.

Considering the psychological complex of which self-hatred is a part,
Clark states that in order to effect a change in blacks' material and psychological status, whites must change in their attitudes and behavior toward

blacks. How is this idea reflected in Wright's novels and how does it illustrate his view of the white image in the black mind?

Perhaps the answer to this question lies in the fact that Wright again and again writes about white characters who are the only ones who understand the black protagonist, even while these black characters remain estranged from other blacks, underlining the uniqueness of the relationship between blacks and sympathetic whites. In *Native Son*, for instance, an obvious example of Wright's use of these figures is Max, Bigger's lawyer, who gains Bigger's trust to the point that Bigger shares his feelings about his life with Max. Furthermore, Jan's visit to Bigger in jail also shows Wright's use of an extraordinarily understanding white character. Jan, whom Bigger had tried to frame for Mary's death, says to the man who killed his girlfriend:

> "I—I don't want to worry you Bigger. . . . I'm not angry and I want you to let me help you. I don't blame you for trying to blame this thing on me. . . . [I]t would be asking too much to ask you not to hate me, when every white man hates you. . . . Though this thing has hurt me, I got something out of it. . . . It taught me that it's your right to hate me. . . . I was in jail grieving for Mary and then I thought of all the black men who've been killed, the black men who had to grieve when their people were snatched from them in slavery and since slavery. I thought that if they could stand it, then I ought to. . . . I said, 'I'm going to help that guy if he lets me.'" (Wright 1940, 266–68)

A similarly strange scene occurs in *The Long Dream*, when, in response to Tyree's attempted justification of his criminal activities, MacWilliams, the reform politician, responds, "Your people have been terribly provoked. There was slavery and then there was hate on the part of the white man for the freed slave. Then your people began to adjust to an unjust situation. . . . Your excuse is valid" (Wright 1958, 376–77). Thus, like Jan's forgiveness of Bigger, MacWilliams absolves Tyree of responsibility for his actions and has complete sympathy for him. Finally, in *The Outsider*, the hunchbacked district attorney, Houston, identifies with and articulates the plight of the protagonist, Cross. Houston's empathy for Cross is evident when he tells him that he is, like Cross and blacks in general, an outsider because of his deformity. Also, like Max in *Native Son*, Houston voices the protagonist's reasons for his crimes. Cross has committed two murders out of his hatred of tyrannical authority figures. Houston understands completely Cross's motivation for killing these two power mongers—his desire to assert his own power and autonomy—"Man desires ultimately to be a god. Man desires to be everything. You felt that what obstructed desire could be killed."[19] An understanding white figure is found in each of these three novels that span the entirety of Wright's novelistic career.

There is an important difference, however, between Max in *Native Son* and the other two characters. In *Native Son*, Bigger was a man who could not articulate the meaning of his life and crimes until the end of the novel. In

fact, in "How Bigger Was Born," Wright states that "due to American educational restrictions . . . the bulk of the Negro population . . . is not yet articulate" (1940, xx). Max, therefore, is a justifiable if, at times, incredible
mouthpiece. Yet, Max ultimately does not truly understand Bigger, for when
Bigger, in their last meeting, validates the positive meaning of his crimes,
Max is horrified. As Robert Felgar points out,

> Disoriented by Bigger's proto-Existentialist affirmation and emotionally in-
> volved with him enough to hope Bigger can become one with himself be-
> fore his death, Max is disappointed that Bigger will not substitute his
> individualist world-view for a Marxist vision. Whereas Max feels that Bigger
> could find serenity by accepting the fact that he is largely a result of a hor-
> ribly racist environment, Bigger . . . cannot accept that he is merely a by-
> product. It is as a social statistic, then, that Bigger is comprehensible to
> Max: but as an individual, he is too nightmarish a figure for his lawyer to ac-
> cept. (1980, 93)

Jan is the character who most truly accepts Bigger, for he sympathizes with
Bigger's criminality and hostility.

In *The Outsider*, in contrast to Jan and Max, Houston seems a superfluous
character, for he is not needed as a spokesman for an inarticulate character.
Cross has, after all, studied philosophy at the University of Chicago and is
acutely articulate about his motives. In fact, his analysis of the murders occurs nearly two hundred pages before Houston's (230). Why, then, does
Wright use this technique of having a white character who is the protagonist's kindred spirit in three of his novels?

One possible answer is provided in "How Bigger Was Born." Here, Wright
states that he was concerned with "the possibilities of alliances between the
American Negro and other people possessing a kindred consciousness"
(1940, xv). Clearly, Wright intended Jan and Max in *Native Son*, Mac-
Williams in *The Long Dream*, and Houston in *The Outsider* to make clear the
possibility that whites could come to understand the experiences of blacks,
instead of dismissing them through the blindness of racism.

Still, this technique has problems—the main one is its incredibility. In
Native Son, for example, it is hard to believe that a man whose girlfriend has
been killed and who then has been framed for her murder would act so
humbly and even apologetically toward the man who was responsible for
these acts. The same is true of the reaction of MacWilliams—the honest
man who wants to fight corruption—to Tyree's long list of illegal activities.
Furthermore, not only is Houston's role as spokesman for Cross's true motives heavy-handed, it is also a contrivance, to the point of ludicrousness,
that Houston should tell Cross that he has insight into the plight of blacks
as outsiders because he, as a hunchback, is an outsider. Scenes like this contribute to what Robert Bone has called the "curious unreality" that sometimes mars Wright's work.[20]

Another interesting aspect of the "alliance between kindred souls" is that blacks in Wright's novels achieve this unity only with whites and never with other blacks. Bigger, as mentioned earlier, is estranged from his family from the beginning of the novel. Moreover, after killing Mary, he feels "cut off from . . . [his friends] forever" (Wright 1940, 102). After Bigger is jailed, although his family and friends visit him, only Jan and Max are capable of giving him meaningful emotional support.

Similarly, in *The Outsider*, only with his white mistress, Eva, and with Houston, is Cross able to have relationships that are meaningful to him. To Cross, his family and his black mistress, Dot, are mere burdens. Furthermore, it is only with Houston that he shares the lessons he has learned from his life of crime and deception: "I wish I had some way to give the meaning of my life to others. . . . To make a bridge from man to man. . . . Tell them not to come down this road" (Wright 1953, 439). Estranged from everyone else, Cross feels that Houston is the only one with whom he has enough of an emotional bond to try to convey the meaning of his life.

Perhaps one factor in Wright's use of this technique is that it shows characters who are the opposite of the racist structure that Wright describes in which whites are felt by blacks to be a force that demands blacks to act in accordance with the dictates of racism and that negates their individuality. Sennett's comments also shed light on this device of employing a white character who alone understands the black character's motives. According to Sennett, "Someone who is indifferent arouses our desire to be recognized; we want this person to feel we matter enough to be noticed. We may provoke or denounce him, but the point is to get him to respond" (1980, 86). Clearly, Wright's motive in writing *Native Son* was to make people respond.

> When reviews of . . . [*Uncle Tom's Children*] began to appear, I realized I had made an awfully naive mistake. I found that I had written a book which even bankers' daughters could read and weep over and feel good about. I swore to myself that if I ever wrote another book, no one would weep over it; that it would be so hard and deep that they would have to face it without the consolation of tears. (Wright 1940, xviii)

In addition to wanting to confront white readers with the plight of blacks, perhaps Wright created Jan and Max—like their counterparts in other novels—to represent his hope that at least some whites could change from being a negative force ruining blacks' lives to being fellow human beings who could empathize with blacks.

This technique of creating white characters with whom the black protagonists have a meaningful relationship can also be illuminated by Sennett's discussion of the "bonds of rejection" (1980, 86). As Sennett explains this concept, when one is confronted with an authority figure who refuses to recognize one,

> A struggle for recognition is set up. . . . [T]he inferior person is bidding for recognition. . . . [H]e wants to be seen as a person by . . . [the authority figure]. . . . This play between recognition and indifference is how the knot [connecting the authority figure and the person under him] tightens. The superior person remains in control of the apparatus of recognition; his or her attention is the prize of disruption. (102)

Perhaps Wright's writings reflect, then, the author's own psychological "bonds of rejection," for three of his novels emphasize the centrality of a black person's being recognized and understood by whites, to the complete detriment of fictional credibility and in the face of the total absence of meaningful relationships with other blacks. In stressing the importance of the protagonists' recognition by whites, Wright shows traces of the mentality he wrote about in *Twelve Million Black Voices*: "In the main, we are different from other folk in that . . . [b]efore we black folk can move, we must first look into the white man's mind to see what is there, to see what he is thinking" (1978, 164). Consequently, Wright's representation of sympathetic whites is not the liberating move that Clark may have had in mind when he spoke about the need for whites to change in order to improve the condition of blacks. It is, instead, a sign of Wright's own psychological chains to whites, for to him they are the requirement for blacks' psychological connection to the human race. Hence, the whites in the eyes of Richard Wright betray the author's own internalization and inferiorization.

It is now time to return to some of the basic issues presented in the opening pages of this chapter. Can one, for example, find the celebratory element in the novels under discussion that Baker states is characteristic in Wright's works? Is Wright to be condemned for revealing and, at times, exhibiting inadvertently black self-rejection and the "bonds of rejection"? To return to a fundamental consideration of this study as a whole, can the representation of a lingering pathological or neurotic condition in the psychology of some blacks constitute a liberating mythology? Readers will certainly answer these questions for themselves. I have only provisional interpretations to offer, not solutions.

If there is a celebratory aspect to the works by Wright under discussion, it is to be found outside of the texts. The degree to which Wright helps readers to understand the complex psychological problems of internalization and the dilemmas that blacks face when they place an excessive amount of importance on whiteness is an important, potentially liberating, and, therefore, celebratory element for readers, whether they suffer from, perpetuate, or merely observe the psychological conditions discussed in the novels. Thus, if one understands the concept of celebration in this context not to mean an infantile state of gratification but to entail the positive aspect of a work introducing readers to such harsh truths, we can find merit in Baker's dissenting message.

NOTES

1. Lerone Bennett, Jr., "The White Problem in America," in *The White Problem in America*, ed. editors of *Ebony* (Chicago: Johnson Publishing, 1966), 2.

2. Richard Wright, *Black Boy* (New York: Harper and Row, 1945), 45.

3. James Baldwin, "Alas, Poor Richard," in *Nobody Knows My Name* (New York: Dell Publishing, 1961), 165.

4. W.E.B. Du Bois, "Richard Wright Looks Back," in *Richard Wright: The Critical Reception*, ed. John M. Reilly (New York: Burt Franklin, 1978), 133.

5. Robert B. Stepto, "I Thought I Knew These People: Richard Wright and the Afro-American Literary Tradition," in *Chant of Saints*, ed. Robert B. Stepto and Michael Harper (Urbana: University of Illinois Press, 1979), 199.

6. Margaret Walker, *New Masses*, p. 200, quoted in Addison Gayle, Jr., *Richard Wright: Ordeal of a Native Son* (Garden City, N.Y.: Anchor Press/Doubleday, 1980), 84.

7. Houston A. Baker, Jr., "Racial Wisdom and Richard Wright's *Native Son*," in *Critical Essays on Richard Wright*, ed. Yoshinuki Hakutani (Boston: J. K. Hall, 1982), 73.

8. Barry D. Adam, *The Survival of Domination* (New York: Elsevier North-Holland, 1978), 89–90.

9. Michel Fabre, *The Unfinished Quest of Richard Wright* (New York: William Morrow, 1973), 78.

10. Richard Wright, *Lawd Today* (New York: Walker and Company, 1963), 124.

11. Richard Sennett, *Authority* (New York: Alfred A. Knopf, 1980), 47.

12. Kenneth B. Clark, *Prejudice and Your Child* (Boston: Beacon Press, 1955), 52.

13. Richard Wright, *Twelve Million Black Voices* in *The Richard Wright Reader*, ed. Michel Fabre and Ellen Wright (New York: Harper and Row, 1978), 215.

14. Richard Wright, *Native Son* (New York: Harper and Row, 1940), 70.

15. Richard Wright, *The Long Dream* (New York: Doubleday, 1958), 193.

16. Stanley Milgram, *Obedience to Authority* (New York: Harper and Row, 1974), 143.

17. Keneth Kinnamon and Michel Fabre, eds., *Conversations with Richard Wright* (Jackson: University Press of Mississippi, 1993), 222.

18. Robert Felgar, *Richard Wright* (Boston: Twayne Publishers, 1980), 128.

19. Richard Wright, *The Outsider* (New York: Harper and Row, 1953), 425.

20. Robert Bone, *Richard Wright* (Minneapolis: University of Minnesota Press, 1969), 32.

—— *Chapter 6* ——

What Is a White Person?

It is now time to return to the question: What is a white person? Moreover, why does it matter?

Langston Hughes once wrote the text for a book of illustrations that cataloged central experiences of blacks prefaced by the phrase, "Black misery is" (for example, black misery is when you go to school and the National Guard is there to meet you).[1] Considering that much of Hughes's text locates whites as the source of "black misery," it is intriguing to think about a catalog of what "white is" based on the literary data on the white image in the black mind. It would contain the following entries.

WHITE IS . . . *WEAK*

As discussed earlier, black literature demonstrates that perhaps no one has disappointed blacks more than the good-hearted weaklings, for they betray blacks by not acting on their progressive beliefs. In her novel *Our Nig*, Harriet Wilson represents this problem in the treatment of Frado, the black heroine, at the hands of the Bellmonts, the white New England family for whom she works in the mid-nineteenth century. Wilson describes the physical abuse to which Frado is subjected by the women of the family while the father, Mr. Bellmont, fails to act. Though Mr. Bellmont is a "kind, humane man," he is passive in the face of his wife and daughter's treatment of Frado.[2] The result of this treatment is demonstrated in a scene where Frado denies pushing the Bellmonts' daughter, Mary, into a stream, earning Mrs. Bellmont's ire for implying that Mary is lying in accusing her. Mr. Bellmont offers a lame critique of his wife's anger. Wilson describes his thoughts and actions:

"How do we know but that she has told the truth," he replied, and left the house, as he usually did when a tempest threatened to envelop him. No sooner was he out of sight than Mrs. B. and Mary commenced to beating [Frado] inhumanely. . . . [W]hile the tempest raged within, Mr. Bellmont went for the cows, a task belonging to Frado, and thus unintentionally prolonged her pain. (1983, 34–35)

In Mr. Bellmont's behavior, Wilson presents whites who sympathize with blacks but fail to act on their good will when in the presence of whites who disagree. Consequently, black people in such situations may know of their white sympathizer's feelings and hope for or even expect such whites to protect them from the hostility that threatens to harm them. It is no wonder then that the collapse of the good-hearted weakling is of great concern to blacks, for this type of white person betrays blacks' hopes for an alliance against the actions of whites who are bigots. Moreover, Mr. Bellmont's doing some of Frado's chores after abandoning her to the cruelty of his wife and daughter is merely a feeble attempt to assuage his conscience and compensate for his abandonment of Frado. Wilson conveys in this incident that such a person as Mr. Bellmont needs to understand that atonement for such betrayals can come only from following through in a meaningful way on his or her supposed care and concern for blacks. Until then, the sympathy of such whites is meaningless.

WHITE IS . . . *A BURDEN TO BLACKS*

Blacks sometimes comment that they are tired of feeling that they have to educate whites in order to enlighten them about race relations to make being around such whites tolerable. This subject of the drain on blacks' tolerance is made clear in John O. Killens's book, *Black Man's Burden*, when he tries to envision a future where white power is no longer dominant (the book was written during the Civil Rights movement and after the collapse of many colonialist regimes in Africa).

What are we going to do about these white folk? . . . [H]ow are we going to integrate them into our New World of Humanity where racial prejudice will be obsolete and the whiteness of their skin will not be held against them, though neither will it afford them any special privileges? How are we going to teach them the meaning of some of the phrases they themselves claim to have invented but never practiced so far as we were concerned—democracy, human dignity, and the brotherhood of man? This is the enormous Black Man's Burden today. There never was a White Man's Burden within this context unless it was his guilty conscience, assuming that he had a conscience where black men were concerned.[3]

Some may feel that Killens's concerns are dated by their historical context, but they are not obsolete because what the author is really asking is whether whites even possess the psychological fiber to be able to progress to a nonracist world. Some key factors, Killens seems to believe, stunt whites' racial progress, including whites' feelings of the centrality of maintaining unearned privileges, as well as the degree to which whites are led, consciously or unconsciously, to believe that merely parroting such words as democracy is sufficient to preclude the actual deeds it takes to enact such a concept. Hence, Killens suggests that blacks would need to teach whites the true meaning of the concepts they have been mouthing for centuries now. Perhaps blacks have accepted "the black man's burden" throughout history; for example, the Civil Rights movement taught whites that blacks would not continue to accept racial inequality. This example supports one of Killens's implications: the black man's burden may involve dragging many whites against their will into a higher consciousness and a better future. Perhaps the motto of this future and of bearers of the black man's burden should be the words of the late Congressman Adam Clayton Powell: "Either let us practice the democracy we preach—or shut up!" In short, as Killens illustrates, whites need to know—and blacks sometimes have shown them—that high-sounding platitudes are not enough; action is what is needed in order to make a better world. Moreover, in this effort, there should not only be a black man's burden in the progression toward racial enlightenment, but a white man's burden (and not in the sense of the cliché) for, as Malcolm X said, whites need to work among themselves to overcome their racial backwardness.[4] Thus, perhaps it is less relevant for blacks to pick up the black man's burden than for whites to pick up the white man's burden: themselves.

WHITE IS . . . *DISMISSIVE*

In *Their Eyes Were Watching God*, Zora Neale Hurston critiques the habit of whites to dismiss blacks whom they do not know as a result of a judgmental attitude that can cause them to be unfriendly and distant. In the following excerpt, Teacake, the husband of the heroine, Janie, comments on this phenomenon. Teacake says to Janie, "It's bad bein' strange niggers wid white folks. Everybody is against yuh. . . . Janie, Ah done watched it time and time again; each and every white man think he know all the GOOD darkies already. He don't need to know no mo'."[5] This passage illustrates that the hostility some whites convey toward blacks is a race-based judgment against them. Hurston also portrays the concern that blacks have of being ostracized and isolated by whites, not as a result of anything that they have done, but as a result of a general distrust many whites have of blacks. In addition, Hurston's words remind the reader that such concern by blacks about whether whites who do not even know them will make their lives difficult demonstrates that racism influences where blacks live and work and whether they will feel comfortable in their home and work environments. In short, Teacake's words exemplify a main aspect of racism: the assumption of the worst about blacks out of ignorance of them.

WHITE IS . . . *OFF-PUTTING, EVEN WHEN FRIENDLY*

Related to the issue of whites' ignorance of blacks is their failure to know how blacks judge them. Langston Hughes presents how this failure can cause many whites to be unaware of how their attempts at friendliness with blacks can be colored by their unacknowledged racism and thus drive blacks away. The white couple in Hughes's story "Slave on the Block," the Carraways, are fascinated by black art and by black people. Nevertheless, their attempts at making friendships with blacks fail: "They were acquainted with lots of Negroes, too—but somehow the Negroes didn't seem to like them. Maybe the Carraways gushed over them too soon. . . . Or maybe they tried too hard to make friends, and the dark friends suspected something. . . . As much as they loved Negroes, Negroes didn't seem to love Michael and Ann."[6] The aspect of racism portrayed in the passage is similar to that in "Poor Little Black Fellow." A key aspect of both stories is that whites who regard themselves as progressive often treat blacks as objects—fascinating objects, innocent objects—but objects nonetheless. Hughes also makes the point that such whites do not question their behavior toward blacks to an adequate degree; indeed, they may become more ostensibly and condescendingly nice—and overbearing—toward blacks precisely in order to sublimate their racism. Hughes's point is clear: whites' overt friendliness may sometimes be a cover for covert racism.

WHITE IS . . . *IGNORANT OF BLACKS' HAVING FIGURED THEM OUT*

Hughes also dramatizes how one of the most basic aspects of the egotism of racism is that it protects the racist from knowing the extent to which blacks are aware of the bigotry of his or her motives and actions. Hughes's story "Berry" dramatizes the way in which the title character is on to the whites who are his superiors at the home for disabled children where he has been hired to work as a cook. "And even if he wasn't educated, he had plenty of mother wit and lots of intuition about people and places. It didn't take him long to realize that he was doing far too much work for the home's eight dollars a week, and that everybody was imposing on him in that taken-for-granted way white folks do with Negro help."[7]

Hughes uses the character of Berry to raise a central issue: the need to know one's enemy outweighs the need one's superiors feel they have to know the subordinate individual. The knowledge represented by Berry's critical attitude toward the whites who exploit him also conveys the fact that he is more perceptive in figuring out his oppressors' character than they are in knowing his true character, for they merely view him as a "dumb nigger." Perhaps Hughes wanted this story to act as a warning to bigoted whites: if you think that blacks are unaware of the racism of your feelings and actions, think again. It would advance your self-enlightenment years to know how your deeds and thoughts truly look to those who suffer from them.

WHITE IS . . . *TO BE AFRAID TO CONFRONT ONE'S OWN BIGOTRY*

A key defense mechanism among racist whites is the mental trick of focusing on blacks as the cause of their bigotry, as if they do not need to examine and challenge their racial attitudes when their prejudice arises. In "Poor Little Black Fellow," Hughes presents the attitudes of the residents of the nearly all-white town of Mapleton toward the black orphan, Arnie, who was taken in by one of the town's leading families:

> Everything might have been all right forever had Arnie not begun to grow up. . . . Adolescence. The boys had girls. They played kissing games and learned to dance. There were parties to which Arnie was not invited—really couldn't be invited—with the girls and all. And after generations of peace the village of Mapleton and the Pembertons found themselves beset with a Negro problem. Everyone was a little baffled and a little ashamed. . . . To tell the truth, everybody had got so used to Arnie that nobody really thought of him as a Negro—until he put on long trousers and went to high school. Now they noticed that he was truly very black. . . . They were extra-nice to Arnie, though—everybody.[8]

In this passage, Hughes represents the way in which whites may accept a black person—to a degree. Charles W. Chesnutt writes in *The Marrow of Tradition* about whites' ability to befriend blacks: "Their friendship for us, a slender stream at best, dries up entirely when it strikes their prejudice."[9] This statement adequately sums up what happens to Arnie. In "Poor Little Black Fellow," we see that Arnie is accepted as a child as an object of pity, but his adolescence makes whites fear his growing sexuality. They isolate him and treat him as the embodiment of the racial problem when their prejudices cannot be avoided. Moreover, they try to sublimate their true racism with an inadequate niceness. Hughes points out that such sublimation of racism only helps to continue it.

WHITE IS . . . *IN NEED OF SELF-ANALYSIS*

Lerone Bennett, Jr., in "The White Problem in America," emphasizes the view that the most important step in making progress in race relations is for whites to confront their bigotry. This action, Bennett declares, is what many whites have avoided, thus causing America to stay mired in the consequences of racism. By examining why the "Negro problem" should be renamed "the white problem," whites would be forced to confront their centrality in creating and maintaining the race problem, which, according to Bennett, could lead to self-confrontation and change.[10] Bennett indicates that as long as whites fail to examine their own actions regarding racism, bigotry will continue and black–white relations will be fraught with distrust and antagonism. Bennett's voice is one of a multitude of black voices exhorting whites to realize that self-analysis is a key ingredient to making racial progress.

WHITE IS . . . *REPULSIVELY, SELF-DENIGRATINGLY, AND SELF-CONGRATULATORILY DISRESPECTFUL*

Maya Angelou, in *I Know Why the Caged Bird Sings*, offers an example of how racist behavior can cause whites to demonstrate their moral bankruptcy even when they attempt to show how superior they are (in their own minds) to blacks. In her memoir, Angelou recalls the poor white children who lived near her family: "When I was ten years old, those scruffy children caused me the most painful and confusing experience I had ever had with my grandmother."[11] Angelou recounts an incident in which the white children taunted her grandmother to show their hatred and disrespect of blacks. Angelou was especially struck by the actions of one of the white girls:

> She simply shifted her weight and did a hand stand. Her dirty bare feet and long legs went straight for the sky. Her dress fell down around her shoulders and she had on no drawers. The slick pubic hair made a brown triangle where her legs came together. She hung in the vacuum of that lifeless morning only for a few seconds, then wavered and tumbled. The other girls clapped her on the back and slapped their hands. (25–26)

Angelou was also struck by the fact that during this spectacle her grandmother was quietly watchful and at one point even sang a gospel song.

The episode described by Angelou illustrates several important points. One clear point is that Angelou's grandmother valued maintaining her dignity even when the children not only acted obscenely disrespectful but also obviously attempted to disrupt her calm and respectable demeanor. Here, Angelou conveys the need many blacks feel to meet such potentially humiliating attacks with dignity, even while whites gaudily and hatefully throw theirs away. Moreover, Angelou's story illustrates that whites may think that their antagonistic actions are something of which to be proud and even happy, as represented by the children's glee. Nevertheless, such people often succeed only in being filthy and disgusting to any rational and sane observer. Hence, the white children's jubilation represents the vanity and self-centeredness of racists, whether their actions are more subtle or even more overtly violent than those in Angelou's story.

WHITE IS . . . *JEALOUS*

Whites' desire for social status can be a main component of racism. The need of so-called poor white trash, for example, to feel superior to blacks has long been thought by many blacks to be a desperate attempt to assert status over a more oppressed group. When this status cannot be asserted, white violence can be used to try to establish it. Langston Hughes demonstrates this combination of insecurity and jealousy in one story "Home" when the poor whites of a small town see a black man, Roy, step off a train when he returns to his hometown after working many years as a musician in Europe: "'An uppity nigger,' said the white loafers when they saw [Roy] standing, slim and elegant, on the station platform in the September sunlight, surrounded by his bags with white stickers. Roy had gotten off a Pullman—something unusual for a Negro in those parts. 'God damn!' said the white loafers."[12] These same whites kill Roy at the end of the story.

The racist feeling among whites who feel threatened by the loss of their real or imagined status in relation to blacks is captured by Hughes at perhaps its most basic level. The poor whites of "Home" are jealous of the clear superiority Roy has over them in experience, sophistication, and economics. In a sense, they want precisely what Roy has. Hence, it is a racialized form of jealousy that causes them to assert the only factor that they possess that they feel is superior to blacks: their whiteness.

WHITE IS . . . *CORRUPTED BY POWER*

Power is clearly a corrupting influence in race relations, according to many black writers. In fact, there is a saying that prejudice plus power equals racism. In *The Narrative of the Life of Frederick Douglass*, Douglass shows the combination of prejudice and power in Mrs. Auld, one of his white mistresses. He recalls on first meeting her that she was "a woman of the kindest heart and finest feelings," who, unlike most whites whom Douglass had been around, did not like the slaves to have the demeanor of "crouching servility" around her.[13] Immediately after introducing her into the text, Douglass writes ominously, "But alas! this kind heart had but a short time to remain such. The fatal poison of irresponsible power was already in her hands" (1982, 81). Douglass declares that slavery was as harmful to her as it was to him. He points out that Mrs. Auld absorbs her husband's harshness toward blacks, which was manifested in her change from teaching Douglass to read to becoming "violently" opposed to literacy among the slaves (82).

Douglass's *Narrative* illustrates important aspects of whites' behavior relevant to the nineteenth century and to the present day. Douglass's nineteenth-century readers may have been impressed by two points in his discussion of Mrs. Auld's transformation: that the goodness of any slave master or mistress is highly questionable and that the social and cultural context of slavery morally corrupted many whites. This latter point is still highly relevant to the influence of bigotry on whites living in a racist society. Thus, Douglass's central assertion—that racism is harmful morally and emotionally to both its practitioners and its targets—should still inspire modern readers to think of how prejudice and the power to exercise it affect human thought and behavior in today's society.

WHITE IS . . . *SELF-AGGRANDIZINGLY SEXIST*

The stereotype of the black woman as a slut (attacked, for example, in bell hooks's *Ain't I a Woman*, 1981, and Michelle Wallace's *Black Macho and the Myth of the Superwoman*, 1978) is a clear attempt by some whites to deny the history of their sexual aggression against blacks and to project it onto blacks. Ann Petry, in her novel *The Street*, shows the racist vanity of this attitude when the heroine, Lutie, who works for a white family, the Chandlers, overhears whites' stereotyping her:

> Whenever she entered a room where [Mrs. Chandler and her friends were] they stared at her with a queer, speculative look. Sometimes she caught snatches of conversations about her. "Sure, she's a wonderful cook. But I wouldn't have any good-looking colored wench in my house. . . . You know they're always making passes at men. Especially white men." It didn't make Lutie angry at first. Just contemptuous. . . . [S]he didn't want any of their thin unhappy husbands. But she wondered why they all had the idea that colored girls were whores.[14]

Petry uses this passage to demonstrate the egotistical assumption made by some whites that not only are blacks hypersexual but also that blacks want them. Few ideas could be more vain and self-flattering. Though in reality these ideas are directed by whites against both black women and men, it is intriguing to examine how whites' invention of the myth of the bad black woman was an outgrowth of white men's rape and sexual abuse of black women during slavery, as documented in many accounts by and about black women in Gerda Lerner's *Black Women in White America* (1972), a historical book of invaluable resources. Such displacement by whites whose sexual behavior was out of control clearly was a defense mechanism meant to deflect attention away from their own sexual exploitation of black women. In addition, Petry portrays white women who accept racist myths about black women as a threat to their marriages as a possible way of not examining their own inadequacies. The insulting nature of these lines of thinking is made painfully evident in the life of Lutie in *The Street*.

WHITE IS . . . *PRESUMPTUOUS*

As stated in the first chapter, liberalism has been critiqued by many as an attempt by whites to be guardians and trustees of blacks. This attempt presumes that blacks want to be led by whites. This meddlesome and egomaniacal attitude is shown in Ralph Ellison's *Invisible Man* by Mr. Norton, one of the benefactors of a black college attended by the title character. The invisible man recalls Mr. Norton as a "Bostonian, smoker of cigars, teller of polite Negro stories, shrewd banker, skilled scientist, director, philanthropist, forty years a bearer of the white man's burden."[15] Moreover, Norton tells the invisible man, "I had a feeling that your people were somehow connected with my destiny. That what happened to you was connected to what would happen to me. . . . Yes, you are my fate" (1952, 41).

For any white person to assume that blacks are complimented by such patronizing sentiments is woefully naive. Norton's words represent the tendency of condescending whites to think that wanting to aid blacks means taking ownership of them in however seemingly kind a manner. This possessive attitude is embodied in Mr. Norton's high-sounding—and presumptuous—words.

WHITE IS . . . *SELF-RIGHTEOUSLY DANGEROUS*

The violence that has been perpetrated by many overt racists is a clear fact of American history. Chesnutt, in *The Marrow of Tradition*, captures this attitude in Captain McBane, one of the most influential citizens in town, in his desire to have Sandy lynched for the unsolved murder of a white woman. "Burn the nigger," reiterated McBane. "We seem to have the right nigger, but whether we have or not, burn a nigger. . . . The example would be more powerful if we got the wrong one. It would serve notice on the niggers that we shall hold the whole race responsible for the misdeeds of each individual" (1979, 182).

As an expression of overt racism, McBane's words show a homicidal race hatred: any black man is guilty of being black, thinks McBane, therefore he may as well die. Perhaps the incident which is most analogous to this passage and is best explained by it is the 1986 murder of Yusuf Hawkins in Bensonhurst, Brooklyn. The incident began when a crowd of young white men gathered to attack blacks who they thought were going to attend a party that night given by a white woman who knew the whites involved in the attack. Yusuf Hawkins, who was only in the neighborhood to look at a used car, was sacrificed for this mistake. After being encircled by a bat-wielding crowd, he was shot to death by Joey Fama. The "lynching" of Yusuf Hawkins in the 1980s is illuminated by the words Chesnutt wrote in 1900, for like Captain McBane, the racist attackers of Yusuf Hawkins wanted "to serve notice on the niggers" that their presence would not be tolerated on "white turf," especially when "the flower of white womanhood" (arrested soon after the murder on drug charges) is part of that turf. Yes, these brutes had "the wrong nigger"—but they obviously were not concerned about being sure that they had the person they were looking for when they killed Yusuf Hawkins. Of course, no racist murder is justified, and every black person is the "wrong one" to meet such a fate. We can see very clearly, therefore, that McBane's hateful ideology lives on at the turn of the millennium.

WHITE IS . . . *CONFUSED*

James Baldwin believed that one of the saddest spectacles is progressive whites' "personal incoherence."[16] This confusion is clear in the character of old Delamere in Chesnutt's *The Marrow of Tradition*. In the following passage, Delamere defends Sandy, his servant, from a murder charge in such a way that shows his enlightenment (e.g., his critique of slavery) and his egotism. Sandy's innocence is explained by Delamere not as a sign of the man's goodness but by Delamere's claiming ownership of Sandy's moral qualities, as if they are inherited from his white boss. Delamere states:

> [W]e thought to overrule God's laws, and we enslaved these people for our greed, and thought to escape the manstealer's curse by laying our souls to the flattering unction that we were making of barbarous Negroes civilized and Christian men. If we did not, if instead of making them Christians we have made some of them brutes, we have only ourselves to blame. . . . But my Negroes, Carteret, were all well raised and well behaved. This man is innocent. (Chesnutt 1979, 211)

In Delamere, Chesnutt presents another in the catalog of blacks' questionable allies. Such an alliance is always double-edged. Certainly, on the one hand, an influential white person in a racist society can sometimes help a black person from being the target of a life-altering bigotry. On the other hand, Delamere's confused racial views mar the integrity of his progressiveness, for he is motivated, in part, by self-interest. His attitude seems to say, "Sandy is mine. His actions reflect on me. That I like him is natural since he is one of my Negroes. Thus, my reputation is on the line where Sandy is concerned." The flaw in such thinking is that it is clearly self-centered and self-obsessed. Consequently, such allies as those symbolized by Delamere may help blacks but sometimes at the cost of their feelings of independence and pride.

WHITE IS . . . *COWARDLY*

Again in *The Marrow of Tradition*, a white reporter, Ellis, in the presence of the black Dr. Miller, reflects on the violence on the day of the white riot:

> In his heart he could not defend the deeds of this day. The petty annoyances which the white folks had felt at the spectacle of a few negroes in office . . . which he knew [was] to be made the excuse for overturning the city government, he realized full well [was] no justification for the wholesale murder or other horrors which might well ensue before the day was done. He could not approve the acts of his own people; neither could he, to a negro, condemn them. (Chesnutt 1979, 291)

Again, we meet the good-hearted weakling. Cowardice in this particular incident reflects racial bonding, for Ellis, while revolted by the whites' actions, feels he cannot be critical of whites in front of a black person. Hence, in this episode, Ellis represents the white person who sympathizes with blacks—but not enough to act. Such people, consciously or unconsciously, place racial loyalty above morals, ethics, and fairness to blacks, ceding the ground to those less conflicted, more honest racists.

WHITE IS . . . *NEUROTICALLY REPRESSED*

Emotional emptiness and unfulfilled lives are an intrinsic part of the representation of whites in Baldwin's *Another Country* and Hughes's "Little Dog." While characters in those works turn to blacks to fill their emptiness, in *Savage Holiday*, Richard Wright analyzes the fear and inhibition of a white man, Erskine, on his retirement from his job. Though black characters do not figure in this story, Wright most certainly implies that the repression and sterility to which Erskine is bound are racial characteristics. In this novel, Wright seems to be telling readers that such whites will bring emotional bankruptcy to all their relationships and most certainly to their interracial interactions. Erskine's neurosis is detailed as Wright conveys his thoughts about retirement:

> He was trapped in freedom. How could he again make a foolproof prison of himself for all of his remaining days? What invisible walls could he now erect about his threatening feelings, desires? How could he suppress or throttle those slow and turgid stirrings or buried impulses now trying to come to resurrected life in the deep dark of him? How could he become his own absolute jailer and keep the peace within the warring precincts of his heart?[17]

Though *Savage Holiday* does not feature the black vs. white antagonism of Wright's other novels, it certainly is not racially neutral. In fact, Wright wanted to convey the psychology of a middle-class white person—someone

whose repression is of a piece with that of the white characters in the aforementioned works by Baldwin and Hughes. In *Savage Holiday*, Wright seems
to want to show the emotional problems that sometimes inform the behavior of whites, whether in intraracial or interracial relationships. Wright implies that it is no wonder that such repressed, emotionally sterile people as
those represented by Erskine would look to others—sometimes blacks—to
add excitement to their lives.

WHITE IS . . . *EXPLOITIVE OF BLACKS IN ORDER*
TO HIDE FROM ONE'S OWN STERILITY

In *Another Country*, Baldwin writes about a problem similar to that dramatized in *Savage Holiday* and "Little Dog." Vivaldo, an aspiring Italian
American writer who lives in Greenwich Village in the early 1960s, regards
blacks as objects of excitement who supply needed adventure in his drab,
unfulfilled life. Baldwin recounts Vivaldo's trips to Harlem for sex with
black women:

> It had been his fancy that danger, there, was more real, more open, than dan-
> ger downtown and that he, having chosen to run these dangers, was snatching
> his manhood and testing it in the fire. He felt more alive in Harlem, for he
> had moved in a blaze of rage and self-congratulation and sexual excitement.
> . . . And, nevertheless . . . the misadventures which had actually befallen him
> had been banal indeed. . . . He must be poor indeed, [blacks] seemed to say,
> to have been driven there. . . . [T]he liberal, even the revolutionary senti-
> ments of which he was so proud meant nothing to them whatever. He was just
> a poor white boy in trouble and it was not in the least original of him to come
> running to the niggers.[18]

Baldwin shows in this passage how whites sometimes use blacks in order
to spice up an otherwise dull life. As bell hooks writes in *Killing Rage*, whites'
interest in black culture "in no way challenges white supremacy when it
takes the form of making blackness the 'spice that can liven up the dull dish
that is mainstream white culture.'"[19] This contention is demonstrated in a
tragically twisted way in the fact that after participating in the murder of
Yusuf Hawkins, Keith Mondello, who would later be convicted in connection with the murder, got together with his girlfriend to watch rap videos.
Such personal incoherence exemplifies that acceptance by whites of the
part of black culture (in this case, rap music) can coexist with rejection
(and even hatred) of black people. Furthermore, relevant to hooks's idea
and Baldwin's novel is the fact that John Lester, who was convicted of murdering a black man, Michael Griffiths, in Howard Beach, New York, simply
for being in the neighborhood, had a black girlfriend. Some whites can dis-
connect the part of blacks that gives them pleasure—and that they can use,
exploit, and control—from the overall humanity of blacks. Blacks, there-

fore, have profound evidence that some whites' use of black people and black culture to entertain themselves can exist simultaneously with their rejecting and hating blacks on the most basic level.

WHITE IS . . . *THE PERPETUATION OF SEXIST RACISM*

Tension between black women and white women sometimes results from the white women's combining racism and sexism to assert white superiority. In her novel *Meridian*, Alice Walker illustrates this issue in the actions and attitudes of Lynne, a white woman who earns the anger of black women by becoming sexually involved with black men with whom they both work in the Civil Rights movement. As a result, the black women

> began to curse and threaten her. . . . And she began perversely to enjoy their misguided rage, to use it as acknowledgment of her irresistible qualities. It was during this time that whenever she found herself among black women, she found some excuse for taking down and combing her hair. As she flung it and felt it sweep the back of her waist, she imagined she possessed treasures they could never have.
> She began to believe the men fucked her from love, not hatred.[20]

Lynne symbolizes the vain white woman who uses her feeling of superiority to black women and her sexual assertiveness with black men as a crutch to hold up her self-esteem.

WHITE IS . . . *GIRLISH*

According to Toni Morrison in "What the Black Woman Thinks about Women's Lib," weakness and artificial vulnerability are qualities some white women have mastered.[21] This idea is echoed in Wright's *The Outsider* when Eva tells Cross of her fears that her association with political radicals may have put her in danger: "I'm so scared—and I'm so much alone. . . . You're colored and you're strong. . . . Have pity on me and let me stay near you."[22] This excessive display of vulnerability disguises a manipulative play for control: strength masquerading as sentimental sweetness.

WHITE IS . . . *NARCISSISTIC*

Interactive narcissism is a foundation of racism. This narcissism is interactive in that the egotism of whites often negatively affects blacks, for it precludes whites from examining and trying to curtail their racist behavior. In "White Man's Guilt," Baldwin explains how whites prevent themselves from progressing in their racial attitudes by clinging to an idealized self-image concerning the history of race relations: "[P]eople who imagine that history flatters them (as it does, indeed, since they wrote it) are impaled on their history like a butterfly on a pin and become incapable of seeing or changing themselves or the world" (1985, 410).

Baldwin's essay argues that until whites look at their own actions to account for racial hostility and conflict, they will never understand their accountability for continuing the cycle of racism, whether actively or passively. Nor will they be able to take steps toward ending the de facto bigotry that is still a pillar of American society. Consequently, we all pay for the narcissism of racists.

Baldwin argues passionately that the failure of bigoted whites to look analytically at the actions that express their prejudice is one of the keys to the continuation of racial antagonism. As Baldwin further points out, such people use history as a mythology that attests to the conquests and civilization of the white race. Yet, I would like to expand Baldwin's use of the word history as a distorted record of the deeds of the white race. Indeed, a main ingredient of Baldwin's essay is that bigots are very often blind to their true nature regarding their own personal history of how they treat blacks. Parnell in Baldwin's *Blues for Mister Charlie*, for example, is so busy patting himself on the back for having a black friend that he misunderstands this fact as proof of his progressive nature. Yet, such a person, Baldwin presents in his play, can use the word nigger when with his white friends as if it is a perfectly natural term for black people. Moreover, as the play and the essay argue, one of the main defenses of such white people against seeing their own bigotry in this instance and others like it is their need to maintain an exaggeratedly high self-image concerning racism, for example, the unconscious refrain, "If I do not think I am a racist, nothing I do can be racist." Thus, many of the very people who perpetuate racism will never combat it in themselves and others because, in their view, they themselves have nothing to overcome or critique in their behavior regarding racism. Such people, therefore, help America stay where it has long been concerning race relations: stuck in quicksand, spinning its wheels as it sinks slowly.

WHITE IS . . . *SELF-DECEIVING*

In *The Rage of a Privileged Class*, Ellis Cose indicates that perhaps the greatest mental trick whites employ concerning racism is the defense mechanism of believing that racism—like death—is something relevant only to others. Hence, the very people who need to learn from blacks' critiques of racism are those who have attempted to absolve themselves of bigotry simply by telling themselves that they are not racists. Yet, such people could benefit from reading Era Bell Thompson's "Some of My Best Friends Are White." Thompson asserts that when many whites tell blacks that they are not even faintly racist, they are, in fact, trying to assuage their guilt over their actual inner prejudice; they protest too much.[23] Thompson's beliefs illustrate that the self-proclaimed freedom from racism is also an indicator of guilt feelings for repressed and unresolved racism which are covered up by a guilt-inspired vanity.

WHITE IS . . . *NICE*

An intriguing theme in black literature is that whites who practice veiled racism use their very "niceness" to act as a barrier to keep blacks at a seemingly polite distance. Such racism is portrayed by Andrea Lee in her novel *Sarah Phillips* when the heroine recalls her treatment at Prescott, the nearly all-white school she starts attending in the seventh grade:

> Classes were easy for me but friends were hard. A few years earlier I'd seen a picture of a southern black girl making her way into a school through a jeering crowd of white students, a policeman at her side. Prescott didn't jeer me—it had, after all, invited me—but it shut me off socially with a set of almost imperceptible closures and polite rejections. If one waves a hand through a tidal pool, one finds the same kind of minute and instantaneous retreat.[24]

The racism encountered by Sarah in her school is the hardest kind to confront because it is hidden. How does one deal with bigotry when it takes the form of whites, in virtually all white settings, organizing a party to which everyone is invited—with the exception of their one black schoolmate? This sneaky kind of bigotry isolates blacks by barring them from social relationships in schools and workplaces. Such whites, as in the situations represented in *Sarah Phillips*, maintain covert racism; if they were confronted by blacks with the racial nature of their exclusion, they would deny that it has anything to do with race and project their bigotry onto the black person, whom they would thus perceive as injecting racism into the relationship. Such thinking is an extension of the narcissism and hypocrisy discussed in previous examples. Consequently, the "nice" racism of Prescott in *Sarah Phillips* represents one of the most frustrating, alienating, and isolating forms of unspoken racism.

WHITE IS . . . *SPIRITUALLY AND RELIGIOUSLY BANKRUPT*

In "The Un-Christian Christian," the Reverend Dr. Martin Luther King, Jr., attacks the ways in which he felt many whites use religion in order to bolster their Eurocentric relationships and beliefs. To King, this was clearly immoral. King was especially troubled by the segregation of many churches, symptomatic of their misuse as places to establish cliques that reinforce a sense of racial tribalism.[25] This misuse of religion causes nominal Christians to ignore Christ's exhortation not to love only their neighbor, but also to love their enemy—people who are not like them. King believed that the rejection of the idea and practice of being concerned for those different from themselves leads to a kind of pseudo-spiritual inbreeding which is a rejection of both Christianity and life. King makes a convincing case that some religious institutions which should cause society to advance actually cause it to regress. He makes one wonder about the failure of many who consider themselves religious (and who are followers of a religion which has love as one of its key ideas) and the arrogance of their inability to entertain the idea that their failure to practice what they preach damages society as a whole. King's message is still relevant to the racially fragmented society in which we live today.

Perhaps this final image of whites best sums up the qualities that many blacks perceive as the embodiment of the true character of good-hearted whites. It comes from Lawrence Otis Graham's *Member of the Club*. Graham tells the story of a white female student in a race relations workshop he attended as a junior at Princeton University. She said that she wanted to befriend blacks but did not know how to do so. "She reminded me of one of my two sophomore roommates—stuck somewhere between good intentions and a total ignorance of others."[26] He told her to treat blacks as she treated her white friends. After the workshop had finished,

> For the next eighteen months during my junior and senior years, I passed this woman on campus and coming to and from our meals at our respective eating clubs on Prospect Avenue. Every time I would open my mouth to say hello, this woman who had argued, with great conviction, that she had wanted to befriend black students, decidedly dropped her head or abruptly crossed the street to evade my salutation. It occurred to me that she was willing to be candid in that meeting when none of her white friends were present but unwilling to practice what had been preached to her once she was outside with her white friends who might not have appreciated her desire to mix with blacks.
>
> She needed some white person—some white leader—to give her permission to do the right thing. But none was there to do it. (1995, 212–13)

This young woman stands as a metaphor for the white problem in all its guises. And, as Graham states in an idea with which Malcolm X would have concurred, whites' progression from such a weak state is, indeed, the white man's burden.

CONCLUSION

To review major aspects of the white image in the black mind, in addition to the characteristics above, one should remember the following as representing recurring aspects of white identity as understood by blacks. According to the tradition of how whites are understood by many black writers, whites are hypocritical, defensive, in denial, arrogant, ignorant, fake, crafty, passive-aggressive, cunning, sneaky, self-satisfied, back-stabbing, silencing, and dishonest.

Why is it important for blacks and whites (and people of all races) to know about and analyze the typology of whites represented by black writers? How can a typology which is mainly negative actually constitute a liberating mythology both for blacks and all who want to become aware of the nature and consequences of racism?

The important and liberating nature of the study of the white image in the black mind is indicated by ideas in Derrick Bell's *Faces at the Bottom of the Well.* Speaking of the need for American society to examine white racist behavior, Bell asserts that it is possible to be prepared for the future only by looking unflinchingly at the past; particularly, one must examine the mentality of white racism in order to come to grips with the way racism contaminates American life.[27] Furthermore, it is a long and perhaps endless quest to comprehend why, in Bell's opinion, blacks have been and continue to be the country's traditionally targeted subjects of bigotry (1992, 13). As enlightened people have been aware, certainly since the publication of Gunnar Myrdal's *An American Dilemma* (1944), the key answers about the nature of racism come from analyzing the character of those who practice it and the particular nature of their neurosis—who better than the target of this neurosis to examine and dismantle its validity? Thus, if we as readers and as members of this society want to transform this race-corrupt nation, facing the harsh truth as understood by blacks is a primary prerequisite.

Ideas from Cose's *The Rage of a Privileged Class* also convey the importance of the need for Americans as a whole to comprehend blacks' understanding of the nature of racism, a major aspect of that understanding being the black interpretation of whites. Particularly relevant to our study is the emphasis Cose places on blacks' response to racism, particularly anger.

> Such emotions do not develop in a vacuum. They arise in response to experiences that many members of racial minority groups share, regardless of achievement or status—experiences preserved as painfully recorded snapshots of moments when racial reality rears and slaps one in the face with stunning rudeness. These moments typically begin long before the age at which one enters the work world, and they accumulate throughout life.[28]

The emotions that are produced by such experiences have been transformed by many writers into literary examinations which attempt to give order to them by analyzing the primary cause, the condition sine qua non of racism: white people.

> [N]o matter how equivalent their backgrounds and personal attributes, [they] live fundamentally different lives. And because the experiences are so immensely different, even for those who walk through the same institutions, it is all but impossible for members of one group to see the world through the other's eyes. That lack of a common perspective translates into a lack of

empathy, and an inability on the part of most whites to perceive, much less understand, the soul-destroying slights [suffered by blacks]. (Cose 1993, 4–5)

After reading much black literature, one could certainly argue with the idea that blacks "cannot see the world through the other's (i.e., whites') eyes." Indeed, Cose's point, as emphasized in the latter part of the passage, is that whites cannot understand blacks' perspective on racism and how it affects their lives. Since empathy is a key to understanding the nature and the impact of racism on blacks, an analysis of the white image in the black mind can sow the seeds of empathy for blacks in white people. For black readers, such an analysis can validate their interpretations of racism and, more specifically, demonstrate how the whites who practice it operate in their lives. Hence, for the analytical reader, pondering black authors' images of whites can be potentially liberating in fundamental ways. For whites, such works can help destroy and prevent interactive narcissism, a mainstay of racism. If this were accomplished, perhaps fewer blacks would be in danger from suffering from tolerance exhaustion. The white image in the black mind is, therefore, a liberating mythology on at least these levels.

Final ideas about the white image in the black mind as a liberating mythology may be illuminated by Henry Tudor's *Political Myth*:

The view of the world that we find in a myth is always a practical view. Its aim is either to advocate a certain course of action or to justify an existing state of affairs. Myths are, therefore, believed to be true . . . because they make sense of men's present experience. They tell the story of how it came about.[29]

To compare Tudor's ideas with the concept of a liberating mythology as discussed in chapter one, the black writers under discussion are most certainly, to be general, advocating a certain course of action: the end of racism. Moreover, the mythology that constitutes black writers' images of whites tells how the blacks' oppressed condition came about by presenting the psychological and behavioral components of white racism. If we, as a society, are willing to face the harsh truths in the works of black writers, perhaps we can begin to transform the hostility and distrust between the races into, at the very least, a dialogue between enlightened individuals of all races. If not, we will continue living in a new century with the same problems that have plagued America for already too long a time. One of the central problems—white identity vis-à-vis nonwhites—is perhaps best summed up in a letter written in 1967 by theologian Thomas Merton, one of the major white thinkers on race, whose ideas are included in *The White Problem in America*. In a letter written to my mother, Ruby Davis, who corresponded with him, Merton declared, "Perhaps much of the trouble has come from the fact that people have been living in a dream world, and have imagined that they had everything under control when they did not."[30] This critique of the source of the white problem and the resultant racial discord stands as testimony to the need for whites to engage in self-criticism and self-analysis, which can best be prompted, perhaps, by an examination of the white image in the black mind.

NOTES

1. Langston Hughes, *Black Misery* (New York: Oxford University Press, 1994), n.p.

2. Harriet Wilson, *Our Nig* (New York: Vintage Books, 1983), 24.

3. John O. Killens, *Black Man's Burden* (New York: Trident Press, 1965), 149–50.

4. Malcolm X and Alex Haley, *The Autobiography of Malcolm X* (New York: Grove Press, 1965), 337.

5. Zora Neale Hurston, *Their Eyes Were Watching God* (Urbana: University of Illinois Press, 1978), 255.

6. Langston Hughes, "Slave on the Block," in *The Ways of White Folks* (New York: Alfred A. Knopf, 1933), 20.

7. Langston Hughes, "Berry," in *The Ways of White Folks* (New York: Alfred A. Knopf, 1933), 174–75.

8. Langston Hughes, "Poor Little Black Fellow," in *The Ways of White Folks* (New York: Alfred A. Knopf, 1933), 133–34.

9. Charles W. Chesnutt, *The Marrow of Tradition* (Ann Arbor: University of Michigan Press, 1979), 194.

10. Lerone Bennett, Jr., "The White Problem in America," in *The White Problem in America*, ed. editors of *Ebony* (Chicago: Johnson Publishing, 1966), 10.

11. Maya Angelou, *I Know Why the Caged Bird Sings* (New York: Bantam Books, 1970), 23.

12. Langston Hughes, "Home," in *The Ways of White Folks* (New York: Alfred A. Knopf, 1933), 35.

13. Frederick Douglass, *The Narrative of the Life of Frederick Douglass* (New York: Penguin Books, 1982), 77.

14. Ann Petry, *The Street* (Boston: Houghton Mifflin, 1946), 41.

15. Ralph Ellison, *Invisible Man* (New York: Random House, 1952), 37.

16. James Baldwin, "White Man's Guilt," in *The Price of the Ticket* (New York: St. Martin's/Marek, 1985), 411.

17. Richard Wright, *Savage Holiday* (Jackson: University Press of Mississippi, 1994), 33.

18. James Baldwin, *Another Country* (New York: Dell Publishing, 1960), 115–16.

19. bell hooks, *Killing Rage* (New York: Henry Holt, 1995), 153.

20. Alice Walker, *Meridian* (New York: Washington Square Press, 1976), 165–66.

21. Toni Morrison, "What the Black Woman Thinks about Women's Lib," *New York Times Magazine*, 22 August 1971, 64.

22. Richard Wright, *The Outsider* (New York: Harper and Row, 1953), 260.

23. Era Bell Thompson, "Some of My Best Friends Are White," in *The White Problem in America*, ed. editors of *Ebony* (Chicago: Johnson Publishing, 1966), 156.

24. Andrea Lee, *Sarah Phillips* (New York: Random House, 1984), 54.

25. Martin Luther King, Jr., "The Un-Christian Christian," in *The White Problem in America*, ed. editors of *Ebony* (Chicago: Johnson Publishing, 1966), 58–60.

26. Lawrence Otis Graham, *Member of the Club* (New York: HarperCollins, 1995), 212.

27. Derrick Bell, *Faces at the Bottom of the Well* (New York: Basic Books, 1992), 11.

28. Ellis Cose, *The Rage of a Privileged Class* (New York: HarperCollins, 1993), 47.

29. Henry Tudor, *Political Myth* (New York: Praeger Publishers, 1972), 50.

30. Thomas Merton, letter to Ruby Davis, July 10, 1967.

Selected Bibliography

Achebe, Chinua. *Hopes and Impediments.* New York: Doubleday, 1989.

Adam, Barry D. *The Survival of Domination.* New York: Elsevier North-Holland, 1978.

Andrews, William L. "William Dean Howells and Charles W. Chesnutt: Criticism and Race Fiction in the Age of Booker T. Washington." *American Literature* 48 (November 1976): 331.

Angelou, Maya. *I Know Why the Caged Bird Sings.* New York: Bantam Books, 1970.

Baldwin, James. *Another Country.* New York: Dell Publishing, 1960.

————. *Blues for Mister Charlie.* New York: Dell Publishing, 1964.

————. *The Fire Next Time.* New York: Dell Publishing, 1962.

————. *Nobody Knows My Name.* New York: Dell Publishing, 1961.

————. *Notes of a Native Son.* New York: Bantam Books, 1964.

————. *The Price of the Ticket.* New York: St. Martin's/Marek, 1985.

Baldwin, James, and Nikki Giovanni. *A Dialogue.* Philadelphia: Lippincott, 1973.

Baldwin, James, and Margaret Mead. *A Rap on Race.* New York: Dell Publishing, 1971.

Baldwin, James, and Budd Schulberg. "Dialogue in Black and White." In *James Baldwin: The Legacy*, edited by Quincy Troupe. New York: Simon and Schuster, 1989.

Banta, Martha. Introduction to *The Shadow of a Dream and An Imperative Duty*, by William Dean Howells. Bloomington: Indiana University Press, 1970.

Baraka, Amiri. *Tales.* New York: Grove Press, 1967.

Bell, Derrick. *Faces at the Bottom of the Well.* New York: Basic Books, 1992.

Bone, Robert. *Richard Wright.* Minneapolis: University of Minnesota Press, 1969.

Bontemps, Arna. *Saturday Review*, 28 March 1953; in *Richard Wright: The Critical Reception*, edited by John M. Reilly. New York: Burt Franklin, 1978.

Bryant, Earle V. "Sexual Initiation and Survival in *The Long Dream.*" In *Richard Wright: Critical Perspectives Past and Present*, edited by Henry Louis Gates, Jr., and K. A. Appiah. New York: Amsterdam Press, 1993.

Cash, J. W. *The Mind of the South.* New York: Vintage Books, 1991.

Chesnutt, Charles W. *The Marrow of Tradition*. Ann Arbor: University of Michigan Press, 1979.

Clark, Kenneth B. *Prejudice and Your Child*. Boston: Beacon Press, 1955.

Clinton, President William J. *ABC World News Tonight*, October 16, 1996.

Cose, Ellis. *The Rage of a Privileged Class*. New York: HarperCollins, 1993.

Douglass, Frederick. *The Narrative of the Life of Frederick Douglass*. New York: Penguin Books, 1982.

Editors of *Ebony*. *The White Problem in America*. Chicago: Johnson Publishing, 1966.

Ellison, Ralph. *Invisible Man*. New York: Random House, 1952.

Erikson, Erik H. *Identity and the Life Cycle*. New York: W. W. Norton, 1980.

Fabre, Michel. *The Unfinished Quest of Richard Wright*. New York: William Morrow, 1973.

Fabre, Michel, and Ellen Wright, eds. *The Richard Wright Reader*. New York: Harper and Row, 1978.

Fanon, Frantz. *Black Skin, White Masks*. New York: Grove Press, 1967.

Felgar, Robert. *Richard Wright*. Boston: Twayne Publishers, 1980.

Gayle, Addison, Jr. *Richard Wright: Ordeal of a Native Son*. Garden City, N.Y.: Anchor Press/Doubleday, 1980.

Ginzburg, Ralph. *One Hundred Years of Lynchings*. Baltimore: Black Classic Press, 1988.

Giovanni, Nikki, *Gemini*. Indianapolis: Bobbs-Merrill, 1971.

Goffman, Erving. *Stigma*. Englewood Cliffs, N.J.: Prentice-Hall, 1963.

Graham, Lawrence Otis. *Member of the Club*. New York: HarperCollins, 1995.

Hakutani, Yoshinuki, ed. *Critical Essays on Richard Wright*. Boston: G. K. Hall, 1982.

Hernton, Calvin C. *Sex and Racism in America*. New York: Grove Press, 1965.

Hill, Mike, ed. *Whiteness*. New York: New York University Press, 1997.

Hogue, W. Lawrence. *Discourse and the Other*. Durham, N.C.: Duke University Press, 1986.

hooks, bell. *Killing Rage*. New York: Henry Holt, 1995.

Howells, William Dean. "A Psychological Counter-Current in Recent Fiction." In *The North American Review*, vol. 173, edited by George Harvey. New York: Franklin Square, 1901.

Hughes, Langston. *The Big Sea*. New York: Thunder's Mouth Press, 1986.

———. *Black Misery*. New York: Oxford University Press, 1994.

———. *The Ways of White Folks*. New York: Alfred A. Knopf, 1933.

Hurston, Zora Neale. *Their Eyes Were Watching God*. Urbana: University of Illinois Press, 1978.

Jefferson, Thomas. "Original Draft of the Declaration of Independence." In *The Norton Reader: The Shorter 9th Edition*, edited by Linda H. Peterson, et al. New York: W. W. Norton, 1996.

Killens, John O. *Black Man's Burden*. New York: Trident Press, 1965.

King, Martin Luther, Jr. "Dr. Martin Luther King, Jr., Memphis Tennessee, April 3, 1968." In *Free at Last*. Audiocassette. Los Angeles: Motown Record Corporation, 1968.

Kinnamon, Keneth, and Michel Fabre, eds. *Conversations with Richard Wright*. Jackson: University Press of Mississippi, 1993.

Lee, Andrea. *Sarah Phillips*. New York: Random House, 1984.

Leeming, David. *James Baldwin*. New York: Henry Holt, 1994.

Locke, Alain. "The New Negro." In *Black Voices*, edited by Abraham Chapman. New York: New American Library, 1968.

Lomax, Louis E. "The White Liberal." In *The White Problem in America*, edited by editors of *Ebony*. Chicago: Johnson Publishing. 1966.

Malcolm X, and Alex Haley. *The Autobiography of Malcolm X*. New York: Grove Press, 1965.

Marable, Manning. *Beyond Black and White*. London: Verso, 1995.

McKay, Claude. *Selected Poems of Claude McKay*. New York: Harcourt Brace Jovanovich, 1953.

Milgram, Stanley. *Obedience to Authority*. New York: Harper and Row, 1974.

Miller, Alice. *For Your Own Good*. New York: Farrar, Straus and Giroux, 1983.

Morrison, Toni. "What the Black Woman Thinks about Women's Lib." *New York Times Magazine*, 22 August 1971, 64.

Parrington, Vernon Louis. *The Beginnings of Critical Realism in America: 1860–1920*. New York: Harcourt, Brace and World, 1930.

Petry, Ann. *The Street*. Boston: Houghton Mifflin, 1946.

Pettigrew, Thomas F. "Prejudice." In *Prejudice*, edited by Stephan Thornstrom. Cambridge, Mass.: Harvard University Press, 1980.

Rogers, Joyce Y. "An Image of Cooperation: White Volunteers in the Civil Rights Freedom Summers Project." Unpublished graduate essay, Stanford University, June 1, 1982.

Schweitzer, Albert. *On the Edge of the Primeval Forest*. London: A. and C. Black, 1922.

Sennett, Richard. *Authority*. New York: Alfred A. Knopf, 1980.

Shapiro, Walter. "Unfinished Business." *Time*, 7 August 1989, 15.

Standley, Fred L. and Luis H. Pratt, eds. *Conversations with James Baldwin*. Jackson: University Press of Mississippi, 1989.

Stepto, Robert B., and Michael Harper, eds. *Chant of Saints*. Urbana: University of Illinois Press, 1979.

Takaki, Ronald T. *Violence in the Black Imagination*. New York: G. P. Putnam's Sons, 1972.

Troupe, Quincy. "The Last Interview." *Essence*, March 1988, 117.

Tudor, Henry. *Political Myth*. New York: Praeger Publishers, 1972.

Walker, Alice. *Meridian*. New York: Washington Square Press, 1976.

Wilson, Harriet. *Our Nig*. New York: Vintage Books, 1983.

Wortham, Thomas, et al., eds. *W. D. Howells: Selected Letters*. Vol. 4. Boston: Twayne Publishers, 1981.

Wright, Richard. *Black Boy*. New York: Harper and Row, 1945.

———. *Lawd Today*. New York: Walker and Company, 1963.

———. *The Long Dream*. New York: Doubleday, 1958.

———. *Native Son*. New York: Harper and Row, 1940.

———. *The Outsider*. New York: Harper and Row, 1953.

———. *Savage Holiday*. Jackson: University Press of Mississippi, 1994.

Index

About the Author

JANE DAVIS teaches in the English Department at Iowa State University. She was a Mellon Postdoctoral Fellow at the Africana Studies and Research Center at Cornell University and has taught at Fordham University and the University of Rochester.

ISBN 0-313-30464-5

9 780313 304644

HARDCOVER BAR CODE